From Riches to Ra
Homelessness

By Matthew Bjonerud

Copyright 2012 Matthew Bjonerud

Published by Smashwords

ISBN: 1469906651

Cover image courtesy of Lars Christensen &
Dreamstime.com
Cover by Joleene Naylor.

The author is donating 30% of his net proceeds from the book to agencies fighting homelessness in Baltimore, Catholic Education, and the Church.

Dedication:

I dedicate this story to all of the teachers and mentors that I have had throughout my Catholic education. Without your presence in my life, I am certain that I would not have had the inspiration, discipline, and guidance to live out this adventure.

To my brother, Eric, for always being there to support me throughout this adventure and all the ones that came before it.

To Dad for showing me what it means to be an honest man who always tries to do the right thing.

To Mom for deciding to look the other way.

Table of Contents:

Introduction

I could hear her sobbing as I limped down West Ward Street. Streams of dark blue eyeliner ran down her cheeks and bright red lipstick smudges covered her chin. As I got closer, I noticed that she smelled overwhelmingly of roses, fields and fields of roses.

"Cheryl, what's wrong?" I asked dropping my duffle bag on the sidewalk.

"They sent me home," she sobbed.

My heart sank.

"Why?"

"My name. It's flagged in the database."

"What for?" I questioned though I wasn't sure I wanted to hear the answer. This wasn't good. This wasn't good at all.

"They won't say. All they know is that I have one week to figure it out or else I'm done."

She looked at me with a pained expression, which I reflected right back at her. We were out of options now, but that wasn't the problem.

I raised an eyebrow, "You don't have any idea what it could be?"

Cheryl sat back, waited for a second, and then answered, "No."

I plopped down on the stoop a step below her and faced out towards the neighborhood. I knew she wasn't telling me everything. If she didn't trust me by now, then would she ever trust me?

I hated to see her cry so I pretended to watch the neighborhood kids play catch. I felt a twinge of sadness at the pathetic sight of kids using a large wad of blue tape for their game. In this neighborhood, households that found themselves with extra money would never squander it on luxuries. A small stout boy wearing his dad's torn wife

5

beater ran out for a long pass but was too slow. The ball bounced off a car windshield and landed in the gutter amidst discarded chip bags and shattered beer bottles.

Cheryl's new situation was a game changer. Unfortunately, I knew exactly why the police had flagged her name. I folded my arms over my knees and put my head down to remember the words that changed everything.

Two days before, my phone vibrated roughly on my desk. The number appeared as unknown, but I recognized it and abruptly jumped out of my chair. I walked briskly down the hall and scrambled to the office lobby to find someplace where no one would hear. There were only seconds before the call would go to voicemail and I doubted that he would leave one. I slammed my body into the brass swivel doors and burst out into the cobbled plaza startling a flock of pigeons.

"Hello," I answered.

"This is Scott."

His voice sounded younger than I had expected.

"Scott, it's good to talk to you. I just---"

He cut me off sharply, "Don't ever send me an email on my work address again. Do I make myself clear?"

"Um, errr, yes," I said, put off by his abruptness.

"Tell me how you found my mother," He snapped.

"I've been living with your mother and father for some time now. I just wanted to let you know that they're okay."

It wasn't until I heard the fear in Scott's voice that I realized he probably thought I was trying to blackmail him. Whenever anyone found anything ugly about a politician or a politician's family, it automatically threatened their career. This was especially true for Scott, who had recently won his campaign by championing family values.

"Do not call Paul my father. That man is not my father," he said almost growling.

" Okay, okay."

6

I had forgotten that Paul wasn't his real dad, but I couldn't be expected to keep track of all Cheryl's marriages. At the young age of 47, she was already on her third, while at the age of 23, I had not yet had my first.

"What kind of program is this? A halfway house?" Scott asked.

"No, it's not a halfway house."

"Who do you work for?"

"No one," I said.

"So, whose house is it?" Scott asked.

"It's my house."

"Well, how on earth did you find my mom and Paul?"

"They were panhandling on the side of the street."

Scott paused for what seemed like a long time, though it was probably only a few seconds. I imagined that his mind was working furiously to figure out what I really wanted.

"You there?" I asked breaking the silence.

After another long pause, Scott finally asked, "Why are you doing this?"

This question prompted an overflow of responses. It would take me hours to sort through all of them, so I used the simplest one I had.

"Because I can."

This answer was followed by a few moments of silence as Scott probably tested it for any kind of malice or ill intent.

"That's nice of you. Yes, very nice." His voice softened and I imagined him wiping his brow with relief.

"They're good people," I said trying to turn the conversation into something positive.

"They're also very dangerous people. You should watch yourself," he said in a stern voice.

7

"Dangerous?" I asked trying to restrain a chuckle. I couldn't picture a little old married couple as being a threat to my safety.

"They're both on the local county's most wanted list. Do you hear me? Their pictures were on TV and everything."

I stopped smiling and stared ahead at the pigeons milling about the square. This was an unexpected comment. He could very well be telling me the truth. As he spoke, I began to realize that he was probably right.

"Why are they wanted?" I asked, hoping for something innocuous like drunken revelry or speeding.

"Among a slew of other things, G.T.A," said Scott.

"G.T.A.?" I asked, unsure of the acronym.

"Grand theft auto."

"Is that a joke?"

"I'm afraid not."

I brought my hand up to my forehead. It was almost comical to think of mild- mannered Cheryl stealing someone's car in cold blood. What did she do? Hold the owner up with a rolling pin?

"There's something else you should know, too."

"What's that?"

"They both have been addicted to heroin. We did everything we could to help them. I spent tens of thousands of dollars on legal fees and rehab."

"And it didn't work?"

"Towards the end, Mom begged us to stop helping. She said that she liked the drugs too much."

"She actually said that?"

I couldn't believe anyone would ever say that. I couldn't tell if Scott was telling me these things to scare me away or to protect me. I decided to change the subject back to the original purpose of the phone call, which was the communication of good news.

"She just got a job at the hospital in the medical records department. It pays benefits and a good wage."

After a long pause Scott said, "I'll believe it after six months of paychecks."

"Well, I just figured you should know. She's trying."

"She's a good woman." Scott paused before saying, "She was a good mom." His voice was cracking. "She could have the world, but instead she hangs out with that deadbeat, Paul."

"She can make it out of this. You'll see."

Scott's voice quivered as he said, "Do you know, they used to live out of a van? That's no way to raise three small children."

"I heard."

"The kids are finally happy. They haven't missed a day of school since they've been with me. They have friends now, and they're even going on a camping trip this weekend. Don't ruin this for them." The uplifting tone of the conversation changed. Again the phone went silent.

"Scott? You there?" I asked, but I knew he was there. I could hear his breathing.

Then he spoke, "Don't take this the wrong way, but I don't want you to ever contact me again. I can't risk having the kids get unsettled again. They don't handle it well." Those were the last words he said before the line went dead.

By now, things had gone off plan so often that events like this were expected. Yet, I still couldn't help but find it funny how a brief phone call could so drastically reshape reality. I sat on the park bench and reflected on how I had gotten myself into a situation where I was accidentally threatening politicians, unknowingly harboring fugitives, and randomly living with heroin addicts in a Baltimore ghetto. If I had to pinpoint the beginning of this adventure, I guess the best place to start would be the day I graduated from a Jesuit University.

It was sunny day, and I could see my parents waving. I nodded slightly. Dad, a large camera around his neck, nodded back, while Mom sat next to him glowing with pride. My grandfather held his camera firmly between his hands with a finger resting on the trigger button. He had flown in all the way from Vegas. Vegas! That's almost a five-hour flight. I figured that there was a good chance that Dad would watch the whole thing through his camera lens and witness not a second in person. Couldn't risk it. He might miss it, *the one moment.* Never! Everything must be photographed. Documented. This was important. A momentous occasion.

At the base of a large eighteenth century stone building, a slender woman with short red hair read aloud from behind a podium reciting names from a long list as my classmates walked across the stage. Large iron bells rang out, announcing the hour from the stone clock tower above. Underneath my black graduation robes, little sweat streams ran down my legs and into my knee-high socks. Time seemed to stand still as the woman took a sip of water and adjusted her circular spectacles.

But then it happened. The woman called my name bringing to an end term papers, final exams, and all-night study sessions. No longer would letter grades rule my life. I was free, free at last. Only twenty-two years old, I now possessed youth, health, and a very expensive education. My whole life was ahead of me, and I had complete freedom to do anything I wanted. Become a sky diving instructor? No problem. Teach history? Great. Work in a large corporate consulting firm? Perfect.

If that wasn't enough, my parents shouldered all of my college debt so that I could concentrate on building a comfortable life for myself devoid of worries or cares. The

Plan was for me to buy a new car, live in a nice neighborhood, and maybe play some golf on the weekends.

My first year out of college did not go according to The Plan. Not at all. And now, after only eighteen months of "complete freedom," I sit here and struggle to explain myself. I am not yet completely sure how the idea came into my head. Maybe I had always dreamed of doing something great, or perhaps I had always wanted to be part of something beautiful and worthwhile. Regardless of the reasons, all I know is that after college, I didn't care about cars or houses or nice neighborhoods. All I wanted to do was to change the world, a symptom, I suspect, of eight years of Jesuit education. My only problem was that I had no idea what to do or even where to start. So, late on a cold September evening, I looked out at the moon and whispered a prayer asking God, who I had heard was experienced at this kind of thing, to tell me what to do. A few days later, I had a plan and set myself to the messy work of saving the world.

Chapter 1: The Warning

St. Vincent's, a small white church, stood alone at the end of a massive, concrete office building. I swung open the wooden door and stepped inside. Light streamed through the windows and illuminated the dust in the air. The wooden boards beneath my feet squeaked as I walked over to the main hall of the church. Cobwebs littered the rafters of the tall bare ceilings and the stained glass windows cast glimmering shapes on the walls.

There was no telling how badly things were going to turn out, but I imagined very badly. Still, if success were possible, it would be worth it. I had, after all, arranged several of these meetings already. All of them had been with other city leaders; all of them had ended the same way: consult Father Lorenzo. When they realized that I had no idea who he was, they did their best to bring me up to speed. They told me he was a one-of-a-kind character and that he was a complete and utter slob. Not a single moment of his day was wasted tending to issues of cleanliness, physical appearance, table manners or the funny business of matching one's socks. I should expect to be interrupted by burps and other flatulence, depending on what he had had for dinner the night before.

Contrary to outward appearances, however, I was also told that he was a genius regarding homelessness. Undoubtedly, he was heralded as the smartest man in the entire city. For over forty years, he had fought for the homeless and for the poor. He had made significant progress, and gained vital experience. Experience I didn't have. Experience I probably should have had. Everyone I met deferred to his judgment and wisdom, and they encouraged me to do the same.

A door crunched open on the far left, and a large man with a big, bushy beard walked into the church foyer.

Almost waddling, he struggled under the weight of his own stomach. His shirt had dried pasta sauce that had run down the side of it, and the hems of his pants were frayed. The man's gut and beard made him look like Santa Claus except that this Santa was wearing a ragged, old flannel shirt and oversized elastic pants.

"Hello," the man called.

"Father Lorenzo?"

"I am," said Father Lorenzo as he walked over.

"Mr. Bjonerud, I presume."

"Yes sir. Good to meet you," I said, as we exchanged a firm handshake.

"Did I pronounce it correctly?"

"Pretty close, but the best way to say it is 'beyond' then 'rude.' Just stick them together and you get 'beyond rude.'"

"Ah, very good then, Mr. Beyond Rude. Just give me a minute to lock up these outside doors," he said. "Some of the homeless tend to wander in here."

The locking of metal bolts echoed throughout the church as Father Lorenzo sealed the front doors.

"Do they ever steal things?"

"Sometimes, but I am more worried that they might use one of the corners as a rest room," he chuckled loudly.

"Has that happened?"

"Sadly, yes. It was a mess."

"Oh," I managed to respond.

After the doors locked, I followed him through a maze of corridors. The church had an old-fashioned house attached to it with a colonial dining room and a somewhat modern kitchen containing shelves that went all the way up to twelve - foot - tall ceilings. The sink was filled with dirty plates and trays. A large window above the sink let in dim rays of light that fell on old newspapers, books and other clutter lining the counters. In the middle of the room stood a large table with a red-checkered plastic tablecloth.

13

Open bottles of jam and a dish of butter, possibly rancid, were clustered in the middle of the table where a thin, grey cat lay on its stomach.

Father Lorenzo maneuvered over towards the coffee pot.

"Coffee?"

"Umm, sure. Well, only if you have sugar," I added.

"Over there on the left counter, behind that dirty pot," said Father Lorenzo, pouring me a cup.

I went over and grabbed the bowl that had an army of ants trailing behind it. I decided that I didn't need sugar, at least, not anymore and pulled a chair up to the table. My fingers stuck to an oily film along the back of a chair as I carried it over. I cringed at the thought of getting oily residue all over my cashmere overcoat, but I sat in it nonetheless.

Father Lorenzo pulled up his own chair, sat down slowly, and began to stroke the cat which now lay sprawled upside down on the table. Then he bit into an English muffin covered with so much jam that it oozed onto his fingers and fell down his shirt. It looked like strawberry jam, though I am not a jam connoisseur. It could have been raspberry.

In between bites he asked, "So, what brings you here?"

"Well, I've been referred to you," I said.

"By whom?"

"By everyone."

"Really?" Father Lorenzo perked up. Some jam had gotten lodged in his beard.

"Anyone who knows anything about this city says that you're brilliant and you have the knowledge to advise me on the best way to accomplish my task."

Father Lorenzo sat back with a slight smile.

"And what task might you have?"

I produced a thick packet of paper from a black leather portfolio concealed in my overcoat, displaying it all proudly on the table. Here was my plan for success with its blank, white sheet for the title page along with plenty of strategies diagrammed with bullet points, pictures, and figures. After reading it, I was sure he would say that it was beautifully done, well thought out, and impressive. In light of his forty years' experience, I trusted he would confirm that my plan was, in fact, foolproof.

Father Lorenzo picked it up and began to flip through its pages. As he read them, his brow would occasionally furrow and then relax. After some time, he tossed the now jam covered packet back to me.

He paused, took a breath and said, "You are an idiot."

I tilted my head but did not respond. How could he have said that? Did he not read the plan? This was so simple. What, I internally raved, could possibly go wrong with renting a house in a dangerous ghetto to live with homeless people? I would invite them into my house and help them get jobs, pulling them right off the corner and giving them a life. Right off the corner! It should have been easy enough. They'd come, they'd shower, they'd eat, they'd sleep, and then they'd find jobs. It was all in the plan! There would be a merit system complete with rewards and punishments, chores and responsibility, goal setting and follow-up. What was so hard about this? Clearly, it was a no-brainer.

"You have no idea who you're dealing with or what you're doing," he said as he eyed my black pinstripe suit, and silk tie.

"I never said I thought it would be easy," I responded, sitting back in my chair.

"I give you two weeks before everything falls apart," said Father Lorenzo.

I remained still, nonplussed by the comment.

15

"Your phone, your fancy clothes, your computer, everything will be destroyed or stolen."

"I'm prepared to take the necessary precautions," I responded.

Father Lorenzo, looking visibly frustrated, slammed his hand on the table and raised his voice.

"When I say everything, I mean you will come home one day and find all the lighting fixtures gone, the wiring ripped away, and the very pipes of your house torn out of the walls."

The cat jumped off the table and ran out of the room. I just stared at the table, shaken by the image in my mind. The walls broken, the house ransacked, the fridge and stove missing -- no, stolen. Everything stolen. The pipes gone, the plumbing sold on the black market. I would find the front door broken, wide-open. No, the front door would be gone, also stolen. The bathroom would be on fire -- no, the whole house would be on fire. Yes, it was possible. Even probable. I'd come home and find it all burning. Everything in ashes.

Father Lorenzo, as though his point had hit home, grabbed the old notepad next to him and began scribbling a list as he spoke.

"This has been tried before, and it's gone very badly for a lot of people. If you were smart, you would take your time, do some research, and live in the city a bit. There's a lot of money being spent to accomplish the same purpose. There are a lot of people doing things in other ways. You should meet them."

He handed me the list when he was finished writing. I glanced over it and saw the names of volunteer organizations scribbled all over the page.

"So, you're saying that my plan will fail?" I asked, filing the list in my portfolio.

"I am saying that things are the way they are for many reasons. You shouldn't think that you can just waltz

16

in and change all of that with the snap of your fingers," he said.

Still, he had not explicitly said "no," so I had heard everything that I needed to hear. Staring into my empty coffee cup, I tilted my head up, looked Father Lorenzo square in the eyes and said, "Well, thank you for the advice."

"Good. Well" -- I was defiant, spurred on by the breadcrumb he'd left me, and I cut him off, declaring, "Unfortunately, the decision has already been made." And with that, I picked up my portfolio and walked out of the church.

As I headed back to work, I couldn't help but wonder if things would have gone better had I dressed down. Maybe if I had worn some jeans and a ratty t-shirt, it would have looked like I knew what I was doing. But I couldn't help it. I worked at a consulting firm where people are expected to wear suits and ties, and I was running late for a meeting.

Later that night, about 15 miles away in the suburbs of Baltimore, in a two-bedroom condo with a bright red door, the smell of sizzling steak wafted through the air. It was a peaceful place, cozy on winter nights and breezy on summer mornings, the kind of place that's relaxing to come home to after a long day's work. Its large master bedroom had plenty of extra space to accommodate the king sized bed, large wooden bureaus, and walk-in closet. It even had some of those nifty electric blinds that opened and shut by remote control. The smaller bedroom, which couldn't fit much more than a futon, had none of these amenities. So it was a good thing that I kept it completely unfurnished. It was in this room that I spent months planning, strategizing, and weighing the risks of the choices I was about to make. The walls were bare, the floor space was uncluttered, leaving nothing to distract me from complete and total focus.

17

The smell of delicious spices filled the living room where a flat screen hung above the fireplace. A mouthwatering scent crept underneath the door of the small bedroom where I lay curled up on a pile of unfolded clothes. I woke up from my evening nap salivating. Drool had run down my chin and had formed a dark pool on my shirt sleeve. After taking a big yawn, I rubbed my brown eyes with balled up fists and scratched my rumbling stomach. Throwing on some mesh shorts, I stood up, patted down my messy brown hair and began hunting for steak.

Emma, one of my housemates, busily added seasoning to the meat in the frying pan.

"Good morning, Matt."

"Good morning to you, too," I responded. It was 6:00 PM.

"So glad you could wake up in time for dinner," she said.

"Well, it's the least I could do," I said, reaching for the frying pan. The steak would be juicy. Tender. It would melt in my mouth and be tummy rubbing delicious. Emma tried to slap my hand away. She missed, and I grabbed a choice piece of steak, a hotter-than-molten-volcanic-magma piece of steak. The grease burned my finger, and I dropped it on the ground. Sir Grady IV, her beloved Brittany spaniel, gobbled it up, and Emma turned on cool water to run my hand under.

"How was your day?" I mumbled from between my fingers.

"It was boring," said Emma.

"Did you do your yoga practice today?" I asked.

"Yes," she said, which started us laughing hysterically.

Last week I had come home early to find Emma in tight spandex lying on the ground sweating while Sir Grady watched from his perch on the couch. His head tilted to the

18

side, confused by the TV where a bunch of scantily clad women and men were all assuming strange positions. Positions I had never seen. All wore spandex while soft, sensual music played in the background. Somewhere between the music and spandex, it dawned on me that I had interrupted an intimate viewing of soft-core pornography in the living room! Mortified, I jumped back outside and slammed the door.

Emma opened the door and put her hands on her hips. It was an exercise tape. An exercise tape? Yes, of course, I knew that.

"So, Matt, when are you getting a bed?" she asked.

"Umm, I'm not sure yet. Soon," I said, shrugging my shoulders. I wasn't in the mood for this conversation.

"Well, at least maybe you should focus on getting a bed or something," she said.

"Yes, I should probably focus on that."

"I mean, you've been here for a couple months now."

"Yeah, yeah, I know," I said in a tired tone.

"I just figured you'd be tired of living out of a bag by now."

Emma had finished preparing dinner and placed the plates down in front of Alex and me as we watched the TV. I plunked down a $5 bill for the food and service. Trained by chefs in a five-star restaurant, Emma prepared excellent dinners, full of flavor and deliciousness.

"You don't have to do that," she said, waving her hand, but I was happy to kick in some cash for a good meal since it was only fair and I was no mooch. In fact, I was a great roommate, filled with appreciation for the services I received, and so I left the money on the table.

After dinner and a few glasses of wine, I took the dirty plates and placed them in the sink and then disappeared into my room. A few minutes later, I emerged clothed in a mud green hoodie and two pairs of baggy grey track pants. On my shoulder hung an old, frayed backpack that weighed down my shoulders. My worn out sneakers made no noise on the hardwood floors as I walked quickly to the front door.

"Where are you going?"

"Out."

"When will you be back?"

"Later," I said before slamming the door shut.

Chapter 2: The Baltimore Mission

Night crept over downtown Baltimore as the temperature dropped below freezing. A group of people huddled on a corner of the financial district and shivered against the back wall of the federal building. Some were talking to each other while others just sat and stared blankly out into the busy streets. Between their coughing, sniffling, scratching and occasional political discussions, they never noticed that they were being watched.

Those in the group saw themselves as separate from all the others. They were unwilling to be identified as part of the "group" and gladly, were not like the others lying next to them. From each of their perspectives, they had nothing in common other than that for tonight they would call the corner home.

They sat under a large roof that protected them from rain and snow. It was conveniently located at the intersection of two major Baltimore streets, making it easy for church groups and kind citizens to drop off food. The area was well lit and provided a sense of security which was conducive to sleeping.

Many built their own bedding by making forts out of cardboard and stuffing them with blankets. The blankets were soft and made for good insulation during the winter months. Sometimes they didn't bother with the forts and would just lie on the cardboard boxes wearing several layers of clothing. They wore socks on their hands when they didn't have gloves and wrapped their worn sneakers in duct tape to cover the holes. It was here on the streets of Baltimore that I learned about the homeless. I observed them, hung out with them, and ate with them.

To their left, out of a dark street corner, I pulled my hood over my face and limped toward them. No, I was not injured. No, I did not have leg cramps, blisters, or pebbles in my shoe. But when I was around them, I limped because it made me look helpless, needy, handicapped. I found that people were always more honest with me when they thought I was worthless. Sometimes I acted aloof or a bit crazy to add to the effect. I carelessly wove in and out of light posts for good measure. Pausing in front of a bench, I watched a homeless man who lay sleeping. Contorted uncomfortably, the man's body found a way to lie around the armrests. Printed across the back slats of the bench, an inscription read, "Baltimore, the Greatest City in America." The homeless man shifted awkwardly, and he started coughing. I kept moving.

As I got closer, I caught Jerry's attention. Jerry stopped arranging his bed and looked up. Waving his hand he called out, "Hey Matt."

Jerry was one of the very few regulars. Everyone else typically stayed on the corner for a few nights before moving on to other places. We talked a lot, and I came to like him and trust him. Black and in his mid fifties, Jerry caught my attention because he was articulate, somewhat healthy, and always up for a conversation, most of which made logical sense. By then, I had known him for almost two months, and I felt like I understood him. I pulled off my hood and stepped into the camp.

"How are you doing tonight?" I asked, extending my arm for a fist pound. Jerry didn't shake hands. Ever. At least, not with me. He was a fan of the fist pound. Loved it. It was cultural, I think.

"I'm doin' just fine. It's mighty cold out," he said, rubbing his hands together.

"Spring is right around the corner," I said, as if the thought might keep us both warm.

Jerry nodded and said, "riiight, riiiight. It's somethin' I'm lookin' forward to."

After months of hanging out with him, I had pieced together some semblance of his life. He had done many things and accomplished a lot more than I had expected. He was the husband to a wife and a father to a child, whom he loved very much, though he spoke of them rarely. He used to own and manage his own hardware store. He enjoyed it, but family came first. To provide for his son – I think it was his son, I'm not sure – he had to start work at a real job with a steady paycheck. He found this *real job* on the assembly line of an auto factory in Georgia. As luck would have it, he became ill and had to spend three months in the hospital. After release from the hospital, he got fired and struggled to find other work. Soon he lost his house and his family with it. Unable to find permanent work, the bills piled up, and he eventually found himself on the streets of Baltimore trying to stay warm. It has been almost three years since he became homeless. I was not sure how he got from Georgia to Maryland, but then again, there were a lot of things I didn't know.

"What've you been up to, Matt?"

"Just getting to know the city," I answered.

"I've been aroun' these parts for some time now. Yo, be sure tuh ask me any questions ya got 'bout things."

I nodded and leaned my back against a wall. I took a red ball out of my pocket and started bouncing it against the ground.

"Well, actually I do have a question for ya," I said, focusing on the red ball.

"I'm listenin'," said Jerry as he pulled out a half smoked cigarette from his pocket.

"Yesterday I stumbled into an area with tons of blue flashing lights. They seemed unusual."

"Blue lights?"

"Yeah, blinking lights on the top of telephone poles."

Jerry's face flashed with recognition and then scrunched together as if he were in pain.

"No, no." Shaking his head back and forth, he repeated, "That ain't good."

"What?" I asked.

"You shouldn't go there."

"Why not?"

"Because."

"Because what?"

"Because them lights are dangerous."

"Dangerous?"

"If you seem 'em, you need to leave." He spoke in a very matter-of-fact way., "You'll get shot, stabbed, and if not, then the cops will arrest you just for being there."

"So they're bad areas?" I asked.

I didn't like the sound of this. If this was true, then I had completely underestimated the danger of those neighborhoods.

"Riiight, riiight. It's a bad idea to be around those places."

"Why do you say that cops would arrest me? That doesn't make any sense, and I don't even think it's legal."

"Them lights are in places so infested with drugs and crime and prostitutes, yuh can only be there for bad stuff. Just last week they did a raid on one of 'em neighborhoods and arrested 30 people."

"Huh."

"Whatcha doin there anyways?" Jerry asked.

"I dunno."

"You crazy or somethin?"

"Naah, I was just exploring."

"Exploring?"

"Yeah, exploring."

"Do me a favor next time."

"What?"

"Next time you go explorin', give me a holla so I can slap you upside the head," he said.

It was oddly moving to see Jerry's paternal nature coming out. Just two months ago we had been complete strangers, and now I felt like he cared about my well being. I began to realize that we weren't strangers anymore.

It was freezing out, and my teeth started to chatter. Jerry rummaged through his duffle bag until he found an extra pair of mismatched mittens. I helped him fit them over the gloves he was already wearing. It was cold, and I thought I could feel the blood in my hands start to crystallize. Next time would be different. I would bring gloves, a scarf, and maybe a hat. A warm hat, the kind with the fuzzy ear warmers and --

"Ya bring that good cheese I like?" shouted someone under a blanket.

"Howard?"

"Yesss sir, brotha," he said, emerging from a pile of blankets and flattened cardboard. I smiled, still bouncing my red ball. I didn't even know where I had gotten this ball. Where did I find it? It was just in my pocket as if it appeared out of thin air.

"How are you doin?"

"It's goin', yuh know. It ain't too bad and ain't too great."

"Well, which is it?"

"I reckon it's right down the middle," he said.

"Gotcha."

"Say, Matt, did you check out any of those other places?" asked Jerry.

"Yup, but it doesn't matter anymore."

"Why?"

"Because I've already found one that I like."

"What's this? A place for us to live?" Howard asked.

"Maybe."

"You should check the church across the street. I know they have an empty basement and I think some showers."

"Nah, I've already got things moving on the other one."

"Really?"

I nodded and then asked, "Say, did that van of church people come by yet today?"

"Uh huh. They were lookin' for ya. They came last week, said you wanted to drive around with them, or somethin," said Jerry.

"Damn it!" I slammed the ball on the ground. It rocketed into oblivion. Space. Outer space. I would never see it again.

I was tired of methodical wandering, hoping to stumble across the city's homeless camps. This church group delivered homemade soup to all the camps. They even delivered food to the homeless in the woods and abandoned industrial parks. They had a van, food, connections, and the locations of all the big camp sites. It was a match made in heaven, yet somehow I had missed them for the second week in a row.

"Yo, ya still have time to catch the mission shelter. They close their doors in ten minutes," said Jerry.

"Do you think I could make it?" I pleaded, as if Jerry had the power to control time.

Jerry scratched his head, "Well it's almost fifteen blocks away. I guess you could...

Before Jerry could finish, I had already taken off running. Jerry flailed his arms and shouted, "I haven't even told you where it is yet!" But I just kept running. I was a machine, a running machine, faster than the wind. I was not even tired. Not only was I going to make it, but I was going to be early.

I already knew where I was going because I had been there before. In fact, I had been there last week; but when I had approached the door, it was too late. I'd had the door slammed in my face. I wasn't even inside the building and then I was asked to leave the stoop. The stoop! That's how I learned that they were very particular about their schedule.

Sprinting down the sidewalks, I ran faster with each step, weaving in and out of benches and bus stops. I was a cheetah, an exotic African cheetah that ran really fast. Refusing to be late again, my hood flapping behind my head, it might have ripped off. Good. It was dead weight anyway and it was holding me back. I sprinted through the cold, frigid air. Rapidly wiping my runny nose, I jumped over a bench, a tall bench, but I cleared it. I turned into an alleyway.

Breathing heavily, I stopped outside the homeless mission and found that the shortcut had worked. The doors were still open, and an old lady in a bright red uniform greeted a line of homeless people as they hobbled into the building. The lady was ancient. She couldn't have been less than 90 years old or more than four feet tall. Wrinkles covered her pale white face, and she looked very frail. She was barely able to stand on her own. I pulled my hood over my head and filed in right behind the homeless under her strict supervision.

"Hello, dear," said the woman.

"Hello," I said, accidentally towering over her.

"I've never seen you around. Will you be in the area for a while?"

"Oh, err...um, I'm just passing through," I said, avoiding eye contact.

My goal was to be invisible, and the last thing I wanted was to be remembered. I needed to distance myself from her before she asked any more questions. It was important that I fit in and observe things in their natural state.

"Well, welcome anyway," she said smiling. "Please find a seat, dear. The service will begin in three minutes."

I nodded and shuffled inside. As soon as I made it through the doorway, I wanted to leave. A gust of hot air blasted over my face which soon gave way to the most unbearable stench I had ever smelled. The smell of feces and urine choked me and caught me in the desperate struggle to keep from vomiting. Taking the first seat I could find, I tried to discretely cover my mouth and nose, but it made no difference. The next several minutes were spent battling the impulse to run out the door.

I found it easier to ignore the smell once I saw what was causing it. My eyes widened as I began to absorb the horror of human suffering that lay before me with rows and rows of seats of people sitting in misery. Their tattered clothes were covered in old food stains, dirt, and other filth. Their beards were long and uncombed. Many scratched their mangled hair. Their shoes were worn out and many of the holes had been patched with duct tape. Most wore at least two layers of pants along with muddied jackets.

A teenage girl laid her head on her mother's shoulder as her mother ran her fingers over top of her daughter's matted hair. A large man in his forties wore several layers of mismatched clothes and a large dirty coat. He sat upright with his head tilted back and quietly mumbled something to himself. To my right, a skinny man with wrinkled and sagging skin rocked back and forth in his chair. One man in the back of the room couldn't stop coughing, not even bothering to cover his mouth. I wanted to chastise him for his lack of manners, but I didn't because it would jeopardize my cover. I could practically see diseases spewing everywhere. Even though he was on the other side of the room, I pressed my sleeve harder against my nose and mouth.

The others were just silent, trying to sleep by curling up on their armrests. There were a few people who sat together, but many were alone. As I looked around, I slouched in my chair and lowered my shoulders. I tried to blend in, but was suddenly self conscious about *not* smelling like feces. Surely someone would catch a whiff of me and be offended. They would know that I washed my clothes with soap, the kind found only in stores. They would know that I had access to toilet paper, and they would whisper to their neighbors, He has toilet paper. Who? That jerk over there! The one that smells like lavender!

At the very back of the room, a bare stage rose above the seating sections. A wooden podium stood in the middle of the stage which was nothing more than a raised section of flooring. Large fluorescent lights reminiscent of hospital lighting exposed the worn out linoleum floor and large tears in the seating.

There was a loud bang as one of the old ladies pounded a large gavel on the podium which caused the homeless man in front of me to bolt up. Soon the moaning died down.

The lady spoke into a microphone. "We are starting now. Please wake up and stop making noise." She adjusted her spectacles and turned a few pages in her hymnal.

"For those of you who don't know me, I am Sister Ann."

She took out a tome of a book and slapped it on the podium.

"Please, open your books to page 164 to "The Love of God."

Her voice boomed from the boxy rectangular speakers on stage. After the sounds of books opening and the ruffling of pages died down, a strange noise started to get louder and louder until it was thundering out of the speakers. I looked around perplexed and decided that the speakers were shorting out. It sounded like a mix between a turkey gobble and the sound a cow makes while giving birth to an unusually large calf.

After hearing this, I concluded with certainty that the speakers were malfunctioning. But then, after noticing a correlation between Sister Ann's hand gestures and the loudness of the noise, I realized the awful truth. Sister Ann was singing. It was abominable and an egregious insult to the authors of hymns everywhere. The terrible squawking stopped only when Sister Ann paused to yell at someone sleeping in the audience. At other times, she would just point, and her nun henchwomen would march over to the transgressor and levy a sharp prodding.

By the time the "hymn" singing ended, I had exhausted myself enduring the miseries of the rotting feces smell and the abominable turkey/cow sound. As everyone began to file out, a short plump man wearing an oversized flannel shirt and two undersized jackets turned around and stared at me.

"You're new here," he said.

I just nodded and began to shift towards the door.

"Do you need directions to a shelter?" asked the man.

"Oh, no, no. I mean, I'm covered for the night, but thanks." I said trying to end the conversation. By the mere fact that this man was speaking to me, I realized that I must have stood out in some way. I pulled my hood tightly over my head to try and disguise my face and avoid being remembered.

"Oh, are yuh jus passing through?" questioned the man as he turned to maneuver towards the door.

"Actually, it seems as if I'm going to be here for a while," I mumbled.

The man gave slight wave of his wrinkled hand and said, "Well, then, see yuh 'round."

Chapter 3: The Beginning of the Adventure

In the early hours of Tuesday morning, the same morning I had left Father Lorenzo, partners of the Firm gathered in the conference room on the top most floor of a concrete and glass skyscraper. Black and white prints framed in cherry wood hung on the walls. The doors had burnished brass handles, and the room's window was not so much a window as a giant wall of glass. From it, one could see all of downtown Baltimore, the tall brick walls of the stadium and the ballpark, and the large yachts bobbing on the glimmering waters of the Inner Harbor.

Six senior consultants, who had all arrived early, gathered around the mahogany conference table and filled all of the black high backed chairs except for one. Leather portfolios lay neatly in front of each of them who tapped and twirled luxurious gold and silver pens. At this particular meeting, everyone was paying a considerable amount of attention. Our region had just received a new regional president, Lucius Muccino, who had called a private meeting with the top corporate advisory group, my group, to discuss strategy and transition.

Lucius was an intimidating fellow with slicked silver hair and a thick Pittsburgh accent. Dressed to the nines in a pinstriped suit and Italian leather shoes, he had impeccable posture. He was rumored to spend his free time power lifting and training in hand- to- hand combat. Words flowed out of his mouth articulately, yet simply, as he laid out his well-crafted plan for success and growth in the Baltimore market. The strategy stressed discipline and hard work as keys to success.

Meanwhile, ten floors down, I tapped my foot, impatiently waiting for the elevator. Nervously, I looked down at my watch. Father Lorenzo's meeting had run longer than I had expected. "I hate being late," I said under my breath, as I tightened my tie. Checking my reflection in the chrome elevator door, I brushed off some half melted snowflakes from my suit. Why did I walk back? That was a bad decision because now I was late for one of the most important meetings of the year.

The elevator arrived and slowly carried me up to the top floor. Once it stopped, I pushed against the doors to get out faster. Squeezing through the not yet open doors, I walked briskly towards the boardroom, trying to make as little noise as possible, but the black marble floors clicked and clacked beneath my wooden soles. I put my hand on the cold brass handle, took a deep breath, and entered the room.

As soon as I entered, Lucius went silent, and then the entire room turned and stared at me. Time stood still. This was very, very bad. I realized I might be fired right on the spot. I could even be killed. Well, not killed, but definitely fired, and then I would have to live on the streets with Jerry, who would have to teach me how to forage for food in dumpsters. We would have to gather cardboard for bedding, and I worried that I might not be able to handle it. I would freeze to death or starve before I froze. Mom and Dad would kill me if, somehow, I didn't starve or freeze. They would use chainsaws and --

A tall slender man sitting at the other end of the conference table broke the silence.

"Bjonerud, you're late!"

That man was Carlyle L. Mansfield, Jr. He ran the entire corporate division for the Maryland region of the Firm and was my direct supervisor. I was still standing in the doorway as his voice pierced my soul and beads of sweat clung to my forehead. Frantically, I searched my mind for some semblance of an excuse that would put me in a good light and help everyone understand why I was late.

"I'm sorry, sir, but I wanted to make a good first impression for our new president," I said with feigned confidence. After my comment dead panned, Lucius just stared and waited in silence for me to sit down. He readjusted his spectacles and continued on in a stern voice.

"As I was saying, your team is strong, and this market has a lot of potential. I know in the past you've been an outstanding reactive Firm, but the future lies in being proactive. We need to anticipate our clients' needs and exceed their expectations," he said, pounding the table. I know these plans sound simple and basic to you, but I believe the fundamentals have to be mastered before we can delve into more complex goals. Perhaps we can start with punctuality?" he said, looking over at me. I gulped and sank down in my seat.

"Carlyle, I'll leave those decisions to you," he said, pushing in his chair before he left. I was worried that Carlyle might chastise me for being late, but instead he got up and followed closely behind Lucius. A situation like this would have bothered me incessantly because I would have seen it as damaging to my developing reputation; however, I couldn't care because at the time I was focused on much bigger problems.

In the suburbs of Baltimore, I had just gotten back into the Columbia condo when I looked at the clock. It was almost 8 P.M. Emma was hanging out on the couch watching an episode of "Friends." She looked comfortable and made me jealous because I knew that tonight the last thing I was going to be was warm and cozy.

"You gonna watch this?" she asked. "I just made some popcorn, too."

"Nah, I'm okay."

I walked into my room and shut the door. Immediately I tore through the clothes pile looking for my hoodie. All the while, I continually flipped glances toward my phone. I was cutting it pretty close. I should have left earlier. I threw on my grey track pants, dirty sneakers, and a worn brown leather bomber jacket. Dragging a small duffle bag behind me, I made my way out of the condo.

"I'll be back in a few," I said, slamming the door shut.

The moon hung low in the sky, and my breath turned into silver clouds against the porch light. I walked down the concrete steps into the chilly, dark night. After I had taken only a few steps outside, the phone in my jacket started to vibrate. I dropped my bag and frantically fumbled around in my pockets trying to grab the phone. Stupid pockets. After a few more frustrating seconds, I yanked it out and saw that I had received a text message from an unknown number:

Meet me in Chinatown in one hour. I'll be waiting in an unmarked cruiser. Near the newspaper stands.

I just stopped and stared into my phone. My heart beat faster as I realized that tonight everything was going to change. There was no turning back now.

An hour later, I emerged from the Chinatown/Gallery Place metro stop. Bent over the escalators, I panted heavily from my run through the station. Around the back of the block, I found the newspaper stands but no unmarked cruiser. I figured that I had mixed up the directions and had somehow arrived at the wrong Chinatown. How many Chinatowns were there? I should have asked someone, but I wouldn't because I was a guy. A man! I wouldn't ask for directions because that was weak and men were strong. Guys always knew where they were, and so instead of worrying about Chinatowns, I decided to inspect the newspaper stands because they looked as though they needed inspecting.

Ten minutes later, a plain white car showed up on the street corner. It bounced around as its passengers shifted in the back seat. The driver was a big husky guy with a buzzed haircut. He was young and wore a large black t-shirt with the word POLICE written across his chest. Stepping out of his car, he walked over toward me with an outstretched hand.

I remembered how the week before he had practically gotten down on his hands and knees to thank me for renting his house. He thanked me for not having a criminal record, for having a good credit score, and for being normal. He said it was too good to be true. I was stunned that he had missed it. Didn't he know? Things that were too good to be true usually *were* too good to be true, but I wasn't going to tell him that. I gambled that by the time he figured it out, it would be too late.

"Dick, good to see you," I said.

"Sorry about the lateness."

"Not a problem."

"Would have been here sooner, but I was dealing with a burglary."

He tapped on the back window as the people in the back seats glared out at us. They looked really angry and then started to struggle. It looked like they were handcuffed, but I couldn't tell for sure. I silently gulped and hoped that I would not end up like them.

"Are those criminals?"

"Umm, I guess that's for the courts to decide," he said, shrugging, " but if I were the jury, they'd be in jail for a long, long time."

"So you like being a cop?" I asked.

"It pays the bills."

"I bet it's exciting."

"You have no idea."

"I figured."

"Good, good. Well, I won't take up anymore of your time," said Dick, slapping the case down on the top of the trunk. He pulled out a packet of about twenty pages saying, "I need you to sign here, here, and here."

I scanned through the documents as best I could, not that it mattered. There were too many pages, and I was not a lawyer, but I read as fast as possible to make it seem as though I knew what I was doing.

"Oh, and remember what we talked about at the place," said Dick. "Don't ever cross me."

"Right, right. You'll beat my ass, break my legs, and then throw me out in the street," I said, still flipping through the pages.

"You bet I will. I don't mean to be harsh, but it's the only way to get things done."

"You'll get your rent money. You can count on that," I said.

"Remember not to wear any iPods outside of the house. Also, the bars I put on the back windows will be useless if you don't lock the doors."

"So I've been told," I said, still flipping through pages.

"Your first day will be in two weeks, on February first."

"Great."

"Very good. Well, sign here, and I'll have a copy of this brought over to you," said Dick, pointing to the end of the page.

It was time. I took a deep breath, clicked the top of my pen, and signed on the dotted line. He smiled, ripped the contract out of my hands and inspected the signature before stuffing it into his briefcase.

Chapter 4: Disguises

A handful of cars sped by me along Interstate 95 as I was on my way back from dropping off the moving truck. My arms and back were sore, but at least all of the boxes and furniture were safely inside my new house. Baltimore's pointed skyline grew taller and taller, extending into the low hanging cloud puffs. Blue patches reflected brightly off of the shiny skyscraper windows, and the top parts of ships docked at the harbor could just barely be seen. I was distracted by the views, and my car drifted to the side, hitting the rumble strip. I needed to turn, but cars were everywhere. I looked out my side window and found a hole in the traffic, though it was a small hole, and I doubted that it was big enough for me to fit through. Surely the cars would make room, but what if they didn't? No time. Accelerating amidst beeps and middle fingers, I swerved across three lanes of traffic, threaded the needle, and made my exit.

The skyline quickly disappeared as I descended down the off-ramp into a very different scene. The trashy rowhouses of West Baltimore lined the streets, all with grey muted exteriors. Many of the houses had boarded up windows, and some were just shells of the houses they used to be. One house had only three walls and needed makeshift buttresses to remain standing. The rotting buttresses extended into the street and blocked off the sidewalk. The place was a dump.

Newspapers, plastic wrappers, and other assorted trash blew in the wind as cars whizzed by. The garbage congregated by the storm drains causing the drains to flood during heavy rain. A white plastic bag from one of these piles caught the wind and swirled through the air while some kids on motorbikes zoomed down the street. The lead kid wore a bright red bandana instead of a helmet, and none of his cronies were much older than fourteen. Those sitting on the stoops turned their heads toward the loud motor rumblings just in time to see the last kid pop a wheelie. He held out his tattoo-covered hand to try and grab the plastic bag but missed. The bag got stuck on the antenna of one of the old beat-up cars parked along the side of the street.

A light ahead turned red, and I slammed on my brakes and screeched to a halt directly underneath a flashing blue strobe light affixed to a telephone pole. It was one of the flashing lights that Jerry had warned me about. I locked my doors.

There was a bar on the corner that served as a local watering hole for the neighborhood. Outside the bar, a man, probably a regular, lay hunched over on the sidewalk. He clutched a liquor bottle wrapped in a brown paper bag. All I could make out was what was left of his long oily hair draped in front of his pale, wrinkled face. He took a few big gulps from the bag while a few men in oversized plain white t-shirts argued in the street. I relocked my doors and desperately pretended to look bored by twiddling my thumbs and yawning in an exaggerated fashion.

An overweight woman in her 40's stood out on the corner ignoring the commotion behind her. She wore an extremely mini mini skirt and a tight Orioles t-shirt. Her shirt was so tight, I wondered if it would be easier if she were to just paint it on. She stared into the windows of the cars driving by and winked at me through my windshield before walking over to my car.

I ignored her wink, re-relocked my doors, and pretended not to see her. *Be cool, Matt. Just be cool. Look away. No, pretend you didn't see her. Maybe she'll go awa---*

GREEN! I sped through the light and became very thankful that my house was only two blocks down the street.

Normally nobody would be outside during the winter, but this was a particularly warm February day. The stoops on this street were crowded with White, Black, and Hispanic families hanging out and smoking their cigarettes, and their children recklessly chased each other up and down the streets. They were spitting images of their parents, the boys with their tattoos and long hair, the girls with face piercings and makeup. A few gave me mean stares, but this time I remembered that my doors were locked.

The contrast from the poor and rich parts of the city reminded me of the differences between the various floors of the Firm. Over at my office, the fifth floor, known as the bowels of the Firm, had nothing on the black marble and mahogany finishes of the 21st floor. Filled with armies of blue cubes, the fifth floor, my floor, was where the analytics group underwrote all the analysis for the Maryland region. The worn carpets with frayed edges ran underneath an eighties era desk piled high with my papers and files. If one was lucky enough to have a window, which I was not, the views were only of other buildings, most of them ugly. For my co-workers, there was nothing redeeming about this floor, but I liked it. Concentrating on work was easier in this environment, and I didn't feel like I was on show or on parade like the other floors. To me it was comfortable and it was quiet.

I walked down the corridor, took a left turn into my section of cubicles, hung my pinstriped coat on its hook, and carefully sat in my swivel chair. It was covered in cheap fabric, which was great because I didn't have to worry about spilling anything on it. It was a crappy chair, and no one cared about it. Leftover Chinese noodles? No problem. A bottle of white out? Great. Dunkin Donuts coffee with vanilla-and-toasted- almond syrup? Brilliant. It would smell like toasted almonds and vanilla and co-workers would ask, "What is that wonderful scent?"

"Who's Febreeze is that?"

"Is that vanilla wafers I smell?"

I would answer, "No, no, that's just my chair."

I loved that chair. Slowly spinning in my chair, I considered the things that needed to be completed for the day: risk ratings, portfolio reviews, and offerings. Some of this work was beyond my training level and my experience level, but I never said a word. I figured that I could learn by reading every policy and studying all historical offerings in their entirety. I would spend hours reverse engineering past calculations until I figured them out.

The blue walls surrounding me were offensively dull, and when I first moved down, I tried to spruce up the place by sticking up post-it notes with windows drawn on them. I powered my laptop on and like clockwork a handful of paper clips came flying over the wall. Things like this happened all the time. I didn't even need to ask. I already knew it was Jacob Fox, one of the younger analysts. He frequently initiated work battles and enlisted spare office supplies in his efforts. Sometimes it was funny, and other times it was annoying. Jacob appeared in my cube and found me pulling paper clips out of my keyboard and my hair.

"You meet the new guy yet?" asked Fox.

"No, not yet."

"I'm glad they hired him. We need more hands around here," he said.

"Yeah, we do."

"And you're only here for a year or so, right?"

"Yup."

"Does it feel weird to do analytics when you were hired for sales?"

"Feel weird?"

"I mean, these are two opposite sides of the Firm. They're completely different worlds," he explained.

"Carlyle said that I needed to know how all this stuff works."

"Yeah, it's fundamental," nodded Fox.

"Fundamental or not, I couldn't take doing this forever," I said, expecting Fox to concur.

"Well, I could," he said dreamily.

Analytics forever? I could never do it. Too much number crunching and too many spreadsheets. It was good that Jacob liked it so people like me didn't have to. Sometimes I wondered if I'd make it through the week, much less a whole year, which was what my manager assigned to me. From what I could see, the sales job was to bring in new customers and generate new business while the analytics role was to deliver value adding analysis to the customer. Sometimes the sales side would fight to onboard customers who might not necessarily benefit from the Firm's select expertise. Often times both sides butted heads which could make getting deals done a bit challenging.

As an institution, the Firm found that salesmen with analytical experience were extremely successful. They could competently navigate both internal politics and Firm policies, and Carlyle stressed that it was important for me to understand how each side worked. He asked me to get into their shoes and understand their thinking because I needed to know what made them tick. So like a covert spy operation, they sent me behind enemy lines to live and breathe analytics.

Back over in the ghetto, I drove around and tried to find a parking spot. Before I signed the lease, my landlord, Dick the cop, told me not to park in or near the neighborhood because "It's only a matter of time before they steal your car." Then he looked me in the face and emphatically said, "Using the club will only slow them down."

I reminded him that his ad clearly said the house came with parking, but he just shrugged. The scariest part was that I didn't even know how my auto insurance would handle this matter. Would they pay me for the whole car? Would they give me another car? Would it be the same color? I couldn't be sure though I figured that it might be a relief if it did get stolen because then I wouldn't need to bother hiding it.

Pulling over into a back alley, I stashed my car behind a dumpster away from the sight of the neighbors. This place would have to do for now until I could find a safer hiding spot. It was important that no one know that I owned this brand new shiny black Acura with leather seats and a kick-ass navigation unit or else I might be seen as "wealthy." Appearing poor and needy was the best way to avoid muggings, robberies, and other violent crimes. To me, it was of absolute importance to do everything possible to hide in plain sight lest I subject myself to unnecessary risk.

It took a few seconds to fish the right keys out of my pocket, but I found them. Quickly unlocking the front door, I slammed and bolted it shut behind me and took a deep breath. I tried to talk myself into relaxing: *That wasn't so hard, see?* I was still alive and was neither assaulted, battered nor mugged. My nervous breathing relaxed as I realized that with a little practice, some tattoos, and a drinking problem, I'd be able to fit in just fine. I slouched against the door and slid my back down until I sat on the ground. There was a lot of work to be done, I thought, as I gazed into the living room filled with piles of unopened boxes and disassembled furniture.

The house was relatively small as far as houses go but relatively large for one person. The drawbacks of the neighborhood made this place surprisingly affordable but, unfortunately, not affordable enough for me. Car payments, insurance, food, gas, and utilities made it impossible for me to afford much of anything those days, but at least I had known these expenses were coming and had spent months saving for them.

Flicking on the light, I leaned back against the door as the ceiling fan above me spun slowly, occasionally squeaking. The carpet on the stairs almost glistened with newness, probably because it was, in fact, brand new. Before signing the contract, I demanded that all the carpets be replaced, much to the dismay of the landlord.

"Yes, I want *all* carpets replaced," I told him.

He complained that he had just had them shampooed, but I didn't care. They needed to be replaced. The old ones were horrible and so unbearably dirty that even after getting shampooed, they violated health codes. Finally, he agreed to replace them, but he raised the rent to compensate himself for effort. I agreed. Maybe I couldn't afford a safer location, but I could damn well pay for new carpets! The rent hike was well worth it because now I had a house I could take pride in. It was a house I would be happy to offer to someone in need.

A lot of things came together to make this progress, and the smell of fresh carpet helped the reality sink in. It was only natural that I got a bit sentimental. Maneuvering through the boxes, I made my way into an empty dining room and stood for a few minutes just staring at everything, trying to take it all in. Walking over to the exposed brick wall, I ran my fingers along it, feeling the rough edges of the bricks and the smooth gobs of uneven mortar. This was going to be my house for the next year. My house. To offer to whomever I pleased.

I turned on a few more lights and climbed the steep and narrow stairway that awkwardly split the living room from the dining room. The stairs led to the upstairs hallway which was the width of a shoebox and stretched the length of the house. Along the corridor were three doors that opened up to three small rooms: a master bedroom and two smaller windowless bedrooms. I sat on the top stair; and from my perch, I could see the whole first level of the house. Then I shut my eyes and conjured up the vision that had led me there in the first place.

Jerry and Howard lounged on the couch in the living room. They laughed boisterously at the television, and I noticed that their appearance had changed dramatically from the park. No longer wearing rags and tattered clothing, they now wore new pants and stain-free sweaters. Their faces were cleanly shaven. Dignity had returned to their postures, and life had come back into their eyes.

The smell of slow cooked beef wafted through the air, as someone set up for dinner. I heard loud clanging and clinking sounds as plates, knives, forks, fresh bread, and glasses found their way to the table. Stubby candles cast dancing shadows along the brick walls as feet scurried rapidly around the kitchen. I imagined someone carefully flipping steaks, draining noodles, and stirring sauces as if they understood what living in that house meant and cherished each moment of it. Even as I sat all the way upstairs, the heat from the oven warmed my face. In the living room, Jerry and Howard looked at each other, smiled, and then pulled themselves away from the television to help with the hustle and bustle in the kitchen. This dinner was no ordinary dinner but would be one of the last ones they would all share as housemates. They had worked hard, formed friendships, found jobs, and helped each other change their lives forever.

My conscience told me that this dream was nothing more than fantasy. Logic demanded that I not allow this dream to continue and that instead I should have probably tried to think of other things, real things, possible things. But it was not just a daydream; it was a goal. Regardless of the probability of reaching it, the vision was significant because it pointed the way to success and guided me like a compass. I could test my decisions and strategies against this goal and make adjustments accordingly. Yet this ideal and vision were not the only ideologies that guided my actions, but rather it was something else entirely. Something bigger, much bigger.

I have found that too often love is reduced to a feeling, as if it were *just* another human emotion. Family and friends extend trust and friendship to each other, a constant reminder of each person's worth, each person's dignity. Most can think of at least four people who love them and whom they love. Even the truly lonely can think of at least one or two, maybe a child, a parent, a brother or sister, a best friend. When you're sick, they're the ones that remain beside your hospital bed after everyone else has left; they travel thousands of miles to visit when you're alone in a new city; they're the first to congratulate you on your big promotion; and when you lose your job, they're the ones that take you in. In a world full of people trying to cut each other down, they always have your back.

The homeless have no one. More alone than the most lonely among us, they are the butt of jokes, the laughingstock of the city. Each day they cry out for help, and each day their cry falls on deaf ears. Every unopened wallet says – hopeless; every averted glance says – worthless. Anger, fear, sadness, and joy are emotions that come and go, but love is supposed to be constant, unwavering. Love is a feeling, but not *just* a feeling or an emotion, love is also a choice. This clarification was extremely important to me because it meant that my actions would not be bound to my feelings, which were always fleeting. I needed this ideology to guide me through the many dark times that were inevitable on a mission such as mine.

My mission was to bear witness to the truth, at all costs. The truth that, homeless or not, successful or not, deserving or not, all people, because of their humanity, should be treated with dignity. Despite my idealistic tendencies, I realized that communicating this truth could be quite dangerous. Battery, assault, muggings, and even murder were a constant threat in a neighborhood overrun with drug addicts and drug dealers. So I prepared myself and took precautions. All unnecessary risks needed to be eliminated, but sadly, I had no martial arts training and so I was forced to develop other methods of defense.

More powerful than any real gun, stun gun, pepper spray, and more effective than body armor was a strategy that no perpetrator would ever anticipate. The strategy, simply put, was to give them everything they asked for. Furthermore, I intended to smile when I did it. Of course, for this plan to be truly effective, I needed to enlist the help of three secret weapons:

(1) - A Nokia cell phone, which three years ago was damaged beyond repair by a teething German shepherd (my iPhone would be locked in a drawer at work.);

(2) An old leather wallet which would be stuffed with cardboard credit cards and a single ten-dollar bill, would serve as a credible decoy; and

(3) Specially designed sandals that opened up into wallets, where my real credit cards and cash would be hidden.

I felt confident that I could avoid most neighborhood dangers armed with these tools, but I still needed to hide my car. Paying rent for a large house left me unable to afford a downtown parking spot so I had to look for free alternatives. After hours of exploring around the outskirts of town and searching online parking websites, I finally found the perfect spot at the Patapsco light rail station which was surrounded by industrial parks. It was in the middle of nowhere and yet, somehow, it was less than thirty minutes away from downtown Baltimore.

I sat on a cold metal bench at the Patapsco station and tugged at my sleeves flowing out from underneath my bomber jacket. My teeth started chattering, and my pants did nothing to prevent the cold from numbing my legs. I looked out over the almost empty parking lot and glanced at the lone police car watching over the station. My car, parked in the corner of the lot, was brand new, powerful, and awesome even though it was covered from wheel to roof in dirt and grime. It hadn't been to a car wash in months purposefully in an effort to hide its new-car shine. One time a few weeks prior, my dad noticed how dirty it had gotten and decided to do me a favor. He unraveled the garden hose and prepared to wash and polish it while I was upstairs taking a nap. But as soon as I heard the water switch on, my eyes shot open. Frantically, I scrambled down the stairs, burst out the front door, and before a singled drop hit my car, I ripped the hose out of his hands. He just stood there with a confused look on his face. I explained to him that he, after working such a long week, didn't need to worry about washing my car when I, who had youth and energy, could take care of it. He shrugged, looked at me funny, and walked back inside.

I knew that if the car had been clean and sparkly, it would have been stolen. Without chrome 22s or tinted windows, it announced to the world that I was *not* a dangerous and powerful drug dealer. Thieves would see the car and instinctively know that I was neither capable of violent revenge nor able to inflict a painful death. Anyone could tell that the car would fetch a good price on the black market, and I was confident that no thief could resist. Surely they would just grand-theft-auto it out of the lot and strip it of all its parts. Various scenarios of this played out in my head. The scenarios involved them taking the car, breaking the windows, stealing the radio, and cutting the leather. After this, I expected them to destroy the rest that couldn't be sold, possibly by setting it on fire, or maybe just driving it into a lake. I wasn't sure. I didn't want any of these things to happen, but there was very little I could do to prevent it. Thieves could be ruthless, especially Baltimore thieves, and the only thing that stood in their way was this lone cop in the parking lot. He was my only hope, and I knew he would save my car or, at least, prevent it from being set on fire.

A light-rail train crunched to a halt on the tracks in front of me, and I got on. The seats were sporadically filled with passengers that looked like thugs or hoodlums. Normally I would have felt nervous or threatened coming across these people in an enclosed space, but they looked so lifeless and sad that I didn't feel the slightest bit afraid. I think it was because I came across them in a well lit train car instead of some dark alley. Grateful for the florescent lights, I took a seat next to the door as far away from everyone else and as close to the exit as possible. I stretched out on the bench and tried to rest up for the unpacking of my house.

The light-rail trip should have only taken 30 minutes, but that estimate didn't account for my innate ability to disorient myself, which added an hour or so to the commute time. Shaking my head, I opened the door and stepped inside where I found a giant pile of disassembled furniture and brown boxes waiting for me in the living room. The stacks blocked my way to the stairs and kitchen. It was a mess and I really wished I had someone to help me, but there was no one.

After a few hours of non-stop unpacking, sorting, building, and rearranging, I threw my exhausted self onto the couch in the living room where I noticed dust on the T.V. screen. I wiped it off and, out of curiosity, I pushed the knobby power button. I flipped channels but still got nothing but salt and pepper static, which I decided, was a good thing. At least now I wouldn't have to worry about my future roommates turning into couch potatoes, which was the last thing I wanted to happen.

Staring into the screen, I allowed the television's static noise to fill the room and thought about how it had been three weeks since I was last at the homeless camp. I worried that things may have changed. Maybe Jerry, the only one I trusted, had moved to another camp or left town altogether. It could have happened. The homeless are known to be transient. And if it did happen, then I would be reduced to asking random people on the corner. Even I knew this was bad. It was a terrible idea and a sure way to get myself killed. Before starting this adventure, I was sure to research the population by reading census reports, homeless agency reports, and other reports. Using various statistics, I calculated the following probabilities about my future roommates:

There was a 40 percent chance they would be mentally challenged;

A 35 percent chance they would be addicted to alcohol;

A 45 percent chance they would be addicted to drugs;

A good chance they were a convict;

And a better chance they were psychotic.

The chance that I'd get a drug-addicted-crazy-psychopathic-murderous-bi-polar convict as my future roommate was 100 percent. Any other possibility was unimaginable. The math had been done and the numbers double checked. Jerry needed to be there; everything depended on it.

Growling noises rumbled from my stomach, and I realized that it was almost 11:00 P.M. Unfortunately, my stupid fridge was completely empty. Opening every box in the kitchen, I found only a bag of dried rice, various spices, and two tubes of cake icing. This was terrible. There was no food, and I felt like I was going to starve, perhaps even to death. Should I go to the store? No, no, it was much too dangerous and it was dark and late, the worst combination.

Not only that, but I secretly worried that the neighbors were waiting for me to leave the house. Obviously, they would be waiting; and as soon as I left, they would get me. Blood everywhere. On the stairs, on the sidewalk, all over the damn door. It would be a complete mess. I knew that I could not let them win. So I grabbed a tube of icing and held it above my head, opened my mouth, squeezed and began sucking down icing for dinner. Was that weird? Didn't matter. I was too hungry to care.

After a few mouthfuls and a massive sugar high, it was time for bed. I chose the smaller windowless bedroom next to the bathroom because it was quieter and easier to keep warm on those cold February nights. Curling up in my thick blankets, I maneuvered myself right next to a large heat vent. The warm air felt good on my back and helped me to relax. I stretched out and stared up into the pitch black of the windowless room. Lying there in complete darkness, it occurred to me that for the first time in a long time, not one family member, nor friend, nor co-worker knew where I was. It felt strange, really strange. I had felt it a couple of times before but only when I was lost. Not the normal kind of lost, but the scary kind like when lost in the wilderness or in a strange city thousands of miles away from home.

I had only been asleep a few hours when a loud rumbling startled me. My room was black with darkness, and I couldn't see my hand in front of my face. Not sure of where I was, all I knew was that I was afraid and that something wasn't normal. Through my bedroom walls, I could hear drunken people hollering outside in the streets. The extremely loud rumbling shook the house. Groping the walls, I found a switch. Dim, yellow light lit the bare spartan room. I looked for my phone but couldn't find it. Strange, I could have sworn it was right here a moment ago.

Someone started knocking and then pounding on the front door. The pounding stopped, silence followed, and then the front window glass shattered. I went rigid, and then I heard someone stomping around downstairs. What sounded like a second person climbed through the window and landed inside with a thud. Amidst the sounds of plates smashing and furniture breaking, I heard hushed voices and something that sounded like laughter, a malicious laughter. I scrambled to find a phone to call the police. I looked under the bed and in the closet but found nothing. Regretting that I had chosen the room without windows, I frantically searched for some form of defense. Too scared to leave, I threw the mattress off the bed and dislodged a wooden slat from the bed frame. Slamming the lights off, I waited. Within moments the doorknob started jingling. My back pushed up against the back corner, and I gripped the wooden slat so hard that I felt my own heartbeat in my hands. The jingling stopped and was followed by a mighty kick. The knob fell to the ground, broken into pieces, as the door flew open. Two men stood outside the door wielding kitchen knives. The hallway lights cast dramatic shadows distorting their faces, but I recognized them immediately.

"Jerry? Howard? What are you--

Letting out a chorus of deranged laughter, they lunged and attacked.

My eyes burst open. Alone, I sat up as cold sweat dripped off my face. I froze and waited for my lungs to catch up with my heartbeat which was out of control.

Months had been spent meticulously evaluating the risks of my new lifestyle. The dream made the fear real. I felt around the floor and found my cell. I touched a button and the phone became an orb of light in my hands. Squinting, my eyes adjusted, and I could see that it was one o'clock in the morning. The walls briefly shook as motorcycles rumbled past outside. It must have been the motorcycles that woke me up. I felt the door handle and found that it was still intact. I got the wooden slat from under the bed and just sat and listened for a long time. Slowly, sleep took over.

Morning came sooner than I wanted. Groggily, I located my toothbrush, soap, and deodorant before marching into the bathroom. Reflecting on the dream, I took precautions and decided that from then on I would sleep in the room with windows. Sure it would be cold and drafty, but at least I would have an escape route. If threatened, I could jump right out the window. Or maybe, if really in a bind, I could dive out through the glass! Of course, I would do a tuck and roll for a soft landing even though shattered glass would fall around me. Somehow, against all odds, I knew I would be unscathed, much to the frustration of my attackers, who would be angrily waving their fists at me.

After showering and putting on my suit, I inspected myself in the mirror. The white shirt, the silk tie, the black pinstriped suit. No, no, no. This was all wrong. All wrong! This was clearly a wardrobe malfunction. The worst malfunction! I couldn't walk around outside dressed like this. What would the neighbors think? The second I stepped out the door, I'd be stabbed, probably in the leg or the hand. Blood all over my shirt, my bag covered. Leaving me to bleed to death on the stoop, they would run inside and rip the pipes out of the walls and take the electrical wiring. Everything would be stolen and the house would be set ablaze. Luckily, I was meticulous and considered all possible ways that I could be attacked so that I would be ready.

I ran back to my room and dug through a pile of clothes until I found my oversized grey track pants and mud green hooded sweatshirt. I dragged out an old Nike gym bag from under the bed, which had seen better days. Littered with holes, the colors had faded to grayish blue, which made it all the more valuable to me. Quickly, I stuffed my suit coat and leather shoes into it and continued changing. After putting on my second layer of clothes, I pulled a hood over my head and went back to the mirror. Still not perfect so I roughed up my neatly combed hair until it looked like I had spent the night in the gutter.

My fake wallet and fake phone I kept in the front pockets of my second layer (ghetto layer). This way, if I were mugged, I could just turn out my pockets and it would look like I had given them everything I had. I hid my real wallet in my suit pants underneath. Later I would use wallet sandals, but that would have to wait until it got warmer out.

Strapping the bag across my shoulder, I headed out the door into the freezing cold morning. The streets were deserted. Shattered glass from a car window lay on the sidewalk, and the sun glimmered over the roofs of uneven row houses. During my trek to work, I kept constant watch over my surroundings. Crossing over into the next block, I made sure to look through the windows of the parked cars. I glanced down alleyways and scanned the streets ahead for any sign of danger. Luckily, the place was a ghost town. I expected to be held up at gun point at any moment, but I didn't bump into anyone. I concluded that everyone in the ghetto was too drunk or too high to wake up so early in the morning.

Forty minutes later, I arrived at the 21-story skyscraper that housed the headquarters for the Firm's Maryland operations. Pulling the hood tightly over my head, I made sure it hung low over my face. The last thing I needed was to be recognized by a co-worker, or worse, my boss while wearing these trashy clothes.

At first nothing stood out as an ideal changing spot, not even a phone booth. But then, I saw it – a glass rectangular box protruding from the plaza. It was the entrance to an underground parking garage.

At this early hour, the stairwell was crowded with people rushing to work. Everyone was walking up the stairs to get outside, except for me. Annoyed people had to squeeze against the railings to make room for me and my gym bag. Some spilled their coffees and grumbled, but I didn't really care. Scrunched up against the metal banister, I felt like everyone in the city had chosen to park in that garage at the exact same time. Things were challenging enough without hoards of under-caffeinated people swarming all over. I only needed a few moments. Surely there was someplace out of sight where I could change away from these crowds. Diligently walking the perimeters of each level, I found nothing promising. Rows of fluorescent overhead lights reflected brightly off the parked cars, and I found that every level was too well lit and too wide open to be of any use.

After six levels of fruitless searches, I finally found something that just might work. On the last floor, deep underground, an irregularity in the wall caught my eye. I had not noticed it on any of the other floors and walked over to inspect it further. Jutting out against the back corner, it was a concrete outcropping, originally built as a service area for garage maintenance. Exposed pipes lined the sticky dirt covered walls, and grey fluffy cobwebs clung to the ceiling. The white florescent lights ignored the corner, shrouding it in darkness. This was exactly what I needed.

Disappearing into the dark corner, I dropped my gym bag and set to work. *Zip, Zip, Swoosh, Zip, Swoosh.* Thirty seconds later, I looked quite absurd, caught somewhere in-between consultant and homeless man. Part consultant with a bright white shirt and yellow power tie; part homeless man with worn out tennis shoes and grungy track pants. As I reached to pull off my outer pants, the sound of screeching tires made my heart stop. The next thing I knew, a silver Mercedes swerved into a spot directly across from me. Luckily, the car parked just far enough away for me to avoid being spotted.

If wearing a suit to the ghetto was dangerous, then wearing ghetto clothes to the Firm was suicidal. If I did, word of my unconventional clothing choices would spread around the Firm in a matter of hours. Minutes even! Everyone would be wondering why I wore thug clothes over top of my suit. Could I not afford a proper coat? They would probably think I was crazy or messed up, maybe both; and even though I would try to explain everything, I had no proof because I did not yet have a single homeless roommate. The company would have me committed to a mental institution, and I would lose my job. Forever then would I be known as the crazy-guy-who-changes-in-underground-garages-because-he-had-imaginary-homeless-people-living-in-his-house. See how much worse that would be? A reputation could not be replaced like a wallet, and a reputation takes longer to heal than a knife wound. And to lose it would be to lose my livelihood.

Suddenly the white backup lights flashed on. Damn it! What was that guy doing? What was wrong with his original spot? Throwing myself against the wall, I got as flat as possible and tried not to brush my white shirt against the wet grime. The Mercedes backed up directly in front of me until break lights flooded the dark nook with red light. *Okay, Matt. Keep it together. Just breathe slowly. Everything is going to be fine.*

Standing as still as I could, I took large slow breathes. There was no reason for the man to come back towards the nook. The stairs were in the opposite direction, and I felt confident that he was just going to get out and walk toward the stairs. Then I felt the hairs on my skin stand up as the deafening sound of a trunk unlatching cracked into my ear.

Uh- oh. I held my breath and tried not to move. Beads of sweat formed on my nose as I watched a tall man with silver hair step out of the car. The man looked slightly familiar but I couldn't be sure. He seemed distracted, almost angry, as he walked toward the nook. I closed my eyes as if that might lower my chances of getting spotted. The man started digging for something in the trunk. He was so close that I could have reached out and touched him. I felt my face turn red as I came to terms with the inevitable awkwardness. But it was okay. When he saw me, I would just tell him the truth. I would just explain that I was going to live with homeless people and had to wear my hoodie and baggy pants to avoid standing out in the ghetto but that I couldn't wear them to work because we have a dress code. So I had to change secretly in a parking garage because I paid more than I could afford for rent and, therefore, couldn't afford a gym where I could change in a locker room like a normal person. Yeah, right, like he would believe any of that. He would probably think I was going to mug him; and in a panic, he would call the police.

Ripping his briefcase out, the man slammed the trunk down and clicked a button on his remote. The car beeped as the doors locked shut. My foot moved and scraped against the concrete floor. He stood still for a second, as if he heard something, then shook his head, turned around, and walked toward the stairs. Breathing a sigh of relief, I wiped the sweat off my face and finished changing.

Another thirty seconds later I completed my transformation into a consultant, decked out in a black pinstriped suit, shiny leather shoes, and a yellow tie. I looked perfect except for some fresh sweat stains, a minor casualty considering things. I combed my hair back into place with my hands and headed upstairs towards the office.

The revolving door swiveled, and I walked into the main lobby. My shoes made loud echoing sounds as the wooden heels met the hard stone floor. Darkly tinted windows stretched up the full height of the 30-foot lobby keeping it perpetually dim. Several six-foot rectangular glass and iron lamps hung by chains twenty feet overhead. Adjusting my tie knot, I walked toward the mahogany receptionist counter. Polished black marble walls extended far overhead and shot into the grooved concrete ceiling. The receptionists and the security guards exchanged 'good mornings' with me as I walked past. Employees filed into the building from revolving doors on all sides. Holding rolled up newspapers and lunch bags, they waited in small crowds in front of the elevators. Many of them were wearing sneakers, and I noticed one pair looked familiar. Glancing up, I was startled to find Jacob Fox standing right front of me.

"Oh, hey Fox."

He looked down at his own shoes and tried to figure out what I found so interesting.

"You like my kicks?"

"What, err, oh, yeah. They look comfortable. I need to start wearing my sneakers to work," I said.

"Yeah, it makes a difference, especially if you have to walk far. I have a 25-minute walk every morning so these come in handy."

It was good that other people wore sneakers. We both boarded the elevator with the rest of the crowd. Stepping off at the fifth floor, we buzzed through the secure glass doors and trudged off to our cubes.

Seeing the red light on my phone, I dropped my shoulders and let my bag hit the floor with a thud. It wasn't even 8:00 AM and already I had voicemail assignments. I sighed, picked up the receiver, and dialed my password. Immediately I reached for a pen and my notebook.

"Hey, Matt. It's Carlyle. How are the analytics going? I hope you're learning a lot down there. Listen, we need your help on a few projects when you have free time. First...now this shouldn't take up all your time. First, we need you to help out with identifying some top prospects."

I scribbled furiously trying to get everything down.

"Second, we need you to review the progress of all the on-going projects for our division. It's imperative that you make sure they were integrated properly.

"Third... now remember this shouldn't take all of your time. Third, I need a full account of those projects coming up for review in the next six months. Come see me when you get this. I have some packets of information waiting for you on my desk. Bye. Wait, a minute, on second thought —" By now, I had given up scribbling. The message became increasingly interrupted with pauses, which were followed by a repetition of the instructions he had just given. This was definitely another symptom of Carlyle's infamous 'multitasking.' Undoubtedly Carlyle left me this voicemail while simultaneously answering important emails, reviewing morning reports, and checking his Blackberry.

"Just, just, worry first about the prospects. Then when that's completed, come see me and we'll figure out the projected revenues. Okay. See ya."

"Oh, Matt, wait. When doing the projections, make sure to include all business divisions. Just come see me when you have a minute. Okay. Bye."

I hung up the phone and powered up my laptop. There wasn't enough time in the day to get everything done, but I would try. Putting on my earphones, I turned up the volume on my iPod. Diligently working through lunch, I put large dents in several of my assignments. Though I made good progress, my productivity slowed as my mind wandered back to the nightmare. Wondering why the dream bothered me so much, I acknowledged that there was no cause for celebration in break-ins, nor does someone rejoice in an attempted stabbing. But those things were not really bothering me. It was something else. Sighing, I turned off my iPod and rested my hands on the keyboard.

I couldn't get Jerry and Howard's faces out of my head. I couldn't get their laughter out of my ears. There was nothing stopping them from taking advantage of me. They were desperate, and desperation makes people unpredictable. The computer screen went black from inactivity and a small Windows logo bounced from side to side on the computer screen.

I decided that it didn't matter. My actions were exactly that. They were my own, and I was gonna do what I was gonna do, regardless of whether it was appreciated or not; whether anyone becomes changed or not. My hands started typing, and the screen saver disappeared.

Sometime in the early afternoon, the unusual sound of laughter pierced through my headphones. I looked over and saw my cube neighbor, Theresa, with her hand in front of her face giggling. She wore a long skirt, and her braided hair was tied behind her head. She always had some type of candy or pastry at her desk and always made a point to throw some my way. Pulling off my earphones, I felt my face turning red.

"What's so funny?" I asked.

"You were dancing in your seat."

"Oh, are you sure?"

"Also, I think I saw you playing air drums."

"Really?" I asked, a bit embarrassed.

"Just now, or err, you were, but now you stopped. You looked funny."

I admitted, "I'm in a good mood today."

"Did you eat something really good for lunch? What could you be so happy about? We still have another three hours until quitting time."

Theresa was only three years older than I, but she already had four children. There were pictures of them plastered all over her cube walls, her desk, and her computer. For her, five o'clock couldn't come fast enough. All she wanted to do was go home and be with her kids. She loved them a lot. She was a good mom.

"Let's just say it's a long story," I said, smiling, as I turned around back to my computer.

Theresa just rolled her eyes and walked on down towards the water cooler.

Today was the day that I was going to invite Jerry back to my house to live, and I had played it out a hundred times in my head. After months of waiting for it, dreaming about it and preparing for it, containing my excitement was impossible, but I decided it might be best not to get too carried away. I needed to stay off people's radar for a bit, and I couldn't afford any more questions. So I tried to focus and get as much work done as possible.

One of the few young analysts, Bobby Crane, appeared in front of my cube. This was the guy that Jacob Fox had referred to earlier. I had never met him, but I had only seen him once or twice at various office meetings. Fairly tall, his dark brown hair curved up right before it hit his eyes. Smiling, he came around and extended his hand.

"Hi, I'm Bobby Crane."

"Oh, nice to meet you," I said, as we shook hands.

"I'm one of the analysts here," he said, leaning up against the wall.

"Are you new here?" I asked.

"No, I just got back from two months training in Pittsburgh."

"Ahh, got it," I said nodding, "I just got here a few months ago."

"I hear you're moving up to sales soon."

"Yeah, I'm not a spreadsheet guy by nature. Just doing a rotation."

Nodding, Bobby glanced around my cube. His eyes came to rest on the blue gym bag.

"Oh, what gym do you use?" he asked, trying to make friendly conversation.

"Umm, I don't," I said, struggling to throw the bag under my desk.

"Well, then, what's in the bag," asked Bobby furrowing his large eyebrows, "And why are you throwing it under your desk?"

I couldn't believe he was asking me all these things. This was my first introduction to his unfortunately voracious curiosity. Once he detected a defensive answer, he knew he had found a treasure chest of information worthy of prying into.

"Clothes," I said, turning back to my computer.

"Why do you have clothes if you don't belong to a gym?"

"I sometimes go for a run after work."

"You just run around the city?"

"I guess you could say that."

Can't a guy bring his gym bag to work in peace anymore? I needed to distract him or change the subject or something.

"Bobby, I notice that you have sneakers in your cube. Do you belong to a gym? Which one? Do you jog? Are you training for a marathon? Triathlon? No? Why not?"

He got the hint.

"Umm, well, I go to the gym across the street. Speaking of which, I need to head over there now. I'll see ya tomorrow."

Before leaving, he slapped what looked like a photocopy of an enlarged dollar bill down on the desk. I didn't recognize the face on the bill, but I knew enough to know that it was not the face of a president.

"What's this for?" I asked, inspecting the bill.

"It's a Shrute Buck."

"Oh?"

"It's for helping us out down here. If you do more good work, you can expect to see these show up as rewards."

"Thanks."

"No problem," said Bobby. He turned back towards his cube.

"What's the exchange rate between Schrute Bucks and dollars?"

"Not good," said Bobby from across the room, "Not good at all."

Pleased with how successfully I had changed the conversation, I posted the Schrute Buck up on my cube wall next to the post-it-note window.

And with that, I shut down my computer, gathered up my belongings, and made my way towards the parking garage. I joined a flood of employees leaving the building. The elevators took forever as they stopped on almost every floor to pick up more and more people. We crammed into the packed elevator, and a woman's elbow caught me in the side. She had very curly blond hair and wore bright orange shoes to match her neon colored lipstick. I tried to get out of her way and pushed up against the back wall, but it was pointless. Several elbow jabs and a few toe stomps later, the doors finally let us out into the lobby.

Emerging from the lobby's swivel doors, I walked towards the rectangular stairwell entrance. Pigeons milled around in large groups, blocking my way. They were pecking the bricks searching for food. Many of them looked sickly with gaps of feathers on their bodies. A few were missing eyes; one of them had stubs where its toes used to be. Feathers and droppings littered the ground with the rest of their pigeon filth. The birds were diseased and gross. I didn't want them flapping their filth all over me so I lunged at them and sent the entire group flying away.

I waited and let other people pass by so that they could walk down the stairwell before me. Then I stood at the top of the stairs and waited for the sound of footsteps to die down and waited a few more minutes to make sure the stairwell was clear. Scanning the plaza, I couldn't see anyone else approaching the garage entrance and knew it was time. Taking a moment, I considered the significance of what was about to happen and wondered if considering the significance made it less significant. I decided it didn't matter. Adrenaline surged through me as I bolted downstairs. Heading straight for the bottom level, I disappeared into the darkness of the secret nook.

Chapter 5: The Invitation

The Firm ran one of the finest training programs in the world, which schooled us in everything from basic accounting to complicated corporate finance. We learned how to identify operational efficiencies, assess industry risk, and analyze financial statements. Not only did they instruct their employees in finance and operational management but also in the life skills necessary to blend in with the upper crust of society. The program brought in a fashion consultant who tutored us in everything from business casual appropriate clothing, business professional inappropriate clothing, to the difference between scotch and brandy, and the proper times to eat asparagus with ones fingers (whenever it's served without sauce). Over the course of several months, one message was beaten into us – we were the face of the Firm and, whether we liked it or not, we represented the company both day and night. At all times we had to act in a professional and responsible way because that's what was necessary to gain the trust of clients. We gained their trust because we acted like them, looked like them and, therefore, we could relate to them. At least, that was the idea. Though I was never explicitly told those things, I read between the lines. It was clear to me that I could never tell my co-workers about my plan to live with the homeless. It was simply out of the question.

I had not yet told my family where I had moved or even *that* I had moved. But telling them had always been part of the plan, and I was getting closer. They needed to know. But my co-workers did not. There was a place and time for all things, all things except divulging my secret life to the company. I knew that the Firm was a place of conservative professionals. An atmosphere designed for the efficient execution of business. It was a place where everyone conformed to a standard image of success. Dark suits, short hair, and articulate speech marked the up and coming bright stars of corporate America. Good companies successfully provided quality products and services. Great companies standardized their service for exponential growth. The Firm was a great company so it sought to standardize everything. My problem was that standardization came through stringent behavioral policies, which guaranteed that employee actions could be predicted and controlled.

And yet, my decision to house the homeless was based on a value system completely alien to Corporate America. Once my employers saw what they would judge a reckless, unreasonable decision, could they really trust me? Trust me to make responsible decisions at work? Not to mention the implications of hanging out with the scum of Baltimore. I was supposed to be busily infiltrating the business community, not spending all my time hanging out with poor people. What value could that possibly add? What accounts could I possibly bring in? I was hired to be the face of the company, but since when did the Firm dress up in rags and sleep with the homeless? No, this was far too strange to fit into the corporate mold. There was nothing to gain from revealing this at work, nothing at all except alienating my co-workers and losing the trust of my manager.

Sticking out like a sore thumb, I pushed my way through the throngs of suits pouring out of the city skyscrapers. Avoiding co-workers, I cut through narrow back alleys towards the corner where Jerry and Howard slept. I hoped they were still there. Emerging from one of the alleys, I was hit in the face by a blast of cold air. My hood blew off and my eyes watered as they clashed with the frigid temperatures.

Bunching my hands in my sleeves, I tried to keep my fingers from going numb. I came to the corner where Jerry slept and found it empty. No. He couldn't be gone.

He just couldn't be. This was bad. Wait. It was still too early. The sun had just set. Ha ha. Of course, he was never there that early. I would wait and just hang out for a bit because he was *definitely* on his way. I sat on a nearby bench and watched the groups of suits quickly dwindle away until the only people left were occasional stragglers.

Back at the house, everything was arranged for Jerry's homecoming. Brand new blankets, fresh sheets, two big fluffy pillows and a warm comforter covered the bed. The nightstand drawer overflowed with tubes of toothpaste, mouthwash, soap, and sweet smelling shampoo. At the foot of the bed, I had placed new tooth brushes, shower sandals, and a deck of playing cards. New fuzzy towels hung for him next to the shower. For the first time in a long time, everything Jerry used would be brand new. No handouts, no hand- me -downs but new -- wait. He was coming. I saw him coming around the bend, and I knew like clockwork all the pieces were falling into place. He had chosen to come back, and I knew that this was meant to happen.

By the time Jerry showed up, my shivering hands had turned a light shade of blue. After leaning a few large pieces of cardboard up against the wall, Jerry began setting up his bed and started sorting through a pile of thin blankets. I couldn't rush things. My speech would have to be perfect and my delivery flawless. If he was distracted with setting his bed up, then he might not listen. He might not hear what I had to say. And so I waited.

Jerry wore his hair short and had a flat nose, which he frequently wiped. He had strong arms, and I could tell there was still a lot of youth in him. The bag he carried had been reinforced with several strips of duct tape. The wool gloves he wore had special flaps that turned them into mittens. Or maybe it was the other way around. I wasn't really sure which came first, the mittens or the gloves, but I guessed it didn't matter. Either way, I considered them a pretty cool invention.

Disappearing behind a dumpster, he re-emerged with several more pieces of cardboard. Jerry didn't trust anyone with his belongings, ever. It's something that happens after being hurt too many times. Dragging the cardboard and blankets over to his spot, he dropped them on the concrete. Unfolding them, he began to reinforce his bed, but the frigid wind started to pick up again with surprising strength. A large piece of the flimsy board started to get away from him. He fought the wind, but it was too strong and he started to trip over his blankets. Just as it slipped from his fingers, a pair of bare blue hands clamped down on the other side. They were my hands, and they were freezing, but they did the job. We fought the wind, and together we anchored it to the ground.

"Thanks, Matt," said Jerry, extending his fist for a pound.

"How's it goin?"

"Fine, Fine. Still haven't heard anything back from my caseworker."

"Oh?"

"I'll find work soon, though."

Jerry had been saying that for the past couple of months. Maybe that could be his first goal after he moved in.

"I've come here for a couple of months now."

Jerry nodded as he bent down to continue making his bed.

"Tell me again why you guys are out here."

Jerry sighed and said, "I've told ya --."

"I know, a million times, right, but tell me again."

"All we need is a toilet, a warm bed, and a roof over our heads."

"Then what?"

"Then we'll be able to get jobs."

"I've heard of programs providing free housing. Why can't you use those?"

68

Jerry sighed and responded, "Yes, but those are for drug addicts, and you're forced to be in programs all day."

"So?"

"Yuh can't find no jobs stuck in programs all day."

"So there's nothing for people who are just down on their luck? Nothing that you've found that can help you?"

Jerry was standing now having completed his bedding. He nodded in agreement saying, "Riiiiight, riiiiight."

I looked down at the concrete and then slowly I looked back up at Jerry, trying to make eye contact.

"Well, I know of something that could work for you."

Jerry was rummaging through his backpack for something to eat.

"What's that?" asked Jerry, still rummaging.

My lips flashed a quick smile before I said, "Well, there's this house."

"Uh huh?"

"Yes, a big house with three bedrooms."

"And?"

"And one of them, is yours."

Jerry stopped nodding and dropped his bag on the ground. His eyes briefly widened. The wind continued to blow, but neither one of us moved. My voice shook as I felt the weight of the words I was about to say.

"It's cold and lonely, and you don't have to be here anymore."

Jerry stared off into the distance, and his brown eyes darted back and forth. Now that the offer was made, I looked down at the bedding. How much of this stuff would Jerry want to take back to the house? He probably wanted to take all of it. I wondered what would people think when they saw two giant headless balls of trash bags and cardboard stumbling along the sidewalk. Anyone physically standing on the sidewalk would have to walk out into the street just to make room. We would probably attract police attention, and maybe even the landlord. That would be a mess. A very big mess. I laughed to myself as I thought of it and almost missed Jerry's response.

"Thank you, but no thanks."

"What?" I asked.

"No thanks."

"But I thought that this is what you wanted. What do you mean no?" I said, completely perplexed.

"I don't want to."

"You don't want to?"

"No."

"It's cold out. The house is warm."

"I've already made my bed. My bed will be warm once I get in it."

"Don't be ridiculous," I said, staring at the trash heap he called a bed. "There won't be any programs. You can spend your whole day looking for work, but now you get a house and a bathroom. Just like you said you wanted a million times."

Jerry just nodded.

"Winter is almost over. Soon it will be warm out. You don't have to worry about me; about us."

"I'm not charging you rent. Why would you not take this?"

"Because, because it's only temporary."

"Huh?" I said scratching my head, "Well of course it's temporary. That's the whole point. But if you use it properly, it will help you get a permanent job."

"I don't want to get used to a warm house again. Out here ain't bad. What's bad is going from a house to the street. It's that change that is the most miserable thing you can go through."

I just stood, staring.

"Remember, I used to live in a normal house, have a good factory job. At one time, I even had my own shop.

70

Then I got sick and lost everything. The misery of living on the street wore off after a few years. And I can't bear to go through that type of transition again. Now this is my life."

I didn't even know what to say. I know that at some point I felt hot liquid form in my eyes. The finality of what Jerry was saying had sunk in. Dumbstruck, I wondered how I had not seen this coming, not even as a remote possibility. The thought of it had never even entered my mind, and I realized that Father Lorenzo was right. I had no idea what I was doing.

"This doesn't have to be your life," I pleaded.

"Yuh don't understand. After so many years, this is normal."

"This doesn't have to be normal."

"My caseworker's gonna call me back soon. Yuh'll see."

"So what? Use the house in the meantime to find work. Then you can get your own permanent place," I argued.

Jerry sighed and in a resigned tone said, "Aright, aright. How about you give me the address and I come check it out tomorrow."

The nightmares were still too fresh in my mind, and I couldn't bring myself to do it. So instead, I pulled a piece of paper out of my pocket and wrote my cell number on it. I handed Jerry the paper.

"If you ever need a place to stay, then call this number. I'll keep a room open for you."

"Thanks," said Jerry nodding.

I turned around and started to walk toward the light rail stop. I got about four steps before Jerry called out.

"Wait, wait!"

"What?"

I turned around and Jerry took a few steps toward me. Removing the mitten-hybrid gloves from his hands, he then for the first time, shook my hand.

"Thank you."

Chapter 6: 40 Days

"Spare a few coins, miss?"

A homeless beggar singled out a middle-aged woman wearing a red coat. She was in the middle of the crowds emptying out of the local office buildings.

"Um, sorry. Not today."

The beggar had a large beard, a ripped North Face jacket, and dirt- covered work boots. He persistently pursued her through the crowds, much to her dismay. The sun was setting and daylight quickly gave way to darkness.

"Ma'am, c'mon. I need to eat. I don't have any money."

"No, please go, leave me alone," said the woman, gripping her purse tightly.

"C'mon, it's cold. I know you have something. I just need a lil' help."

He continued to follow her as those around cleared out of the way crossing the streets or turning down alleyways. They didn't want to become a target for this man's begging.

"All I want is a few coins, some change. Is that too much for ya?"

He was becoming belligerent and then stood in her way to stop her from walking forward. By now everyone had moved away. The sidewalk was almost completely deserted except for me. I just happened to be there, leaning up against a wall, and I wasn't very happy. My search hadn't been going well; and after being rejected a couple times that night, I was ready to go home. I was taking a quick break as I made up my mind whether to quit for the night or not. Once I saw this guy harassing this woman, I couldn't resist.

The woman was shaking and with feigned anger whispered, "Please, leave me alone."

"Ma'am, all I want yuh ta do is—

My hand firmly gripped the man's shoulder; and with a quick movement, the beggar was suddenly facing me. I looked him dead in the eyes and said, "Why don't you ask me?"

He was extremely confused and seemed afraid, but I let go of him and extended my hand.

"The name's Matt."

The distraction bought the woman in the red coat enough time to get away. She mouthed the words *thank you* right before she turned and hurried off.

"I just need a few dollars," said the man.

"What for?" I asked.

"I'm hungry."

This happened all the time. I had heard the same answer from countless homeless guys. But I knew that few people starved to death anymore, at least not in America. There were enough soup kitchens, enough churches, enough kind souls, and it was always possible to find food; maybe not the best food, but food nonetheless. Time and time again they told me they were hungry, but sometimes they just said they wanted money. I had fun with it.

"That's it? That's all you want, just a few dollars for food?"

The man looked at me and shrugged, unsure of what I wanted him to say.

"I can give you more than just food," I said.

The man's brow wrinkled and he looked extremely puzzled. I saw his mind race trying to identify some trap, to figure out what I was talking about.

"Umm, uh, I just want a few dollars for food for--"

I interrupted him, "Where do you live?"

"Uhhh, on the street."

"Well, you're in luck," I said, opening up my bag. "I've got some food and a spare room for you in my house."

Rummaging around, I found some sandwiches and fished them out.

"Umm, thanks, thanks, but I really have to be someplace. I, uh, uh, just remembered, I gotta be there now. Seeya."

The beggar took off almost running and left me standing alone with my sandwiches still in hand. This was just one of the many rejections I received over the next several weeks.

Back at work on the fifth floor, I brushed aside the files on my desk and took a moment to think. I reflected on how the past couple of weeks had not gone well. In fact, they had been miserable, and I became concerned about the increase in my "recruitment failures." I hoped my boss never found out about them and how I couldn't sell a house to a homeless person. A *free* house to a homeless person. This was a sad, sorry state of affairs for an aspiring business development officer like myself. Evidently my sales skills left much to be desired, and I needed to make sure that my boss never knew. Ever. Then my phone rang and Kristen Whitworth's number flashed on my caller ID.

I picked it up on its first ring. She was a senior corporate consultant and our group's unofficial social coordinator. I could picture her at her desk, reclining in her leather chair, stiletto clad feet up on her mahogany credenza, probably twirling some of her long blonde hair on her finger as she gazed out her large window.

"Are you coming to the happy hour tonight?" she asked.

"Umm, oh, right, happy hour." I responded, clawing for my desk calendar. I had forgotten about it. I hadn't even bothered to write it down.

"Did you forget? Matt, I sent you the email a month ago."

"No, no, I'm coming. Of course, I'm coming," I said. It's not like I had any plans, other than, of course, wandering around the city, striking up conversations with random homeless people, and inviting them to live with me. I could reschedule. I would push it off until tomorrow. No big deal.

" Okay, well, I'll see you at the bar then," she said before hanging up the phone.

This was a good thing. It would be good to have a night off from my search. Beers were good. They would be delicious and refreshing, a great way to relax after a long day's work, and I was looking forward to them. There was no time to waste. I packed up my things and closed down my computer for the night. I had my hoodie, pants, and sneakers already stuffed in my gym bag and was all set to leave, but then thought -- I have no place to store my bag. People couldn't just bring big, bulky worn-out gym bags into the bar. It would look weird and raise too many questions. Maybe I could just leave my clothes in the office. But what if we went bar hopping? In a few hours the office would be locked and then I wouldn't be able to get my stuff. And then how would I get back to work the next day? Wear a suit? Ridiculous. In my neighborhood, I'd get shot and mugged within minutes. Clearly, I would have to bring them with me and store them somewhere at the bar. Perhaps under a table? No, no, much too obvious. People would notice and comment. Then I remembered that I had been in this bar before, and it had a very large coat rack. Yes! I'd just throw it underneath all of the other coats. No one would see it. After that, the only thing I'd have to worry about were thieves, but thieves probably wouldn't be interested in an old gym bag filled with ratty clothes and a worn-out pair of sneakers.

Confident of my plan, I put on my suit coat and made my way over towards the bar with my gym bag in tow. I walked along the gum-covered sidewalks and noticed that the traffic was heavy. An ambulance tried to make its way down one of the congested streets as cars and trucks did their best to move to the side. In the end, it would have been faster for the medics to get out and walk. The angry sirens were extremely loud, and I could barely hear myself think so I walked faster. I turned the corner, and up ahead I could see the bar at the end of the block. Decades ago it used to be an old bank building but just recently had been transformed into a classy restaurant bar with the vault used as a private dining area. I opened the heavy wooden door and walked inside. The ceilings were almost two stories high, and I noticed the hardwood floors had unusually wide planks. The walls were soothing to look at, all painted in dark red, yellow, and green colors. Brass chandeliers hung down low, and the bar was lined with tall stools covered in burgundy leather. I walked into the reception area, dropped my bag on the floor, and suavely slid it under the coat rack with a swift kick. I walked into the main dining area; and the next thing I knew, I was surrounded by a large group of co-workers. Bobby Crane clapped me on the back and handed me a beer. A cold, delicious refreshing beer.

"Here you go, buddy."

"Thanks, Bobby."

Kristen came running up behind me. She always stood out, in a good way, at office events. I wasn't sure if it was the blonde hair or that she was a woman. Either way, she attracted attention.

"Matt! You made it." She exclaimed.

"Thanks for reminding me."

"Well, I figured that you might forget, especially down on the fifth floor."

"Yes, well, we're kinda insulated down there."

Kristen took a sip from her glass of white wine, and I couldn't help but notice the ring on her finger. It had a large rectangular diamond in the middle, which was surrounded by several other smaller diamonds that sparkled even in the dim light. To her right stood her extremely attractive brunette friend, and I noticed that her hand had no such ring.

"This is my friend, Laura."

"Hi, Laura."

"Matt, nice to meet you. So, you work with Kristen?"

"Yes. She's fun around the office."

"I bet. I've known her for years," she said.

Kristen glanced over at the clock and grimaced.

"What?" I asked.

"My parking meter just ran out of time."

I offered to put change in it for her because I was a nice guy. A gentleman, a high-class individual, who was always willing to help a damsel in distress.

"I'll come keep you company," said Laura.

"Okay, cool."

" Yeah, Laura will show you where I parked," said Kristen.

The second Laura and I got outside, Laura popped a cigarette into her mouth.

"I think the car is that way," she pointed.

Somehow, on the short walk to the car, I must have charmed her. We found the car, put change in the meter, and returned to the bar. As soon as we stepped inside, Laura announced that she wanted to go to a club. A fancy club. A club with bottle service and dancing, and fireplaces. Gas fireplaces. Kristen agreed wholeheartedly so we all chugged the rest of our drinks and piled into her Beamer, the one by the meter which I had just refilled.

"We can't go straight to the club yet," I said.

They both complained. "What? Why not?"

"I need to drop off my bag, and I need to change." I was still wearing my suit clothes. Somehow Kristen and Laura were both dressed up for going out. I was not sure when that happened, but I still needed to change. I knew it was a risky bringing them into the neighborhood, but I had to change. I had to! If they freaked out and asked questions, I would be vague with my answers because being vague was better than lying. I would be mysterious. It might even make me more alluring. Yes. A mysterious, alluring gentleman who worked at the Firm, put money in parking meters for damsels in distress, and lived in the dangerous part of town. It didn't get more bad-ass consultant than that.

"That's going to take forever," she complained.

"No, it won't. My place is not that far."

Kristen agreed after a deep ,sigh; and within fifteen minutes, we had entered into my neighborhood.

"What on earth are you doing living here?" shrieked Kristen as she locked the doors.

"Well, I live here," I said as innocently as I could.

"With who?" exclaimed Laura.

"Umm, well, I'm currently looking for roommates."

Kristen and Laura were peering out of their windows and continuously making sure that the doors were locked. They did not appreciate the stares from the people hanging out on the curbs. They did not like the flashing blue lights. In fact, they started really freaking out. I worried that they might get too scared and turn around, but they endured a little while longer until we got to my place.

Half chuckling, Laura asked, "You live here? Oh...my...god."

"For Pete's sake, hurry up, Matt!" yelled Kristen.

"All right, all right, I'll hurry."

"I don't want to get attacked tonight," she yelled and looked out her window.

I bolted out of the car and ran up the stoop. The car window was half open; and as I fished the keys out of my pocket, I could hear them make comments about my place.

"What the hell is he doing living in this part of town?" asked Laura.

"I swear, I didn't know he lived here."

"Doesn't he work at your Firm? Don't you guys get paid?"

"He must not have known about the area before he rented this place."

"How could he not know?"

"I don't know."

I got the door unlocked and ran inside. Rapidly, I unbuttoned my shirt, threw it in the corner and took off my pants while scaling the stairs. There wasn't much time. The neighbors would surely see a Beamer outside of my house. They would think that I had wealthy friends, friends with things to steal. I knew exactly what would probably happen next. This is what would happen: I would be kidnapped and ransomed, ransomed for the Beamer. A note would probably be delivered to Kristen's house saying something like, *If you want your friend alive, hand over the keys! Ha ha.* It would be written with cutout magazine letters, varying in size, shape and color. The letters would be stuck on lined notebook paper, and she would have five days to respond. But she'd forget to put it on her Google calendar. Her life was on that stupid calendar. She would forget and then they would kill me. Blood everywhere, all over the --

My foot got stuck in my jeans' pant leg. Standing still, I tried to coax my foot through the pants. I took three hops, but it didn't help, and I crashed onto the floor. Betrayed by my own pants, I momentarily lay there dazed and confused before getting up. I finished changing, and five minutes later I was getting in the car. Kristen and Laura had stopped arguing, and I assumed that peace had been made.

"Okay, off to the club," I said shutting the car door.

In a low voice Kristen said, "We have to drop Laura off first."

"Why?"

"Because she's not feeling well…anymore."

80

Slowly I realized the cause of her sudden illness and looked out the window.

"Oh."

"I'd like to go home now," she said.

"You don't want to go to the club?" I asked.

"No, I don't think she wants the club tonight," said Kristen.

And it was confirmed. I lived in a giant piece of birth control. Birth control! But there was nothing I could do or say. And that was that. We dropped her off on the other side of town and proceeded to the club without her. This situation bothered me, but I knew I shouldn't have expected anything less considering the circumstances.

Throughout many months of research and preparations, I discovered that the hope of the Baltimore ghetto did not lie in landing the perfect dream job, but rather in landing the perfect lawsuit settlement. Almost everyone I talked to was waiting on some kind of settlement, usually from his or her employer or a wealthy individual. I knew I needed to protect myself from this. This mission was no joke, nor was it a simple service project, and I was well aware of the dangers that lurked around every turn.

If the homeless thought that I was wealthy, then I figured they would try and find a way to steal from me, extort from me, or just outright sue me. So I needed to convince the homeless and the neighborhood that I was poor because no one sues someone they think owns nothing. Unfortunately, the risks of the neighborhood were not the only obstacles to my success in this project. If my parents were to find out about this, they would be furious. They had ways of being extremely persuasive, and so I needed to convince them that I still lived at my old place because no one intervenes in a problem they don't know exists. Friends told me to avoid spreading this around work. There was too much downside and no real professional upside. So I needed to convince my co-workers and clients that I lived a normal life. No one trusts someone they don't understand. Furthermore, no one hands over their consulting relationship and business decisions to someone they don't trust.

I knew very well that this double life couldn't last. Both lives were simultaneously true but unnaturally separate. I couldn't keep things from everyone for too long without causing damage. Permanent damage. I needed enough time to claim some measure of success. Some sign of hope that this plan could work. So for a time, I would balance a life of luxury and a life of poverty.

The dazzling blue lights of my polished black Acura blinded the hotel valet as the car jerked to a stop on the front entrance cobblestones. The valet opened the passenger door and helped Kaitlyn out of her seat. Garbed in a black lace dress, her auburn hair hung low down her back. She was comfortable yet elegant. A red shawl around her shoulders did little to protect her from the cold. Dressed in a black suit and red tie, I came around and took her arm, escorting her inside. The lobby held throngs of men dressed in suits and women draped in evening gowns. Their high heels clicked and clacked along the hardwood floors. A pianist wearing a black suit played what sounded like one of Mozart's finer pieces from a grand piano at the far end of the ballroom. The lighting shone brightly on the smooth marble columns, and the furniture looked as though it had been imported from modern French castles. It was the grand opening of the Inn at the Colonnade Hotel in Baltimore.

"Oh, wow, this does look good," said Kaitlyn.

"Yes, I'm impressed," I said, admiring the floors and the decorative ceilings. "They really did a nice job."

I had met Kaitlyn in college and quickly found her to be of extremely high intelligence. She read books for fun, wrote many essays, edited the school paper, published articles for popular websites, and studied all the time. Knowledge that great needed to be shared, especially with me, and so she helped me through four years of English and psychology classes. In return for helping me study and editing my papers, Kaitlyn requested that her name be placed on my diploma. She was serious. I thought about writing it in myself, but I had no experience with calligraphy; and even if I had, I didn't think she would have been pleased because she wanted it to be official.

We walked through the hallways until we came to a great room with gold chandeliers. It fit almost one hundred guests who ate and chatted loudly.

"Uggh, I'm not the best at these events," I grumbled.

"Why?" she asked.

"I never have anything to say."

"You? You never know what to say? Honey, that's not your problem." Her earrings glimmered as she shook her head.

We checked our coats and followed the crowd of newly arrived guests into the main party room. A six-piece band filled the air with music, playing violins, violas and flutes in the other back corner. Waiters wandered around the room with platters of pastries and other assorted hors d'oeuvres. I reached over and plucked a crab ball off the tray but dropped it on the ground. Damn. I looked down and saw that it had smashed all over the floor and my shoes. When I looked up, a flash of light caught my eye. What was that? I forgot about the crab ball. The guests blocking my view started to move out of the way, as if controlled by my mind. Could it be? Was it? Yes, I think it— Craning my neck, I saw it -- light emanating from a giant block of ice carved into the shape of a bar. An ice bar! It was carved to fit various forms of alcohol bottles. Lit from inside, it shot little glimmers of blue and green light into the crowd. A man dressed in black stood behind it pouring mixed drinks.

"I'm going over there," I said, pointing.

"You do that," responded Kaitlyn, following behind me.

Approaching the bar, I couldn't decide what I wanted. It all looked so good. I spoke with the bartender at length about various methods of ice carvings, how to fit the lights underneath, and the amount of time before it was fully melted. After, I walked over and brought back glasses of red wine for myself and Kaitlyn. We strolled over to one of the large windows and looked out at the moonlit courtyard.

"So what's left to do for your house?" she asked, taking a sip of wine.

"I have everything moved in. A friend loaned me some furniture. So now all I have to do is find some roommates."

"That's it?"

"Well, I guess I also have to avoid getting shot or stabbed in the process," I said shrugging.

"Yes, do try and avoid those things," she said with a heavy dose of sarcasm. Then she stopped drinking and just stared into her wine glass.

"How are you going to do it?" she asked.

"Do what?"

"You know, lead both of these lives."

"I'll find a way." I paused. "And I don't think it will be two lives."

"Well, you want to continue your job at the Firm, wining and dining clients during the day, and then you're going to go home and wear rags and hang out with homeless people at night."

"And?" I took several more sips of wine.

"Well, first, it's absurd."

I set my almost empty wine glass down and looked out the window.

"But it isn't."

She furrowed her brow and spoke with an increasingly frustrated tone.

"You've been really lucky with your crazy schemes in the past, Matt. Your luck won't last forever."

"Then it's a good thing I'm not counting on luck," I said in a soft voice. I picked up my glass and led her back into the crowd.

"Now we really should try to meet some of these people."

We went on to meet interesting doctors, lawyers, architects, and developers who regaled us with tales of their various projects in the city. The banquet was a nice hiatus from my nights on the streets.

I spent the next couple of weeks trying to invite the homeless back to my house. But I failed. Sometimes it was because I was too scared to ask; other times I was too tired to search, but surprisingly many of the homeless rejected my offer outright. I just couldn't figure out why every homeless person I met was turning me down. At this point, I was asking random people off the corners to follow me home. No one was buying it. I found myself getting worn down mentally. How many more times would I have to be told "no" before I got it? I thought it might be good just to get away from it all for a day or two, perhaps gain some perspective. So that weekend I agreed to go down to Georgetown to visit some friends from college.

By the time I made it over to campus, it was dark out and the yellow street lamps had already been burning for a few hours. I met up with a number of friends one of whom was Wyatt who had gotten me through freshman economics and a few other college classes. Born and raised in Alaska, I could always count on him to play Frisbee in the dead of winter. Between the two of us, we had gotten into a lot of mischief. He exhibited a "can do" attitude when it came to adventures or crazy ideas. We concocted one thrill-seeking scheme after the other. Over the years, we had been thrown out of stores (CVS specifically), created new drinking games involving exotic hot peppers, and went mud sliding during hurricanes. In fact, I have only seen his I'll-do-whatever-whenever-even-if-it's-3A.M.-in-the-morning-on-a-school-night-before-a-big-midterm attitude falter once. It was the night that I had decided to explore a one –hundred- year -old abandoned school building. He said that it was a really stupid idea and that we would die. I probably should have listened, but I thought he was being a bit overdramatic. Later that night I fell through a rotted hallway and broke my back and foot. It was a good thing I didn't learn my lesson about risk taking then; otherwise, I might not have dared to embark on this latest adventure.

After an hour or so of laughing and exchanging post college stories, Wyatt turned to me and asked, "Anything else new happening other than work?" But I had no intention of bringing up my plans in front of everyone. There were too many things to explain; and even if I did, it would be awkward. Somehow I suspected that Wyatt already knew, probably from my brother, but I wasn't sure.

"Nah, just the usual same old stuff."

"Uh huh," said Wyatt, skeptically.

"How's your job search coming?" I asked.

"Still submitting applications here and there," he said. "I may go back and work at the hedge fund in California."

After another half hour, I looked at my watch and saw that it was time to leave. I said my goodbyes and maneuvered over to the door. Wyatt followed me outside where it had gotten darker and colder.

"Wait a second," said Wyatt, shutting the door behind him. The yellow glow of the street lamp lit his face with a dull yellow tint. I was already on the sidewalk so I just turned and leaned against the corner light post. He had a weird look in his eye and looked like he was going to say something awkward, and I knew he knew.

"What's up?" I asked.

"I heard about what you're planning," he said.

"Oh."

"What do you think you're doing? I mean, have you thought this out? Do you have an idea of who will be staying with you?"

"I've thought it out," I said.

"Well, do you know of anyone who's done this before?"

"Not really," I said, looking at the bricks in the sidewalk, refusing eye contact.

"Well, I've heard of someone doing this before." His face got more serious. "There was a girl in Alaska who brought in a homeless woman to live with her. She gave her a bed, her own room, and everything."

"See, that's great."

"I'm not done yet."

I just stared at the sidewalk and said, "Oh."

"So she takes in this woman and gives her all this stuff, but she finds out that the woman won't get off drugs. The girl was essentially enabling this woman. So the girl made her leave the house. She had the locks changed so the woman couldn't come back."

I shivered as the wind picked up speed. Leftover dead leaves from fall were tossed into the air and bounced on the silver Mercedes behind me.

"Well, that's sad, and hopefully that won't happen," I said, zipping up my brown bomber jacket. Wyatt, wearing only a t-shirt and mesh shorts, must have been freezing, but he stood barefoot on the cold stone stoop and continued to tell his story.

"I'm still not finished," he said. "The homeless woman did come back. She broke into the house and then she stabbed the girl to death."

I continued to stare at the ground.

"Tell me how what you're doing is any different," he said.

I said nothing.

Wyatt continued, "You can't expect that these people are just going to listen to you and go out and get jobs."

"I know," I said, glancing back to the sidewalk.

"There are some people who refuse to be helped. They want their drugs and their beer, and that's it."

"I know," I said.

"Some people just want to take advantage of every situation. They're desperate. This isn't a Disney movie, you know."

"I know."

"If their families and their friends can't help them, then why do you think you can change them?"

"I don't."

"You are going to waste your education, your talents, and your job on people who don't deserve it or want it."

"Yes, I am."

"Is there anything else I can say that will convince you not to do this?"

"Nope," I said and started walking away.

Wyatt shouted after me.

"Don't be an idiot! There are a lot of people who are going to be pissed if you don't come back."

The alarm pierced the silence of my afternoon nap and startled me. I woke up, grimaced and let out a great big yawn. Napping after work was not one of my normal activities, but on this particular day, I was simply too tired to continue searching. As I sat up, rivulets of sweat ran down my face as if I had just stepped out of a swimming pool. I realized that I had just had the nightmare again, the one where Jerry and Howard stormed in and attacked. Feeling around on the floor, I found an old shirt lying next to me and wiped the sweat from my eyes.

Removing my blanket, I sat and stared into the blackness and thought about the landlord, the lease, the furniture, my job, the secret nook, and how everything had fallen eerily into place. Well, not everything. Of course, something had to go wrong -- Jerry had said no. Something always had to go wrong, but why couldn't it have been something simple like a small house fire or a plumbing leak? Even getting my car stolen would have been better, a lot better than this. I started hitting my pillow as I thought about it. I threw it across the room and it slammed into the wall before landing to the ground with a light thud.

According to the census count, the city conservatively estimated that about 3,000 homeless people lived in Baltimore. Surely, I could find at least one to live with me, but I was turned down over and over again, and I was starting to get pissed. Rejection, fear, and the bitter cold took their toll on my will. After all these days of failure, I was on the brink of exhaustion and debilitating disillusionment. Now back in my room I contemplated terminating the lease. I would say that I had made a mistake, explain that the neighborhood was too dangerous, which somehow I didn't realize at the time even after seeing the hookers, crack heads, or blue flashing lights on the corners. Maybe I could say that a friend needed help with his mortgage payments. Yes. That would be best. I would *have* to leave, and there would be no way around it. It would be a sacrifice for a friend, a friend in trouble. Though the landlord would be pissed, he would come to understand or maybe even empathize with me. Of course, I'd give him two months' notice, which was more than ample time to rent the house, and surely everything would be worked out. But was that what I wanted? For once, this was something I didn't want to give up on.

Some of my friends had recently come to visit. Among other things, they were disgusted by my icing dinners. I ate very large lunches, I explained. Sometimes they were big enough for three people, yet I ate them all by myself. I explained this many times, many times! They didn't listen and would ask silly questions like, "Why haven't you gone grocery shopping?" I told them what I always had told them, which was that I had only one thing on my mind -- the search. They decided to drop off a bag filled with deer meat to help sustain me. I sat in the kitchen and stared at the little packages wrapped in white butcher paper. I poked the meat with my finger and frowned as I came to the realization that I didn't have a clue as to how to cook *a* meal, much less a meal consisting only of deer meat. In the event that neither a mom nor a chef could be found, my idea of a home cooked meal deteriorated quickly into mac 'n cheese from the box and precooked hotdogs. Realistically speaking, I am not a five star chef, and I admit that now. But even if I were a gourmet cook, I would have failed before I even began due to the sorry fact that my kitchen lacked the basic cooking staples which I have categorized as "unfortunately necessary," a category, which among other things, included such cooking staples as oil, butter and salt. As one might expect, I went to sleep hungry that night.

The next day after work, I emerged from the parking garage outfitted with street clothes and roughed-up hair. It was the forty-first day of living in West Baltimore, and I made a commitment to myself that I would not return home without a roommate. I might have to spend the whole night outside, or maybe spend the night at a friend's house, or perhaps sleep at the office. But no matter what, I was not coming home without a roommate. If I failed again, I decided it was time to move on with my life. I would shut the house down, move back to my old apartment and live a regular life again. What was the point of prolonging this misery? This was getting stupid, living in the house alone, in constant danger with death lurking around every corner, not to mention no food, no car, and no money. Roommates were the key. Without them, all of this effort was simply not worth it.

Armed with gifts of bottled water, I set out to find my people and, of course, it was like every other day, full of rejection. In fact, it was a bit worse as the first couple of homeless refused to even accept the bottled water, not even bothering to look at me. I bit my lip and kept moving. I understood that they were working. Any minute spent talking to me cost them donation money. But then as rejection came over and over again, which got old fast, I felt the urge to quit. No. Yes. No. Yes. Maybe. Maybe? I didn't know. I didn't know! It had been over forty days, and so I started thinking that maybe it was not meant to be. I was done, washed up, no hope, not even a chance. Maybe it was for the best. I couldn't tell, and, at the time, I was too angry to entertain such optimism.

As the war against giving up waged on in my mind, I kept asking people to come live in the house anyway, but I got rejected by everyone. The guy under the bridge; the guy on the grassy median; and even the crazy guy by the hospital. All I wanted to do was to help. All I wanted to do was give this gift. But for reasons that were unclear to me, no one would accept it. And it killed me to think of the warm beds, clean towels, running water and then to see these people choosing to be miserable. I couldn't stand it. I couldn't understand it.

The temperature dropped with every passing hour, my feet were sore, and the bag around my arms got heavier and heavier. I didn't have much left. Just when I was about to throw in the towel, I came across a short man with a pronounced limp. He looked like many other of the homeless I had met, complete with a bushy, matted beard. He puffed heavily on a cigarette that seemed to be floating in grey facial fuzz. I had never heard of this, but wondered whether beards could catch on fire. I guessed it could happen, especially with his cigarette so awfully close to a few of his stray hairs. What would happen if it just lit up? I wasn't aware of any way to put that out quickly. I remember in kindergarten we were taught to stop, drop, and roll if caught on fire, but those scenarios only involved body fires. Perhaps the same tactics could be applied to face fires, but as I thought of it, I was less and less convinced. It simply would not work. Having him drop and roll on his face sounded painful, and he'd probably prefer to have his beard burn off instead. I didn't know, I just didn't know.

Wearing old jeans, an army cap and worn out boots, he hobbled among stopped traffic. He looked to be in his late fifties, possibly sixties. Glancing up from the traffic, he caught me watching him from on top of the grass-covered median as cars whizzed past.

"Hey, sir, you got any spare change?" He asked. I produced a dollar from my pocket and handed him a bottled water from my gym bag.

"Here ya go. What's your name?"

"My name's Paul."

"I'm Matt."

He took a sip of water and stuffed the dollar into his jacket.

"How's the night been going for ya?"

"It's goin. Just trying to make enough for dinner, that's all."

"Can I ask you a question?"

"Shoot," said Paul as he gulped down the water, some of which spilled on his beard.

"What was the last job that you had?"

"I'm a construction guy by trade."

"Are you still in construction?" I asked as if I was talking to him at some networking event. I couldn't believe myself making small chat like that when obviously he was no longer in construction or any line of work for that matter.

"Ahh, umm, a few years ago I fell out of a building, shattered my foot 'n lost my job and couldn't really find one since."

I eyed him up and down assessing his potential for work. He looked like he still had a few good years in him, and I was encouraged.

"You can walk now. Why haven't you found another job?"

"Well, when ya don't have a house or a bathroom or a phone, you can't find a good job."

"And if you had those things?"

"I'm on a list somewheres, but it kinda takes months and years to get into a house."

"But could you get a job if you had it?"

"Well, I'm damn sure; 'course I could!"

"Paul, listen carefully to what I am going to tell you."

"Huh?"

"I have an offer that could change your life."

He just stopped and stared at me. I figured I had his attention so I continued.

"It's only temporary, but if you accept it, you can make it into something permanent."

His beady eyes widened briefly.

"I have a house for you with many rooms. If you live in it with me, I'll help you find a job and secure your own place."

I wanted him to say yes so badly and scanned his face for any sign of hope. Accept. Accept, damn it! I had gotten to this point with many others, but none of them ever worked out. Like the others, he would say no. I knew it. I had a sense for these things.

"That's sounds great. Only…," said Paul trailing off.

I gasped. Out of all the past conversations, I had never gotten anyone to say that my idea sounded "great." Hope came rushing back into my world and brightened it with the possibility of the unimaginable. My heart pounded deeply in my ears. But I wanted it to stop beating; I needed to hear what he said next. What if he asked something I couldn't accommodate? What if he asked to use drugs in the house? What if he asked to bring his gun collection? What if he asked for the keys? What if he wanted me to pay him? Why would he ask me to pay him? I don't know. I don't know! What if I couldn't do what he asked and then I never found anyone else? I would regret it for the rest of my days, and every morning I'd wake up and curse my decision.

"Only what?" I asked, trying to hide the desperation in my voice.

"I have a wife. Do you think she could come, too?"

I did not expect him to ask that, but it seemed like an easy request considering the circumstances. Even though I had been against having women in the house for a whole slew of reasons, I was desperate, and so I gladly compromised.

"That's fine. Where is she?"

"She's in our tent under the bridge."

"Is that far?"

"Nah, a few minutes' walk or so."

"Not bad."

"Lemme go tell her and we'll get ready.

"Get ready?"

"I gotta pack."

"Oh, yes…your stuff," I said, trying to remember that he was a normal human being with possessions just like the rest of us.

"Yeah. Jus' 'cause I don't got a house don't mean I don't got stuff."

"Yes, yes, I know. It was a joke. But out of curiosity, how much stuff?" I asked, envisioning mounds of furniture, boxes of trinkets, and piles of clothes. Maybe even a rusty shopping cart with a missing wheel.

"Not much. Just a bag or two."

"Sure, sure. Well, by all means go pack."

"Both of us'll be back in an hour," he said.

"Great. While you do that, I'll run home and pick up my mess."

"Yuh don't gotta do that for us, but suit yourself," said Paul.

"So I'll see you back here in an hour?" I asked.

"Yeah, yeah."

"Good."

"My wife's had a tough time with everything, and this'll make her so, so happy. Thank you, thank you."

"Please."

"What?" asked Paul.

"Please, don't thank me."

Back on West Ward Street, I burst through the front door and went running up the stairs, stripping off my inner suit layer as I went. Running all over the house, I raced to clean everything up. I washed the dishes, folded the blankets, and threw out the long-expired deer meat that I had left in the refrigerator. This was a new experience for me, and I wasn't sure what to expect, so before I left, I hid the two kitchen knives on top of the fridge, just in case things got out of hand.

Putting my hoodie and track pants back on, I raced out the door and jogged, no, *ran* up the sidewalks, which was an uncommon practice for the neighborhood. No one ever jogged around these parts unless it was to get an extra 40 ounce before the bar closed. Exercising was a mark of privilege because it meant that you neither worried about rent payments nor had a smoking problem. If one had to exercise, it would be best to do those things in private so as not to raise suspicion. Jogging was a sure fire way to get oneself labeled as an outsider, but I didn't care anymore, and I ran full speed down to the corner because at long last I had found roommates!

Meanwhile, Paul was busy over at his tent waking up his wife, Cheryl. Later, she filled me in on how it all went down --- Paul frantically unzipped a mud splattered tent door.

"Honey, wake up. Wake up!"

A middle-aged woman buried in a heap of tattered blankets let out an annoyed groan. Light from the sunset shone in through the mesh window coverings, and tall yellow weeds surrounded the tent, keeping them hidden from the street.

Paul whispered, "Cheryl, wake up. I found us a place. We're finally getting outta this dump."

Cheryl sat straight up and brushed her tangled golden brown hair out of her face. The sleeves on her shirt were much longer than her arms and hung past her hands. Her denim jacket had holes where her pockets used to be.

"What? You did what?" she whispered rubbing her droopy eyes.

Paul excitedly whispered back, "I found us a place to live with a shower and everything."

96

Cheryl began to grasp what he was saying and then started convulsing.

"A place to live? A house!" She excitedly screamed.

"Shhh. Sssshhhh. Quiet, Cheryl! Everyone will hear you."

The last thing they needed was to share this house with the rest of the homeless camp. Cheryl covered her mouth and tears started to pour down her eyes. Paul described my invitation as she sobbed after every word. Tears poured everywhere and dripped all down her shirt, and then she just started laughing.

"Get yourself together, Cheryl," said Paul, disgusted. She told him that she couldn't help it. She wiped her eyes and then helped Paul pack their clothes into a large trash bag.

An hour later, I arrived back at the corner and waved to Paul. He was hobbling around a cluster of cars waiting for the light. Across the street I saw a downtrodden woman, who I presumed to be Paul's wife, Cheryl, and walked towards her. She held out a sign and stood next to a very large and very full trash bag. Facing away from me towards the traffic, she waved her sign at the cars, but I could tell that she wasn't putting any heart into it. Her sign faced her leg more than the traffic and she didn't exactly wave with enthusiasm. To make sure this was his wife, I caught Paul's attention from across four lanes of traffic and pointed to her. He nodded, and I walked the rest of the way up the median until I stood directly behind her.

"You're Paul's wife, aren't you?" I asked.

She hadn't seen me coming, and I expected her to be startled by my voice, but she wasn't. Instead she calmly turned around and briefly scanned me from head to toe.

"You're not what I expected."

"Sorry?"

97

"It's dangerous out here, ya know," she said, looking like a concerned mother.

"I know."

"There are some real crazy people out here."

"I think I've met some of them," I said, putting my hands in my pockets. For a minute, we just stared out at the traffic. The cars stopped at the light, but she didn't approach them. If anyone had wanted to give money, they would have had to leave their cars and walk to the middle of the median.

"Paul says you have a spare room for us."

"He's right. I do."

"We weren't always like this. We're regular people like you, yuh know."

"I know."

"We just need a lift up from nice folks like you."

"Happy to help."

"Thanks for doing this."

"Please don't thank me."

"Yuh wouldn't b'lieve the way people live out here. It's just awful."

"Cheryl." I said looking at her worn shoes.

"Yes?"

"Can I ask you something?"

"Yeah?"

"What do you want?"

"Huh?"

"You know, what do you want?" I asked a bit softer.

She paused for second and then slowly in a quivering voice answered, "I just want my life back."

Grinning, I said, "That's all that matters."

"Really?"

"Yes."

Her eyes watered and her mouth quivered into a smile as a few stray tears fell.

"Oh, thank you."

"You don't have to thank me."

"Yeah, I do."

"Well the house is only a short walk from here. Lets get a move on."

I turned around to lead the way back, but Cheryl didn't follow.

"Can't leave yet," she said.

What does she mean -- *can't leave yet*? I thought. Why not? What more could you need? I was offering a house, food, heat, and privacy.

"Why ever not?" I asked innocently. While she hesitated to respond, I began to think that, of course, this was too good to be true. Surely, Cheryl was just finding the words that wouldn't hurt my feelings, maybe trying to let me down softly.

"Paul won't leave until five at eight comes," she answered.

Confused, I wondered what the hell the five at eight was. Of all my time in the street, I had never heard of this term. I suspected it might be gang jargon or drug lingo, but I wasn't sure and assumed it was probably both.

"What's the five at eight?" I asked.

"It's the woman who drives by around eight and gives him a five dollar bill."

"How much longer will we have to wait?"

"Depends. Maybe an hour; maybe more."

"Maybe an hour, maybe more?" I blurted out.

I couldn't believe she just said that. Well, this was just ridiculous. What did they think I was doing here? What the hell did they think! It's not like someone comes around and offers a free house every day. Why wait? Especially when it's exactly what they needed, what they wanted. Such a mighty, generous, rare, once-in-a-lifetime gift should never be kept waiting. I had a good job at the Firm. I could, no, should be spending my free time getting ahead in my career. I could be using my money to buy a house in a nice neighborhood, a nice house with big windows and granite counters and large, spacious rooms, rooms with skylights. Skylights! But 8 years of a Jesuit education have a way of overriding my knee jerk reactions to things.

"We can leave right after she comes. We're all set to go," she said tapping her trash bag.

"Sure, sure, sure. No rush. I'll just wait on the other side of the street. Take all the time you need," I said, in the softest, most understanding voice I could muster.

Being asked to wait was a slap in the face, but I wasn't about to let them get away. Maybe they didn't think I was serious, but that didn't matter. At long last I had finally found them, and there was no way that I was going to let them go without a fight. I would fight them, fight myself, fight everyone to pull them out of this hell they were stuck in. If they thought they were going to shake me that easily, then they had no idea who they were dealing with.

The corner happened to be right next to Ravens stadium so I walked over to it and sat against one of its tall brick walls. Sitting down Indian style, I played with the shoe strings of my worn out sneakers to try and pass the time. Occasionally I looked up to make sure they were still there. It was good that she brought the bag. I took it as a sign of commitment and evidence of her intent to follow through. But then I thought maybe this wasn't as good as I thought; in fact, this could be really bad. Good? Bad? Good? Bad? Definitely bad! Why would they agree to come back with me? Everyone else refused and sometimes refused adamantly. I started to realize that the only logical reason Paul and Cheryl agreed to follow me home was because they wanted to kill me. They would wait until we got back to the house and then they would stab me. Blood everywhere. They would probably bury me in the backyard and then live in my house. They would sell my stuff and use the money for drugs, alcohol, strippers, and other pleasures. But then I thought that maybe I was worrying too much. Even though they wanted to kill me, they would need weapons and, luckily, I had hidden the kitchen knives. They wouldn't have expected that, and when they ran for the knives, they would find only spoons! They would never think to check the top of the fridge; and even if they did, they were too short to reach it. They would be forced to use the spoons; and, try as they might, they would not be able to stab me.

As I was thinking these things, I was startled by the appearance of a pair of shiny black shoes. They were attached to a security guard who, I'm pretty sure, was carrying a police baton. I looked up at him, and he informed me that I was loitering. Illegally loitering. I looked around and thought that this might be a joke. Perhaps this was a guard with a sense of humor. I looked to the left and saw what appeared to be tumbleweeds and sheets of discarded newspapers blowing across the empty parking lot. I looked to my right and saw hundreds of yards of deserted sidewalks. There wasn't a person for miles except, of course, for Paul and Cheryl on the corner. The guard stood with one hand on his baton, and I started to explain that I was waiting for the five at eig-- I stopped. Dumb. A stupid explanation, and he wouldn't care. It would take too long to give the explanation, so I gave up. Sighing, I agreed to move over towards the bushes growing on the side of the street. He nodded and then tapped his foot on the ground while he waited for me to stand up and leave.

After an hour passed, Paul waved his hands over his head to signal that the woman had come. I saw him stuff the five-dollar bill into his pocket. Shortly after, we all assembled on the grassy median before we began the trek home. Paul and Cheryl picked up their baggage and followed me as I led the way back through the neighborhood streets. The sun had set an hour before, and it was very dark; but with the clarity of midday, I saw that this was a turning point not unlike the Rubicon. We were crossing the Rubicon, or maybe the Delaware, and it was a beautiful moment.

People define beauty based on a variety of standards, sometimes based on relativity, where beauty lies in the eye of the beholder, and other times based on objectivity, where beauty depends on rarity. Still others define it spiritually, concluding that all things touched by God are inherently beautiful. I was not sure which of these was most accurate, but it didn't matter to me. And on this seemingly ordinary winter night, to anyone watching us walking home. We looked like the farthest thing from beauty imaginable, with me wearing ratty clothes, Paul's matted beard, and Cheryl's torn, dirt-covered denim jacket. From outward appearances, we looked to be just a random group of hobos hobbling around, hauling trash bags, probably searching for a good sidewalk to urinate on. But I knew the truth, and Cheryl and Paul knew the truth. The truth was that this was good, rare, and touched by God. This was a beautiful moment.

If human events had taken their normal course, we all never would have met unless through a half open car window. I considered how something unnatural, no, supernatural must have happened to set our impossibly opposite paths, mine from corporate America and theirs from the streets, colliding into one another. In that moment, all of us had been knocked wildly off course and into a direction where nothing could be predicted. Despite all of the unknowns, I was certain that God knew Paul and God knew Cheryl, and still He loved them. I was certain of this, and I was certain that they needed to know.

If it hadn't been so dark, we probably would have aroused the neighbors' suspicion as we hobbled down the broken sidewalks. All of us scuffling along, Paul and I limping ahead, with Cheryl hauling her overstuffed trash bag. We were a motley crew indeed. Despite my questions, and I'm sure their questions, we hiked to the house mostly in silence lest any of us say something that might ruin it.

I had dreamed of this day for so long that I could scarcely believe it was real. Everything had come together, and now it was time to start the messy work of second or third chances, whatever the case may be. I had not yet found out what had brought them to the street, but I didn't want to ask and preferred that they tell me when they were ready. Just because I was offering them a house didn't give me the right to pry into their lives. Also, I didn't want to answer too many of their questions either. As we walked, I had no idea what they were thinking; though a little bit later, Cheryl spilled her guts. She told me that they were terrified, literally scared speechless. They had fleeting thoughts that I may try to kill them; or worse, that I might want to sleep with them. Desperate, they had no choice and figured it was a chance worth taking. They were new to this homeless thing (four months) and didn't know any better.

I gave them a tour of the house and relished pointing out the toiletries and new bedspreads in their rooms. They ooohed and aaahed at all the appropriate times which pleased me. Appreciation was a positive sign; and not only did it make me feel good, but I figured that it would help them along their way to recovery. If they could grasp that this opportunity was a once-in-a-lifetime kind, then they might believe themselves capable of a once-in-a-lifetime result.

We toured the rest of the house, which in total took no longer than four minutes, maybe three, and explored everything from the bathroom, to the guest room, to my unfurnished room and barebones closet. Afterwards we came back down to the kitchen and sat around the table. To my surprise, everything was happening as I always had hoped it would. I had not yet been stabbed and, somehow, they seemed ready to listen to me.

Downstairs I poured them glasses of water, the only thing we had to drink. Quickly, I gulped down my entire glass as I composed my thoughts on what I would tell them. It was time for me to outline expectations and rules for the house, and I decided to start with my favorite subject: food.

"I will buy the first load of groceries for us; but afterwards, you will be responsible for the food," I said.

"We can do the food," said Paul, nodding, while Cheryl's cheeks flushed with red. She got excited and was practically jumping up and down. It seemed as though she was still taking in the big picture and was not yet ready to handle the joy of details.

"It's a real house," she said, looking around the kitchen, "It's not a halfway house or a shelter but a real house!"

"Yup, it sure is. That's kinda what I was going for. But let's try and stay on topic." I said.

"Okay, lets get this over with. Where's the paperwork," asked Cheryl while getting out a pen from her tattered pocket.

"What do you mean?"

"You know, registration paperwork and stuff like that," she said, looking from the empty table to the bare counters.

"Oh, right," I said.

She looked at me expectantly.

"There is none."

"What?" asked Paul.

Slowly, I repeated, "There…is…no…paperwork."

Now both Paul and Cheryl were just staring at me, but quickly averted their glances to the floors and walls trying to hide their surprise, not wanting to jinx their good fortune, as if their reactions would indicate a mistake on my part and cause me to suddenly pull out spare paperwork which I had stuffed in a drawer waiting for just these occasions.

"Well, there is one thing that you must fill out, but it's not exactly paper. I don't expect you to do it today."

I walked over to the dining room, which wasn't really a dining room but more of an extension of the kitchen. In fact, the whole downstairs was really just a large rectangular room, separated by a very awkwardly placed staircase that ran perpendicular across the width of the house. This one room served three purposes – living room (front part), dining room (middle part), and kitchen (back part), but their supposed "non-paperwork" would take place on a wall in the living room/middle part. I rested my hand on a large blank white board, which was about two by three feet large, and affixed to the exposed brick wall. On it in large black letters I had drawn the words *Wall of Want*.

"This is the 'Wall of Want,'" I said pausing for a second before continuing. "On it you will write your goals. But you should only do this when you're ready."

"Goals?" they asked.

"Goals for your time in this house."

"Anything? Whatever we want?"

"You just gotta make them inspiring."

"Inspiring?"

"Yeah, inspiring. You know, exciting enough to get you out of bed every single morning of the rest of your lives."

Paul and Cheryl just looked at each other.

"You must never forget why you're here."

"I think that's a good idea, don't you, Paul," said Cheryl.

"Yup, yup," said Paul nodding.

"Oh, and before I forget, there are, of course, rules that must be followed," I said, pulling a folder from a nearby bookshelf which contained a packet of paper with a blank white cover. It was the same packet that I had

105

presented to Father Lorenzo over forty days before. It contained the strategy for getting jobs as well as the expectations and rules for living in the house. Part of the strategy included a merit system where acts of good behavior received merit points and bad behavior received demerit points. A system based on military behavior modification. I figured if it worked for the military then it would work for Paul and Cheryl, who may or may not need their behavior modified.

After three weeks, if they achieved a certain number of points, they would receive a key to the house and could come and go as they pleased. Until then, they were to leave in the morning before 8A.M. and could return after 6P.M., which gave me ample time to get back and forth to work.

"We shouldn't have any problems with those rules," said Paul. "My wife's a neat freak and we'll keep --

Cheryl excitedly interrupted, "I love to clean. I can't stand a dirty house."

"Great, so we're good then."

This was going well, and I was surprised there was neither push back nor any attempt of negotiations of any kind. They seemed to love everything I said, and so I did my best to take advantage of the momentum.

"In addition, there are four cardinal rules that must never be violated. Ever. Any violation would be grounds for instant eviction. If violated, I will physically throw you out the window."

I explained to them the following cardinal rules:
No drugs (including marijuana);
No alcohol;
No visitors or guests or family in the house, ever;
And no stealing.

I reiterated that these were the four rules that must never be broken. Both Paul and Cheryl nodded in agreement. They understood and still did not complain. I expected complaints, at least some kind of attempt at negotiation, but they accepted them all. This was going just great and so exceeded my expectations that I began to wonder if I was, in fact, a pessimist.

"Also, I would appreciate it if you refrained from speaking with any of the neighbors. Try to stay out of sight, and don't cause attention to yourselves. The landlord knows them; and if they find out about you, they will probably tell him."

"Paul and I smoke cigarettes. Would it be okay if we smoked them on the front stoop?" they asked.

"Use the back porch. I'm serious about the neighbors."

Cheryl nodded, "Okay, the back porch it is."

Locking and relocking my door, I prepared for the night by filling my suitcases with clothes and used them to create a barricade against my bedroom door. I wrapped myself in blankets, curled up against the barricade, and drifted in and out of sleep. I realized that I never searched their bags or pockets. Considering things, I probably should have checked for weapons. A mistake. The lock might not hold and could easily be broken down, but maybe my barricade would hold. After all, I had built it with my bare hands so I knew it could withstand the initial attacks. I reassured myself by remembering that I wasn't relying on just physical barriers to defend myself. In addition to the barricade, I made sure that they saw how empty my room was with nothing in it but an old particleboard desk, some ratty clothes, and a thin blanket. I didn't even have a bed. I found it hard to believe that they would have any reason or desire to come in after they knew I had nothing to steal. Unbeknownst to them, all my suits were at work, carefully hidden throughout the office. It was important that they not know that I wore a suit to work. Otherwise, they might think I was important or something, maybe think that I had money to steal, or at least got paid more than I had let on. Then they might have motive to sue me or kidnap me, or find ways to extort from me, which were all things I didn't want to risk.

Across the hall, Paul and Cheryl spent the night in the corner of their room with their own door locked. Not entirely sure what to expect, they told me that they made their own barricade but still had trouble sleeping. They said that they expected me to break in at any moment and then force myself upon them. After I heard this, I thanked them for their confidence in my character and decided that I needed to work on my first impressions.

Chapter 8: Jimmy the Rapist

The next three weeks passed by in a surprisingly normal way. The dishes were cleaned, the counters wiped down, and carpets vacuumed. In fact, it was so normal that by the end of those weeks, I threw out the merit system and handed them a key to the house. Their civility and manners were most unexpected and, again, made me question my morbidly low expectations where I anticipated being stabbed and left for dead by the end of the first week. Contrary to all of the warnings from the community, friends, family and my own common sense, we lived in harmony.

Cheryl reported on her job search, application time frames, and obstacles to getting hired. I made sure to keep pressing her to send in applications even if she didn't think she was qualified. Paul continued to panhandle but brought back all sorts of food and clothing. He never mentioned how much money he made; and when asked, he would answer vaguely, but I didn't care. I knew how protective people could be about money. I was the last person who could make comments considering how I kept my suits at work, my car at a light rail stop, and my computer at my parents' house, all in an effort to make myself look poor. Things had turned out much better than I had ever imagined. By now, I had expected to be in court, in jail, or dead and was shocked that it had lasted so long already. But no matter how great things seemed, I knew all too well that this honeymoon period would never last.

I rounded the corner of my neighborhood block, looked down the street to my house, and felt a pit form in my stomach. I stood almost fifteen houses up the street and could see what appeared to be a large gathering of people hanging around my stoop chatting. Getting a few houses closer, I began to recognize most of them as neighbors.

Why would they be standing at my house? I figured that someone must have gotten hurt, maybe even shot or stabbed. But I quickly realized that couldn't be the case because if that were true, then there would be an ambulance or, at the very least, a police presence. Why no ambulance? Perhaps it just happened a few moments ago. But, no, everyone appeared entirely too calm to have just witnessed a crime…unless it was a cover up! Maybe everyone was involved in a sick twisted group murder. By now I was almost five houses away and made sure to walk with an exaggerated limp, which helped me fit in with the area.

As I hobbled along, I spotted a police car zipping through a nearby intersection and thought of the landlord. What if he showed up? I craned my neck but couldn't see his car, though he usually parked around the corner. I wouldn't be able to see his car! I wasn't sure what catastrophe had happened, but I was sure that I wasn't ready for this. I pulled on my hood extra hard so that it covered my dress shirt collar.

Only two houses away, I scanned the crowd trying to gauge their emotional state, but everyone looked calm. My nerves eased after I couldn't spot any injured people, dead bodies, blood, or landlords. But I did see something right there in the middle of everyone that infuriated me. At the center of a group sat none other than Cheryl! I couldn't figure out what the hell she was doing. I specifically told her not to talk with the neighbors. They would tell everyone and ruin us. I had only been gone for a few hours, and now she was practically hosting a neighborhood block party. The only things missing from this happy gathering were cheese dip and checkered tablecloths. The nerve.

"Hey, Matt! You took your time getting back today, didn't ya, hon," she said.

"Yes, yes, I did," I said, making intense, disapproving eye contact.

She ignored me and kept on talking. I could never have guessed what she was about to say next.

"Hon, I want to introduce you to some of the neighbors," she said, putting her hand on my shoulder. The neighbors all stopped talking and looked at me.

"Everyone, this is Matt, my son," she said gesturing before the small crowd in front of us.

Your son? Your son! Unbelievable. Uncalled for! Right there in front of everyone, in a type of sick public commitment, Cheryl signed me up for another fake life, another sham existence without even checking if I was okay with it. She sought to fool the entire neighborhood, and we were going to get caught. There was just too much to balance. At this point, on any given day, depending on the time, I was either a consultant, a homeless person, a son to homeless parents, a son to non-homeless parents, living alone in a house in West Baltimore, and/or living with my yuppie friends in suburbia. There were simply too many balls in the air, and I realized that no amount of caffeine, which usually solved most of my problems, could keep me on point.

I went around and shook everyone's hand and then disappeared inside the house. I had no idea what else she had told them; and the longer I remained outside, the greater the chance of accidentally exposing her lies, which would be a disaster. She would be embarrassed, and the landlord would be told. It would be the talk of the town. It needed to be prevented at all costs. I waited inside and composed myself in preparation for operation Damage Control. I decided to confront her the minute she walked in the house which I expected to happen within moments. Two hours later, Cheryl walked through the door smiling. After waving goodbye to everyone, she shut the door.

"We have such nice neighbors," she said, plopping herself down on the couch.

"You told them I was your son?" I said, shaking my head.

"Well, what did yuh want me to tell them? The truth? Like they'd believe that."

I opened my mouth to say something, but then surprisingly I realized that she made perfect sense. Kids around the neighborhood just grew up and then stayed home. It was only normal that they live at home with their parents so Cheryl's explanation actually worked.

"Now we fit in with everyone else. Kids around here just grow up and stay home," she said.

"I guess," I sighed and was angrily surprised by her brilliance. Though I disapproved of her lying, she had bought us a lot of time. Time we needed.

"Anyways, they all claimed that they could see quite a resemblance between us," she said, chuckling. I laughed awkwardly and looked down.

"So did you learn anything interesting about any of them?"

"Not really. The house across the street has seven, eight people living in the basement. And I think there are a few of 'em drug dealers around."

"Just some drug dealers and a few illegal squatters?"

"That's about it," she said.

"Who was that small guy on your left? I've seen him biking around."

"Oh, Jimmy. Yes, Paul and I met him down at the homeless camp. He and Paul are good friends."

"What's he doing here, Cheryl? You know I don't feel comfortable with guests from the homeless camp coming around to the house."

As calmly as if she had been talking about the weather, she said, "Oh, he's a rapist."

Matching Cheryl's calmness, I gently brushed imaginary dirt from my arm, and I slowly repeated, "Oh, he's a rapist?"

"Yes. The others say he got picked up for molesting some girls at a playground, but he recently got out of prison. He's done his time."

"Interesting, but why is he here?"

"Oh, I think he likes me. He came over to find out if I was interested in 'gettin' it on' today."

I had not expected this answer because it was too *expected*, too stereotypical. Shocked, I blurted out, "You guys got it on?" I wasn't balking at the thought of marital infidelity nor was I surprised at the idea of sleeping with a known sex offender. Rather, it was the sheer mechanics of it all. It boggled my mind considering how Cheryl was taller, rounder, four times heavier, and twenty years older than Jimmy. There's just no way I, or anyone else, for that matter, could reconcile the differences.

"Heavens, NO! I am a happily married woman and have been for the past sixteen years," she said, acting insulted that I even mentioned the idea.

"Okay, Okay. That was a joke, I think," I said, with an uncomfortable chuckle.

I lifted myself out of the chair and headed out of the living room.

"Where are you going?"

"I'm going up to my room. I may take a nap," I said, climbing the stairs and forcing an audible yawn. I shut the door and leaned back against the wall and allowed myself to slide down until I was sitting on the floor. Yes. That just happened, *that* being the fact that today I shook the hand of a rapist, a rapist who was *good* friends with Paul and who tried to hook up with Cheryl in my own house. My roommates must never, not ever, under any circumstances, multiply with the neighbors. This was easily the worst thing that could ever happen. How did I forget to include this in the list of forbidden rules? A dumb mistake. Stupid. But maybe I could fix it with an amendment. Yes, that wouldn't be so hard. I would amend the rules, write a decree, and nail it to their bedroom door! I would force them to memorize it and repeat it every morning before breakfast and once before dinner. Perhaps our house could return to the time when it held the prestigious award of world's biggest form of birth control. A badge of purity I once cursed, I now realized, needed to be preserved and protected at all costs.

Later that night, Cheryl and I met in the living room to watch a few NBC sitcoms. Cheryl always let me have the dish chair. A sign of respect. It was the most comfortable chair in the house, and she gave it up to me willingly while she took the less comfortable couch option. I had no problem with this. A rerun came on, and she scowled. This happened often as we were in the midst of the writer's guild strike. No new shows anytime soon, only reruns. I didn't care because I was never a big TV watcher. However, those days I watched it a lot because it was a way to spend time with Cheryl and Paul. I found that Cheryl often told stories about her life during the commercial breaks. A shame. I enjoyed the commercials more than the sitcoms, especially the commercials involving woodland creatures, specifically the kind that could speak English. I don't know why, but I loved those crazy animals; they made me laugh.

During a particularly entertaining commercial, Cheryl started reminiscing, which was the worst of times for such an activity. A commercial involving a fuzzy squirrel had just started. It was on right in front of her. Couldn't she see it? Was she not entertained? The squirrel looked to be selling auto insurance, an assumption I made on account of the squirrel nearly getting hit by a speeding car which swerved off the road and hit a tree. The squirrel must have taken this near death experience personally because it became very angry and he or she, I can't tell the difference between squirrels, jumped up and down waving its tiny paws while shouting at the driver. The driver, who looked angry himself, got out of the car and walked menacingly toward the squirrel who held up its paws in balled fists. They were on the verge of a brawl. I sat on the edge of my seat shaking in anticipa--

"I remember I used to throw large holiday parties for my family," she said.

"How many people was it for?" I asked, before turning and facing her. This was important. I decided I would YouTube the commercial later and watch it over and over again until I was sick of it or until I had bought the car insurance, whichever came first. I needed to be there for her. Paul wasn't exactly an active listener, and it's not like she had anyone else to listen to her.

"We have a large family. Almost twenty people," she said.

"That's a lot of people."

And where was her family now? None of them could help her? Out of twenty people? I find it hard to believe that none of them would try. What could she have done to turn them all away? Though all of these questions swirled in my head, I never asked her. Cheryl broke eye contact with me and just stared as she spoke, completely absorbed in her memories of better days.

"I used to make so much food. I'd cook and cook. Everyone loved my pigs- in- the-blanket appetizers, my hams, cheese balls, salmon cakes, lasagnas..."

"Sounds delicious."

"Yeah. I put on a big production and decorated the buffet table with candles and flowers and sparkly things."

"I love sparkly things."

"The children would go running under the tables, and sometimes they would even sneak some of the cheese slices before dinner started."

I chuckled and looked over at Cheryl. The dark room was lit only by the TV, but I could see tears sparkling in her eyes.

"They would get in trouble with their dad."

"Kids," I said, as if I understood.

"No, they weren't *just* kids. Not at all."

I sat there watching her. Her light brown hair hung below her shoulders. Barefoot and wearing capri khakis, she sat on her hands as she told her story. As if she were trying to control her emotions.

"They were the most wonderful children in the entire world. Innocent, sweet, darling children," she said. Her eyes shifted away from me as her mind dived into a treasury chest of warm memories.

I wasn't sure what to say so I silently nodded, encouraging her to continue.

"We used to throw these great Thanksgiving dinners. With two huge turkeys," she said.

As she spoke, I discreetly lowered the volume with the remote wedged between the chair cushions.

"I miss them," she said, quickly brushing tears out of her eyes.

Family, food, children were the greatest of things. I wanted her to continue because it was a vision of what she wanted. I wanted her to see that these things which were once lost had impossibly come back into reach. But before she could finish -- SLAM.

The door flew open, and Paul crashed into the living room. I jumped out of my seat, petrified. I thought the door was locked, but I guess it wasn't. Cheryl flipped on the light. Paul looked terrified and started shouting and yelling.

"They took it! They took it!"

"Paul, calm down," yelled Cheryl.

"Cheryl, they took it!"

"What did they take?" She asked.

"Everything."

"What? Did you get mugged?" I asked.

"Yeah, Yeah!"

"By who? Who would mug a homeless guy?"

I had never heard of this. I had never heard of homeless people getting mugged.

"There were three of them," said Paul.

"Three of them?"

Paul paced back and forth, fuming.

"Three huge, massive black guys."

"Where?"

"A block away. They stole the forty dollars I made today."

"Just calm down. You're lucky that's all they did," I said.

"Its hard work walking back and forth all day. I got bad knees!" he whined, almost crying.

"Paul, relax," said Cheryl.

"I need that money. I need it!"

I knew he had no expenses and so clearly he was being a drama queen. Though after he almost started crying, I figured he must have been shaken up pretty badly. Later, Cheryl explained that he had been a fighter in his youth, and he was not transitioning well into old age. He had a lot of pride, and I guess he couldn't stand to lose a fight.

"I could have taken them. If I were a few years younger and I didn't have such bad knees. I could have pounded their heads into the sidewalk. They never would have— he yelled, practically frothing at the mouth. The whining went on a bit longer before his voice trailed off. He thrashed about and balled up his fists and swung them in the air as if performing a poorly executed interpretive dance.

Eventually he got tired and stomped up the stairs before slamming his bedroom door.

"He's pissed," I said, stating the obvious.

"I know. He hates being handicapped," Cheryl said, turning her attention back to the TV.

A few seconds later, he came half the way downstairs, poked his head into the sitting room, and asked me a question.

"Can I ask a favor of you?"

"Umm, sure," I said, humoring him. I was opposed to any favors. I felt that I had done enough.

"Can I borrow $40 off of you?"

I hesitated for effect, as if I were actually thinking about it. But Paul became uncomfortable with the silence and started speaking.

"I'll pay you back over the next week in $5 payments. I can leave it on the kitchen table every night," he pleaded.

"Why do you need it?" I asked.

"I just do."

"Well, there's food in the house and you have a bed and a –

He cut me off.

"The truth is I wanted to get Cheryl a professional haircut for job interviews."

"Oh," I said a bit surprised. I had not expected such a good explanation so full of concern for his beloved wife. It could have been true; it's not like I knew Paul well enough to make a judgment, but either way it didn't matter.

"She has a right to feel good about herself," he pleaded.

"Paul, I'm sorry, but I don't carry cash."

"None at all?"

"Nope."

"Oh."

"Sorry."

"There's an ATM at the bar a few blocks away."

"Paul, she can't get a haircut tonight. It's 10 PM," I said raising my voice.

Paul's eyes darted left and right until he just sighed and trudged back upstairs. He didn't come out of his room for the rest of the night.

"That was nice of him to want to get you a haircut," I said, doing my best to hide the sarcasm.

"He's a sweet man. It's why I married him."

"Are you angry that I don't have the money?"

"No, we know what it's like to have too many bills to pay."

"Yeah, too many bills," I said, sinking deep into my chair.

We watched TV for another hour until I got sleepy and headed for bed.

"Goodnight," she said.

As I climbed the stairs, I reflected and realized that this was the first time she wished me a good night. The awkwardness of the first few weeks was fading away, and it felt good, really good.

"Goodnight, Cheryl," I called back from the top of the stairs.

We didn't have a lot of ways to entertain ourselves in the house. Our TV only had three channels and one of them was blurry so it was more like two channels. For amusement, Paul and Cheryl often told me stories about their past, their families, and their children. We never sat down and conducted a full interview from start to finish, but after weeks of little vignettes here and there, I was able to reconstruct a good portion of their story.

Before I found them, Cheryl and Paul had been living under a bridge, which they called home, for about four months. Before that, they lived out of a van; and before that, they lived at friends' houses. In short, their existence was nomadic at best. However, almost a few years ago, they lived a completely opposite life. They lived what most would describe as a normal life, a great life. They practically lived out the American dream in a normal house in Glen Bernie in the great state of Maryland. Paul worked construction jobs for the union and other contractors, while Cheryl waited tables at local restaurants. She also worked as an administrative assistant for a doctor's office. Two paychecks provided them with more than enough money to take care of themselves and their three 12-and-13-year-old children. They had family barbecues, went fishing on the Chesapeake, and took the family on camping trips. Everything was going great until life dealt them a few bad cards.

Soon they were out of their house and forced to rotate living between family and friends. But that wouldn't last forever. One day Paul and Cheryl woke up and found themselves living out of a van. To make food money, they collected scrap metal and sold it for cash. I didn't ask where they found the metal because I didn't want to know. As any parent could guess, van life was unsuitable for raising kids. The children missed days and then weeks of school, and they were miserable for it. Cheryl's 30-year-old son agreed to take in his two younger siblings and raise them as his own children. Paul and Cheryl would have to figure themselves out on their own.

When the van's transmission gave out, they left it for dead on the side of the road. Making their way to the homeless camp under a bridge, they borrowed a tent and started panhandling. Their situation looked grim, especially after their children left, and they had nothing else but each other. They scrambled to come up with a strategy to pull themselves out of this downward spiral and eventually developed a plan: Wait for a miracle.

Drinking one last sip of hot chocolate, she set her cup down. Cheryl stood up, left the living room, and walked over to the wall next to kitchen table where she lay her hand on the smooth, blank, white board hanging on the brick. It had been almost five weeks since they had moved in. I sat facing her and leaned my chin on the tall back of the chair. Staring into the board, she looked ready and had a twinkle in her eye. I could tell something really cool was about to happen and goose bumps formed all over my arms. Paul had already left to go panhandling. It was a shame that he wouldn't be here for this.

"I've always dreamed of going back into the food business again," she said wistfully.

"Nothing's stopping you."

"I know, but, hon."

"What?"

"I need benefits. My health..."

"Waitress on the side," I said, still leaning on the back of my chair. "Work at a company for the benefits; waitress on the weekends."

"Yeah, that could be good," she said, nodding excitedly, "That could work."

"If you want, you could do it."

"I know."

"It's been several weeks," I said, fishing something out of my pocket, "Are you ready?"

"Ready for what?"

I pulled out a marker and, when she saw it, the ends of her mouth briefly curved into a slight smile.

"Yeah. You know, I think I am," she said before taking it from me. Indeed, this was the passing of a baton, a big moment which had been four weeks in the making. I had taken it as far as I could, and now it was her turn. This is what I had been waiting for. She was doing great, wonderfully even. Her hand went up and down moving the rest of her arm with it. The pony tail she had tied behind her head jingled as she scribbled in large purple letters. After a few minutes, she stopped writing, shook her wrist, and admired her handiwork. Satisfied, she stepped back so I could see. Scribbled on the wall, in purple magic marker, was the finish line to the race. In outstanding penmanship, she had started her list with "a job" and ended it with the words "my family together." There were many other things written in between, but the first and last were the most important.

Over the next few weeks, Cheryl made significant progress. She had even gotten her old waitressing job back, but we didn't consider this a "big win. She had already worked there before, and it didn't pay nearly enough to make a proper living. On top of all that, she didn't even get a prime shift. But it was something, and something was progress, a stepping stone that made me hopeful and should have made her hopeful too, but she was disappointed. I could tell by the way she hung her head low whenever she spoke about it. There was no future there; and even with free housing, she couldn't make ends meet. I reminded her that this wasn't going to be easy. I told her over and over again that good things don't come easily and she must never give up. I prodded. I nagged. And she listened.

After waitressing, she came home and sent applications everywhere. The next fourteen applications ranged from catering jobs and temp agencies to painting gigs and office assistant postings. She even walked door to door in the neighborhoods marketing herself as a cleaning woman.

In the beginning, no one took her seriously. Even though she had an address, she had no email nor did she have a phone number. I was thrilled to hear her excuses because I knew that the faster we got to the issues, the faster we could make progress. Not having proper contact information was only one of the many walls blocking her to success. Every one of these walls would have to be identified and every wall would have to be torn down.

And so it began. I purchased a pay-as-you-go phone, complete with 200 minutes for both of them. Cheryl and Paul agreed to buy their own phone cards after the initial minutes were used up. Outfitted with phone and address, Cheryl received several callbacks. She went to interviews; but because of the recession and credit crisis, an actual job offer never materialized. Still, I thought this was great because it was working, we were getting traction, and sooner or later something would pan out. This was all a numbers game, and quitting was not an option. I made this clear. And she listened.

She sent out more applications, attended more interviews, but still endured more rejections. She started getting disgruntled, but, again, quitting was not allowed so she sent out more applications, walked door-to-door asking for work, and received more rejections. Remarkably, she kept at it and filled out yet another round of applications, one of which was to a job at a local hospital. She did not particularly like working in hospitals, though she had hospital experience from working in an E.R. a few years back. She explained to me that one day she witnessed a thirteen- year- old boy die in front of her. The boy reminded her of her own 12-year-old son, and she couldn't handle it. She quit and ran all the way home where she dropped to her knees, hugged her two kids and didn't let go. She was a mom and she loved her children and couldn't bear to think of anything happening to them. While holding them in her arms, she swore off working in hospitals ever again. But now she was desperate; and with her experience, she had a good chance of getting the job. I pushed her to take anything with benefits no matter how low the salary. She submitted her application; and within a few days, they called back and requested to schedule a time for an interview. She went to the interview and reported that they liked her references and would call her back soon.

"Are you sure I should take it?"

"Cheryl, take it."

"But they said that only the late night shifts were open."

"Who cares? It's a job!"

"They said that I could get the 4 A.M. shift."

"If they offer you this job, I will personally escort you to and from the hospital."

"Really? But you hate getting up early."

"For this, I would become nocturnal."

"Are you sure?"

"I'll get three extra loud alarm clocks. I'll go to bed at 6 PM. Before bed, I'll down eight glasses of water to make sure I wake up to pee. Anything! Anything to make sure you get back and forth from your job safely."

"Okay, okay. I get it."

A few days passed without any word, and I became anxious. Then it happened. They called back with an answer. After such a long wait, I expected bad news, but it wasn't. Ecstatic, Cheryl blurted out that she got the job, and I was in a momentary state of disbelief. She got the job? She got the job! Training started in one week. She jumped up and down with tears going everywhere. I gave her a high-five, but nothing more. I may have given her a pat on the back, I can't remember, but certainly nothing more than that. A high five was enough, at least for now, because it was important that she realize that the hardest part was not getting the job but *keeping* it.

Three weeks. All celebrations would be delayed for three weeks. But inside I could barely contain myself. Rejoice! Now was the time to celebrate, and I wanted to go nuts. Crazy! Jump up and down, perhaps streak through the neighborhood, or maybe buy a cake! It took four months, but we made it, damn it! Impossibly, we had made it. A taste of victory, sweet, sweet victory. With all odds beaten and every expectation surpassed, I wondered what Father Lorenzo would say now? What would the world say now? Paul was a deadbeat, I agreed, but so what if he took advantage of everything? Cheryl was worth it. She had found work and a future and had done everything herself. She had found openings. Sent applications. Interviewed.

Pulled her weight and became a living triumph of hard work and dedication. I wanted to shout from the rooftops --- Cheryl got a job! Cheryl got a job! I'd tell the whole world maybe with a megaphone. Yes, I would use a really loud megaphone because everyone must know. She had done it.

We had finally made it, but despite my excitement, I didn't do any of these things. Instead, I went home to my parents where I said nothing at all. How could I? I saw them every weekend, and they still had no idea that I had moved. I talked incessantly about the smallest things and purposefully left very little time to say anything else. It was all part of The Plan. But of all the weekends, this was probably the one which I would willingly spill the beans. Cheryl had a job, a good job; I was still alive, employed, and happy. Measures of success that proved, at least for now, that The Plan was working.

Before walking through the front door of my parents' house, I slapped on an extra goofy grin. The kind of grin that says "guess what!" I expected them to ask, and that was fine because I would tell them everything. Sure they'd be pissed, furious, livid, but only at first. They'd get over it.

I opened the door and immediately frowned. This may not have been the weekend to tell them after all. The house was in complete disarray. Trash bags, paper towels, and disinfectant spray lay entangled by a large vacuum hose. The hose snaked around the entire floor and roped around the banisters up the stairs. A couch was turned over, the rugs were rolled up, and the washing machine, dishwasher, and dryer all ran simultaneously.

It was not unusual to come home to a cleaning operation like this. Mom had been a nurse for many years. She knew about microbes. Knew too much. Much too much. Germs, disease, and illness, were all enemies that posed a constant threat to her beloved family. Ever vigilant, she read up on all the latest outbreaks, both new and ancient viruses. Often, she sent emergency medical update emails complete with pictures to my brother and me. Horrifying emails, many of which displayed decaying flesh and blood. She did this late at night, right before I went to bed. These updates would keep me up for hours worrying. Whether it was from mosquitoes carrying West Nile virus, kittens carrying leukemia, or not washing ones hands after emptying the trash, the family faced constant danger. In the Bjonerud household, few days passed without a near death experience.

"Mom?"

"Matt? Is that you?" she called from the top floor. I heard the vacuum turn off and then the footsteps echoing in the upstairs hallway.

"Yes. What's with all the mess?" I called back.

She came down the stairs in a jogging outfit and sneakers. I knew this as her cleaning outfit. She also carried a basket of cleaning supplies, her prematurely silver hair tied back behind her head. She wore a pair of bright yellow plastic gloves, gloves that were used for handling the most toxic of chemicals. She stood on the third from the bottom step so that she could look me in the eye.

"If you answered your cell phone, you'd know by now, young man," she said, wagging a bright yellow finger.

"What happened?"

"We were attacked!"

"Attacked?"

"Oh, it was horrible."

She told me the story of the attack. It was 10:00 P.M. when the initial strike occurred. No one saw it coming, not even our young, spry shepherd, who lay faithfully at the foot of the bed. Mom and Dad sat innocently watching television. Laughing at Nick at Nite shows, they relaxed, unaware of a predator lurking behind their bedroom door. The next thing they knew, a bat swooped into wreak havoc in the bedroom. They finally won the battle by pillow knocking it right out the bedroom window. But it wasn't over.

She told me that earlier that morning, she woke up to find another bat. It lay dead on the floor in the living room in a small grey heap. She said she called animal control but found out that they only come for live animals. Luckily, while she was on the phone with them, she saw one of the wings move. After an initial shriek, she told the animal control dispatcher about it, and they reluctantly agreed to come over. They sent one of their department's finest to take care of this animal emergency. Carrying a large animal control pole and wearing a thick beard, he stood an impressive 6'5", and filled the entire doorway.

"You arrived quickly."

"Well, with these live animals, we don't always have a lot of time."

"Of course."

"Where is the beast?"

"Follow me."

Mom led him through the hallway into to the living room. She pointed at it but stopped three feet from it and refused to move any closer.

"Oh, I see."

"What's the problem?"

"Well, er."

"Can't you just remove it?"

"It's not that. It's --

The man stopped speaking and poked it with the pole.

"It's just that—

Crossing her arms she said, "What? Just get rid of it, please!"

"It's just that I think this is a ball of dust."

"Oh."

He poked it again.

"Yeah."

"It's a ball of dust?"

"Yes, Ma'am."

"Oh, well then -- really?"

"Yes."

"I'm terribly sorry."

"Happens all the time, Ma'am. It'll just be between us."

"Thank you."

In light of the rabies disaster, I couldn't figure how to broach the subject. Mom would not like to hear that I had moved, especially that I had moved into the Baltimore ghetto. Mom would not be able to bear the fact that I shared a bathroom with homeless people. A germ-infested war zone that would probably result in numerous midnight emails. I had no words of diplomacy worthy of mitigating the risks that she would all too accurately identify. No way to make things "sound better." These were not the conversations one has with someone preparing for rabies injections which were quite painful. An explanation of my recent activities would have to wait.

Almost every night Cheryl, Paul and I conducted intense powwow sessions about job progress. I made them explain their plan for success. We would discuss objectives. All I wanted was a little effort. I demanded effort. These conversations were good because I felt like everyone had a plan for success. However, after a few weeks, I noticed an ugly side effect had developed. Good days were good only if they resulted in progress, while bad days resulted from job activity failures. Few would have seen this as a *problem*, but I hated it. My house was supposed to be supportive, not overbearing; and more importantly, my goal wasn't to get them jobs in the first place. My goal was to give them dignity. Dignity, damn it! For once I wanted them to know what it felt like to be rare, special. Focusing on getting work was good, but too much focus turned it ugly. They were more to me than a success story, and I would make sure that they knew this. They needed to know that I *enjoyed* their company and valued them as human beings. They needed to know that jobs were simply a language to communicate something words could not.

I walked through the automatic doors of a CVS. Pausing, I reminisced about a time when I had gotten thrown out of a CVS in college. A friend and I had gotten into a pushing brawl in the women's aisle among tampons, pads, and eyebrow wax, the aisle that guys just weren't meant to be in. There was nothing for us there. So naturally, we had tried to shove each other into it. Tampons and pads flew everywhere. Everywhere! The row of shelves wobbled. It would have hit the other shelves and caused the shelves to fall on one another like dominoes. The store would have been ruined which was a fact not lost on the security guard. Within a minute, we both were escorted out into the streets.

"Board games."

"Excuse me?"

"I am looking for your board game section," I said.

"Oh, aisle five," said the clerk.

I walked over to the board game section and took stock of their selection. Last week Paul said he liked Yahtzee, used to play it with his friends. Reaching down, I picked up the Yahtzee box and walked back over to the checkout counter. The clerk started to ring it up. Wait. I thought to myself, what if *I* didn't like Yahtzee?

"Wait one minute. I forgot something," I said.

A minute later I reappeared with a pile of games between my hands. I dropped the stack of games down, and they collapsed all over the counter like a bad game of Jenga.

"Well, now."

I reached into my pocket for my wallet. Handed the card to the cashier.

"Sir."

"Yeah?"

"Seriously?"

"What?"

"Every game in the store?"

"Yup."

The clerk looked suspicious.

"Oh, I get it."

"What?"

"Drinking games?"

"No, nope. I wish."

"You volunteering at the senior center?"

"Nope."

Chapter 9: Job Progress

Years ago, Paul had worked as a construction laborer, skilled in carpentry and home repairs. Cheryl said he could build anything. She went on and on about some wooden spiral staircase that he spent weeks crafting. Its spindles were delicate and the wood varied in texture and color. Made of cedar, mahogany, and iron, it was the most beautiful staircase she said she had ever seen. I wished I could have seen it, or any of the other things he made, but I never had the chance.

In a past life, neighborhood kids had loved Paul because he built them tree houses. Large tree houses, which were really more like tree mansions, every one custom designed and each with state-of-the art amenities such as electric lighting, glass windows, refrigerators, and ceiling fans. I thought that I had a good childhood, but after hearing this, I realized that I was raised on the other side of the tracks, specifically the less-than-privileged-couldn't-afford-a-large-tree-mansion side. Back when I was growing up, I was forced to build my tree house with my own two hands. Not only that, but my tree house was not even up in a tree. I wasn't allowed. Mom said that it was too dangerous and that I would surely fall out and break a leg or an arm. So I played on the ground, in the dirt, much like a barbarian child.

I built my tree house out of sticks, leaves, and trash bags, which were necessary for waterproofing. Really, I built them out of whatever I could find. They had no windows, no furniture and, at the end of the day, were nothing more than dirt huts. They were a far cry from Paul's famed tree mansions, but it wasn't my fault. I blamed my workers. Well, my one worker. That's right. I forced my brother into hard labor. It was allowed because I was older, thirteen months older, to be exact. As the elder, it was my responsibility to show him the ways of the world and so I immediately placed him under the yoke. Nothing like manual labor to make someone grateful and appreciative for his blessings, I always thought. Though he would be doing the manual labor, I would be the brains behind the operation, responsible for drawing up the plans to create an impressive awe-inspiring feat of architecture. Neighbors would come from near and far to gaze upon its aesthetically pleasing appearance and design. With my brains and Eric's brawn, we would build a mega fortress of awesomeness. At the time, I thought it would be amazing, perhaps the eighth wonder of the world, or maybe even the ninth. No, it would be the eight *and* ninth wonders of the world! But things did not go as planned, and Eric did terrible work, just awful. Trash heaps. They looked like big trash heaps, which were nothing like the plans I had prepared. The neighbors commented, I think, and Dad got angry. Every weekend Dad mowed the lawn, did the weeding, and planted trees in a three-piece suit. Unlike the other neighbors, he would not hire a lawn service to do it for him. He took pride in his yard work and so any transgression against his lawn, trees or flowers, was taken personally. Needless to say, having large trash heaps in the backyard drove him to buy us tents, large collapsible, throwaway tents. The tents were fun, but I would have loved a tree mansion. Cheryl said that the neighborhood kids had felt the same way and considered Paul a hero for making the houses for them.

Unfortunately, Paul's tree mansion building days didn't last forever. Standing on the side of some scaffolding, he lost his balance, fell three stories, and shattered his heel. As if the pain weren't enough, medical bills drained the family savings. Walking became painful and, soon after, he lost his job. The doctors couldn't repair his foot because floating bone fragments were no easy fix.

After six years and three surgeries, Paul had never fully healed.

One night, he was telling me the story of his fall and decided to remove his shoes to help him tell the story. The moment he loosened his shoe laces, I could smell the fresh air slowly become polluted with the odor of blue cheese blended with rotten eggs. In order to explain his injuries beyond words, he then removed his sock, which was not originally brown. I could tell. He pulled the sock completely off his foot, and that's when I saw it. Knobby bones protruding under his skin, knobs all over his heel. His foot was deformed and looked almost inhuman. It made me want to barf.

"Uuugghh. That is so gross," I complained.

"Yeah, well, yuh get used to it."

"What's worse is them rotten egg smells," said Cheryl, fanning her hand to disperse the smell.

"How were you supposed to work with a broken foot?" I asked

"Ya don't."

"So, if you couldn't work, what was your plan to make money?"

"Well, Cheryl still brought home a paycheck, but there was no way we could pay all them bills."

"Then how else did you pay them?"

"We didn't, hon," sighed Cheryl, "But we had hope."

"In what?" I asked perplexed.

Paul smiled, "I've applied for disability. I'll be hearing any day now."

"Really?"

Cheryl nodded. Paul had applied for disability somewhere between two and ten years ago. I could never get an exact time frame because it was complicated, always complicated. If approved, he would receive thousands of dollars in back dated payments. That part was clear. One large lump sum, kind of like a golden parachute. After waiting at least two years, he figured it couldn't be much longer. He said it was a blessing waiting to happen. But I knew it wasn't. If only he had known, things would have been different. I tried to tell him. I tried. But he wouldn't listen. No matter what I said, I simply couldn't convince him that it was hopeless.

His comment about 'getting it any day now' had been repeated daily for over a year. After his back dated lump sum of several thousand dollars, he would receive a check of about $600 a month, which he said was enough to get him through the rest of his life. A legitimate job, he believed, would ruin his chances of qualifying. Any work he did would have to be under the table. Illegitimate and temporary side jobs that paid in cash were acceptable. Checks were laughable. Healthcare was out of the question. If he had healthcare, then why would he need disability? Healthcare was the enemy, and he would do everything he could not to have it. This disability bailout was his motivation and reason for living, a reason for hope. It's why he stood on the corner every single damn day. To make money, while at the same time maintaining his eligibility for disability. Powerless, I couldn't persuade him otherwise. I tried. I tried!

After a long day of work, I stepped out of the revolving doors and walked into a cluster of pigeons hobbling around the plaza. The lazy birds fed on the crumbs that fell off lunch tables scattered about the square. Incapable of surviving in the wild, they were completely dependent on discarded sandwiches. Thriving on handouts from tourists were their only means of survival, and it made me sick. Sometimes when they got too close, I worried that I may catch one of their diseases and so I would wave my hands around to scare them away. They would fly and send feathers everywhere, but I waited for them to settle on the ground before walking through. It had been a long day of work, and the last thing I wanted was to inhale pigeon feathers, which would surely result in my contracting some terrible lung illness. I disappeared down into the parking garage and re-surfaced outfitted in my street attire.

I wanted to threaten Paul with eviction, maybe put a little fire in his belly, but Cheryl, she had a job and they were a package deal. I wouldn't risk her progress. Pulling my hoodie tightly over my head, I kept walking and made it home in under thirty minutes. I walked quickly because it was too hot to walk slowly. The sun beat down on me, and I sweated through my clothes, saturating my suit. When I got home, I found a dubious surprise.

Large boxes of what appeared to be bottled water greeted me on the other side of the door. It had been a long day, and I was tired and very, very thirsty. The water looked tempting in a forbidden kind of way, but I couldn't tell what brand. What brand? This was important because without the brand, I couldn't tell how badly I wanted one of them. The labels had been torn off, but why would they be torn off? Strange.

"Cheryl," I called. "Cheryl, are you up there?"

Upstairs a door opened and the floorboards squeaked.

"Yeeahh?" she called back. Groggy eyed and puffy cheeked, she slowly trudged downstairs. Apparently she had just woken up from her afternoon nap. She was wearing some old khaki shorts and an oversized pink t-shirt.

"Cheryl, where did all this come from?"

She rubbed her eyes, sat down on the couch in front of the waters and stretched out.

"Oh, yeaah, those are Mitchum's. He brought 'em here after work today."

More name-dropping. Our house has a horrible name-dropping problem. They spoke to me as if I knew them their whole lives along with their entire social network, but I didn't. I needed explanations and context and maybe an introduction or two. These people they referenced, I had no idea who they were.

"He should be back any minute now to pick them up."

"What does he do?"

"He works across the street at the factory."

"Across the street?"

"Yeah."

"Did Paul apply there?"

"I told him to go."

"Did he?"

"No."

I inspected the cases. Cheryl turned the television on and sat down to start watching TV. But, just as she hit the couch, I heard a strange ringing noise from what sounded like a Nextel walkie-talkie phone. It came from right outside the front door.

"Speak of the devil."

"Huh?"

"There's Mitchum now," she said, getting up out of her seat.

I sprinted past her and bounded up the stairs. I still had my suit underneath my street clothes and needed to change. Upstairs I put on my new summer uniform. Designed to help me stay cool, it consisted of a pair of old frayed cargo shorts and an oversized faded blue t-shirt and, of course, my wallet sandals. I picked this shirt because it had no labels and no obvious brand markings. Brands. They helped people determine how much they wanted something. Brand-less meant valueless unless, of course, it was me. Then brand-less meant priceless because it provided me with protection, safety, and the invisibility that I needed to maintain a low profile. I pulled my shirt down and stretched it below my knees, as was the custom in the neighborhood.

Coming downstairs, I found the front door open and a very large black man sitting on the front stoop with Cheryl. In a stern voice, he shouted at someone through the phone.

"Lequita! I don't have time for your dilly dally! I need the truk her' now!...uh huh...uh huh....nah....yeah...I got me sum vitamin waters that need tuh be brought'n home."

Cheryl lit up a cigarette and just stared out into the neighborhood. I looked over at her and tilted my head. She shrugged and mouthed the word "girlfriend."

I mouthed "Oh" back.

"I don't care what happened to mama's pork n' beans, just put it 'n the fridge. Now, get in yur truck 'n get over her'! Devil banshee woman, don't you cross me!"

The phone made several successive 'blupe' sounds as Mitchum lowered the volume, successfully muting Lequita's enraged response. Hopping down from his seat, Mitchum dusted off the stairs so that I could sit.

"It's good to finally meet you," he said, shaking my hand rapidly. It was then that I noticed he had very large cataracts. Once I saw them, I couldn't stop looking at them. They were so spherical and so perfectly glazed that they glistened in the sun. They formed around the outside of his eyeballs. I couldn't stop staring at them, but luckily staring at cataracts results in perfect eye contact.

"You work at the factory?" I asked.

"Yup."

"What's it like?"

"Yuh basically just stand all day and load bottles into boxes."

"Got it."

"Say, your mom said I could keep them boxes around."

That's just like "Mom." Opening up a house to complete strangers. Allowing them to stow their goods in the living room. Just move their stuff in, whatever it was, whenever they wanted. If it had been anyone other than Mitchum, I would have been pissed, but I liked this guy. He had a calm demeanor and fantastic looking cataracts.

"That's fine with me," I said.

"I'm givin ya one of those boxes for helping me out."

"Really?"

"Yeah."

"Thanks!"

"Sure."

"What brand are they?"

"Vitamin waters."

Way to go, "Mom." You just scored us a free water deal, and I wasn't even angry. I was impressed. He was employed and seemed to be an upstanding hard-working citizen who had his own place to live, a girlfriend, and brought us gifts. He seemed like the perfect role model for Cheryl and Paul, and I hoped he would come around more often. Maybe he could even help Paul get a job at his factory.

"You're welcome to store 'em here anytime," I said.

I was impressed by his friendliness, especially after listening to Lequita's tirade.

Cheryl finished her cigarette and threw it on the sidewalk where Mitchum stamped it out.

"Can I get ya both sumthin' ta drink?" she asked.

"I'm good."

"Nutin' like a cold glass of water on a hot day," he said, as Cheryl nodded and went back inside. I noticed that Mitchum's hands had bruises and cuts all over them. His knuckles were completely bashed open. I wondered why I had not noticed these injuries until now.

"Hey, Mitchum, you get into any bar fights recently?" I joked.

"Huh?"

"Look at your hands, man. They're all cut open."

He looked at his hands and then chuckled to himself. He smiled, stood up a little straighter, and pushed back his shoulders.

"These are from my son," he said triumphantly.

What? I couldn't believe I was hearing this. No doubt he bloodied his knuckles in an abusive beat down. Through friendly conversation, I had stumbled into a confession of child abuse right here in broad daylight. The sick criminal was practically beaming with pride that he beat up his own son. His arms were huge. I noticed now. They were massive. I realized that I was talking to a dangerous, dangerous man. A dangerous man who beat his own kids until his knuckles ran red with their blood. I understood at that moment that I needed to do everything and anything to stay on Mitchum's good side.

"My son's stronger than a bull," he continued.

"I bet, just like his dad."

"He and I wrastle all the time, but last night he got me good."

"He got you good?"

"Too good."

As Mitchum spoke, he got very animated. His hands flapped rapidly, and he stomped his feet on the ground. Thrashing about, he retold the story of this epic beat-down.

"I had him in a hold like this, and then he got my leg here and pulled me completely off my feet."

Convinced now that this was not a case of domestic abuse, I relaxed. He was just doing some playful father-son activities.

"My knuckles got pretty bashed as we wrestled on a concrete floor."

"Concrete?"

"Yeah."

"Oh."

"But then he got me in a headlock, good. I was waving about, but I just couldn't break free."

I just nodded in response.

"He got my genes fo' sho'."

Mitchum's phone beeped again. He looked down at the phone and then up at me. Rolled his eyes to signal it was Lequita and walked around the block out of sight. Cheryl came out with his glass of water and set it down on the top step before popping another cigarette in her mouth.

"I think he likes you," she said.

"He's very friendly."

"You would never know it based on the way he talks to Lequita," I commented.

"Don't be fooled. He loves her."

"Are you sure?"

"Every couple has their spats, but the strong relationships always get through them."

"I guess."

"Trust me. I've been married three times. I know."

"No arguments here, but I was wondering how did you meet Mitchum anyway?"

"I bumped into him last week."

"Where?"

"Here."

"Where?"

"Here," she said opening up her arms.

"Here? On the stoop?" I asked.

"Oh, yeah, all sorts of people sit on these stoops all the time."

"Really?"

"Many times they don't even live in the neighborhood."

"Where do they come from?"

"The factory, the bars, stuff like that," she said, blowing out a puff of smoke. Mitchum came back around the corner. Slouching a bit, he hung his head low and looked a little sad.

"Lequita can't make it today."

"Oh, that's fine." I said.

"Really?"

"Yeah"

"We'll pick it up later this week."

He looked at his watch and said his goodbyes. He gave me a hearty handshake, and I took one last good look at those massive pulsing cataracts. Then Cheryl and I watched Mitchum disappear around the block.

"Where's he going?"

"Bus stop, probably"

"Oh."

"He's the nicest maximum security ex-convict I've ever met," she said.

"Wait. What?"

"Didn't he tell you?"

"No…it didn't come up."

"Oh."

"What was he in for?"

"Drug dealing."

"Ah."

"Where do you think his bullet wounds came from?"

"I didn't notice any bullet holes."

"Are you blind? There're some on his arm and on his legs."

I sat and hung my head in my hands. So much for Mitchum setting a good example. So much for the 'upstanding citizen.'

The next day I arrived at the plaza surrounding my office at 7:30 AM, about an hour before the deafening blaring of angry horns from the morning gridlock. I noticed that at least one or two pigeons had smashed into the clear glass windows of the Firm's skyscraper. Sometimes they flew away, and other times they hit the building so hard that they fell dead to the sidewalk, feathers and other bird parts splattering across the cobbled plaza. I stepped over the streams of water created by the city cleaning crew as they hosed down pigeon remnants littering the sidewalks. They raced to clear unpleasant sights before the morning rush without a thought of the lifeless birds under their brooms.

I got to my cube and switched my sneakers for my polished leather shoes. I selected a blue tie from the cabinet and tied a large knot around my neck; but without a mirror it, took a few tries. Unbeknownst to me, Rupert, my analytics manager who had also arrived early, stood and watched me make the final adjustments.

Rupert had been with the Firm seven years and yet was in his late twenties, which made him an experienced and relevant mentor for me. He looked well fed, but not overfed, and had a very dry sense of humor, which took me two months to decipher. Upon first meeting him, I took everything he said literally, which was a big mistake that caused me to miss many witty remarks. Professionally, he was among the most respected managers in the Maryland region because he knew all the Firm policies inside and out. Many high-ranking managers sought his advice on the most complicated deals. In short, he was a walking encyclopedia for the Firm's best practices.

Sighing, Rupert startled me by knocking on the wall.

"Can I see you in my office?" He looked concerned, almost worried.

"Yeah, sure. Uhh, I'll be there in a sec," I said as I hastily folded down my collar.

Managers were charged with making sure that offerings were underwritten properly and according to policy. Each manager was given signing authority to approve deals. Rupert needed to feel comfortable with the financial analysis, the industry analysis, the policy exceptions, and deal structure before he would ever consider signing off on anything. As most managers had to be, he was a perfectionist. Any error, no matter how small, would need to be corrected, completely rewritten, recalculated, and all without regard for timelines.

His primary objective was to protect the Firm, even if it meant losing a deal. I was new at underwriting implementation strategies, and it was only natural to make mistakes. I had come to expect almost daily summonses from Rupert where he would inform me of various sections that needed redoing. He would tell me these things in a monotone. Over the months, I noticed that the errors he found were getting less and less significant. In fact, the majority of his errors were grammatical, which led me to believe that I had learned the fundamentals. Regardless, there were still things I needed to learn, but these meetings always happened only in the afternoon. We never met in the morning because he needed ample time to dig in and review everything, especially the grammar. He used the time to catch every error, every imperfection, and every out of place comma. I wondered how badly, probably horrifically, I had messed up this past report to warrant this crack-of-dawn-early-morning-before-I've-had-my-coffee meeting.

I found Rupert in his office sitting behind his desk and staring into his computer. He wasn't moving and didn't bother to look up when I knocked at the door.

"What's up?" I asked.

He took off his spectacles and placed them down before resting his folded hands on top of his dark wooden desk.

"I have to ask you something."

"Sure, err, umm, is it the debt service coverage ratio? I can explain if-- He cut me off mid sentence.

"Excuse me for being blunt, but are you living out of your cube?"

"What?"

"You heard me."

"Please reword."

"This is not a difficult question. Just look at your work space."

"I've seen it. Yes."

"It looks like a walk-in closet."

I laughed uncomfortably, "Oh, that's just my dry cleaning."

"Dry cleaning?"

"Yeah, just some dry cleaning I haven't taken home yet."

Frustrated, Rupert used his hands to accentuate his frustration.

"Matt, you have three suits, six shirts, two pairs of pants, two sets of shoes, an overcoat, and a leather jacket hanging in your cube right now."

"You're right. Too much," I nodded, backing out off the office.

"And?"

"And I'll bring them home."

"When?"

I stood behind the door threshold and continued the conversation from the hallway.

"Soon."

"Today."

"Can't today."

"Has to be today."

"Why?"

"Some of the bigwig executives are flying in to tour our market. Everything needs to be put in order for their visit."

"Oh."

"I don't care what you do with them after they leave, but while they're here, the clothes must go."

"I'll fix it. Don't worry."

Hanging my head low, I walked back to my desk. Maybe I could hide them on another floor, perhaps find a spare closet and dump them in there. No, there were no closets. Space was tight and every nook and cranny was already used. There was random stuff everywhere, but maybe the stairwell could work? Yes. Perfect. Nobody uses the stairwells anymore, especially not since the invention of the elevators. But wait. What if there was a fire, or worse, a fire drill? As part of the Firm's safety precautions, drills happened often, and I couldn't risk having hundreds of people getting tangled in my clothes and falling down several flights of stairs during one of the un-damn-predictable fire drills. Could I sneak them home? No, Yes. No. Maybe. No. Yes. Certainly not. Cheryl and Paul would see my suits and belts, and they'd think I was rich. Clearly, Paul and Cheryl would steal my clothes and either wear them or sell them. One day, I knew I would come home and find everything stolen and just like that, *they* would be gone with all my clothes. As if having my suits stolen wasn't bad enough, I realized that I would have nothing to wear to work and I'd be forced to go naked, well, maybe not naked, but it would be annoying and expensive to fix my wardrobe problems. There was no way I was dealing with that mess. I would never bring my clothes home. Never!

That night, I stayed late and waited for my co-workers to clear out and for the cover of darkness which was the perfect time to conduct my secret moving operation. Normally staying late was not an issue, but this was Cheryl's first day at her new job. Her training had ended the previous week, and she was fully trained, ready to go, and excited about work. Dying with curiosity, I wanted to know how she liked her co-workers, her manager, and her actual job. She had tried so hard to get the position, and I needed to make sure she was happy. I heard the last person leave to go home as I finished up some extra work, and that's when I folded up my laptop and began my search. Despite my efforts and systematic method of searching, I could not find any spare space even after I wandered all over the floor. Finally, after inspecting every closet, I gave up and stuffed all of my clothing into four large filing cabinets. Sure, they would get wrinkled, but I figured it was better than having them stolen.

After my clothing storage fiasco, I descended down into the parking garage, disappeared into the darkness, and changed. Outfitted in ghetto attire, I felt my heart pump faster. I climbed the concrete stairs to the plaza surface and thought of Cheryl's success. I hoped that she had made a few friends, perhaps even the non-convict type. I was ready to be happy for her, and I walked briskly back home to receive her report.

Curiosity was killing me as I left the downtown skyscrapers and glistening towers for the boarded up windows of the ghetto row homes. It was getting dark, and I held my gym bag closer as I crossed over MLK Boulevard. A few blocks from the house, I saw a small bearded man who was riding a sorry excuse for a bicycle and couldn't seem to steer in a straight line. Even though it was dark out, the streetlamps and blue flashy lights produced ample light. There was no excuse for this lackluster bike performance, but then I saw the condition of the bike and reconsidered. The rusted frame could barely stay attached to the wobbling front wheel, but the man kept pedaling. As he got closer, I could tell by his matted, unkempt beard that it was Paul. He skidded to a stop when he saw me flagging him down.

"Paul."

"Howdy."

"How are you? How's Cheryl? Did she like her work today? Does she like her boss?"

"Whoa there. Calm down, bud. Cheryl didn't go to work today."

My heart sank.

"Why not?"

"She got her period on the walk over to work."

"What?"

"Yeah, it was awful. She needs to go see a doctor."

"A doctor?"

"She bled all down her legs."

"Gross."

"It soaked into her shoes. I ran home and got towels to help clean it up."

"Well, did you call an ambulance?"

"No."

"Why the hell not?"

"She didn't want to."

"She didn't?"

"Nope."

"If she's sick, she's going to the hospital."

"She's resting."

"Where are you goin'?" I asked.

"Gonna try and make some money off that corner."

Paul got on his bike and rode away. All I could do was just stand and watch him go. I found myself wishing that I had some leverage to force him into real work, but he was attached to Cheryl who was doing everything that I had asked. There was no way for me to enforce any ultimatums without risking her progress. I had nothing to threaten him with, nothing to encourage him with. I was stuck. But I guess it didn't matter because I considered Paul's obstinacy worth enduring. I could handle it.

When I got home, I found two purple and pink scrubs lying on the couch. The scrub pants had elastic waists and seemed big enough for Cheryl to wear. I took it as proof that she had, in fact, intended to go to work before her crippling medical emergency. I had many questions, but she had already gone to sleep, and I did not disturb her.

Later on I learned that while hosting one of her neighborhood block parties, Cheryl had mentioned her new job. One of the neighbors also worked at the hospital and happened to have several extra sets of scrubs, the pink and purple kind. The neighbor knew how hard it was to keep a job, and so they bonded. She came over to the stoop, shared a cigarette with Cheryl, and offered the scrubs as a gift.

Now this was the last neighbor anyone would have expected to be so kind. Her name was Margery, and she was a short, stubby black woman who regularly terrorized the block with her ferocious Rottweiler. This terrorizing took place about twice a day, usually in the mornings, shortly after 8 AM, and in the evenings sometime after 5 PM. The dog's name was Spike, I think, but if for some reason it was not, then it should have been. Overly aggressive, Spike lunged at everyone and continually bared his fangs. White froth perpetually dripped from his mouth, and he freaked the hell out of us, us being the neighborhood. On top of all that, Margery carried a large wooden club which was about four feet long and so heavy that I doubted she had the strength to lift it. Typically, she just dragged it behind her which, by the way, made her look ridiculous, as if she were wandering into some kind of caveman battle.

At first I suspected that she might be a Teddy Roosevelt enthusiast, an enthusiast who literally interpreted his foreign policy advice, "Walk quietly but carry a big stick," which surprisingly worked to her benefit. No one would ever have dreamt of mugging her unless they had a death wish. Ironically, I later found out that the club was not exactly for *her* defense but for everyone else's. Cheryl told me that once, when Spike got out of control, he tried to attack a neighbor. As legend had it, Margery sprang into action. Adrenaline-infused super-human strength surged through her body, and she lifted the mighty club. As Spike lunged for the neighbor, Margery smacked him on top of the head repeatedly before jamming the club between his jaws. Single-handedly, she had saved the neighbor's life and confirmed that her dog Spike was truly a nightmare.

Chapter 10: John the Epileptic, Weed Smoking, Crack Addict.

Dawn's first light hit me in the face around 6:30 in the morning. It came right through the shades which were crooked, bent, and practically worthless. I rolled over and stuck my head in the pillows where I continued snoring. Outside the tree buds had opened and miniature bright green leaves dotted the branches. Birds chirped and sang morning songs to the neighborhood. As the temperatures rose, overcoats were shed, and boots were replaced with flip-flops. At work some employees sported sharp seersucker suits and brightly colored sport coats. In West Baltimore, people swapped out their hoodies and baggy pants with wife beaters and jean shorts to cope with the heat.

The ceiling fans in the house spun perpetually as the days progressed from warm to hot. Rubbing my eyes, I sat up and looked with curiosity at the silver and green tints covering the ceiling. The flashes of color distracted me for a second but then I remembered that I was supposed to be angry! Cheryl had missed her first day of work. Right. I was annoyed, furious even. Who misses their first day of work? Ingrates. Ingrates who don't know how good they have it. Dumbasses miss their first day. Her employer was a reputable business that surely had protocol against this type of laziness. Obviously they would rescind the offer on account of zero tolerance for first day tardiness, a no-dumbass policy. Companies don't care *why* someone missed work; they just care *that* someone missed it. My alarm clock went off. BEEP BEEP. Damn clock. BEEP BEEP. I explained this to her a million times. BEEP. If she couldn't be there, then they'd just find BEEP someone who could. BEEPBEEPBEEP. I rolled over, grabbed the clock by its face, and threw it against the wall. Silence.

150

I showered and got ready for work. I made little, if any, effort to keep quiet as I marched, no, stomped down the stairs. Halfway down, I spotted Paul sleeping in a chair and wondered what on earth could he have done to Cheryl to be forced to sleep out in the living room? I couldn't make up my mind whether or not I wanted to find out what happened. Sleeping like a baby, he smelled badly, like old garbage bags that had been left out in sun. Curiosity got the better of me, and I kicked his chair, kicked it hard, and he jolted awake. Stretching out his arms, he gave a great big yawn that filled the room with bad breath.

"Mornin'."

"You and Cheryl have a fight?"

Groggy, he spoke with a slight slur in his speech.

"Ahh, naaah, I's just waiting for ya."

"Why?"

"I wanted t'ask ya a question."

He scratched his grey beard as I maneuvered over towards the door.

"Okay, but be quick. I can't be late."

He sat forward in his chair.

"A really, really good buddy is getting evicted today."

I rested my hand on the door knob.

"That's very sad."

"He's got nowheres to go."

"Does he need the name of a shelter or something?"

He stood up and took a few steps towards me.

"I told him that it might possibly be okay if he stayed in the spare room."

He spoke in a tone as if we had already discussed it, as if this had always been part of the plan.

"Can we talk about this tonight?"

"Why?"

"Because."

"Because what?"

151

" Maybe I don't want any more people here."

"But he's a really, really, really good friend of mine. And he has a job installing carpets."

"We'll talk about it later," I said, stepping outside onto the stoop.

Paul kept pleading, almost shouting now.

"I wanted to be like you and help him out. I wanted to be like you!"

"He has a job. He'll find someplace else," I responded.

"Well, he hasn't and –

"Paul! I have to go."

I slammed the door. We were not in a position to have any more risk. Taking on a new houseguest would be impossible and downright reckless, stupid. But it was strange how desperate Paul sounded, and I began to wonder. Could he have already offered the room? He acted as though he had. No, no not even Paul was that dumb, I thought to myself. He knew better, and I dismissed these worries as unsubstantiated paranoia.

In the bowels of the concrete skyscraper, I spent considerable amounts of time cleaning my cube. I stacked files, filed papers, and removed the clutter from the walls. I took down all the papers and printouts, except for the Schrute Buck. I liked the Schrute Buck and it made the cut to remain on my wall. Normally, I didn't clean. Ever. But the bigwigs had just flown in from H.Q. and they would probably tour the floor. Hopefully, they would be disgusted and maybe order renovations, at least new carpets. Though this was very unlikely. They had bigger fish to fry like handling the painful deterioration of the economic climate.

They gathered us together and comfortably sat forty of us around the giant boardroom table. Grey haired and potbellied, the executives sat at the head of the room and explained to us that the global economy was a war zone. With their sleeves rolled up and slightly loosened ties, they looked like they had just come in from the front lines. They began systematically outlining the good and bad straight from the battlefield. I sat at the back side of the table next to Bobby and Jacob and nervously listened to the end of the economic world as we knew it.

The bad news was that the world was heading towards a global recession, the worst in seventy years. Over the past few months, hundreds of thousands of people were laid off. Unemployment approached double digits, and companies that had existed for decades went bankrupt. Some of the largest, strongest, and most prestigious banks failed. Great institutions, some of which had lasted nearly a hundred years, collapsed overnight with more massive layoffs, and it seemed as if no one was safe. Liquidity markets everywhere had frozen up, and even the strongest of the remaining companies had trouble accessing the credit they needed for payroll and other basic costs.

The good news was that our Firm had sold off their risky business units and closed down their high-risk projects years ago. They had been more prudent than others, and their customer base was well diversified. The market had once called them boring, but now they were one of the few who could still continue to grow, which made them relatively exciting. While everyone else was doing riskier, sexier deals, this Firm stuck with what they knew best, and it paid off. Not only was our Firm okay as a whole, but they considered Maryland a growth market which meant that all necessary resources would be given to us. No massive layoffs were planned; and, more importantly, my group was vital to further these growth objectives. The jobs of the people in the room was more or less safe, and breaths of relief were audible.

After the meeting, I returned to the fifth floor with Jacob and Bobby. We were a bit shaken as the meeting looked similar to nightmare meetings happening all over the country. Our friends at other places told us about them and reported horror stories where entire conference rooms of people were fired. At the beginning of the meeting, we had thought for sure we were next. It was all set up for the perfect firing. The execs, looking disheveled and tired, flew down and gathered us together in one large group, corralled us into a board room, and sat us down to discuss the future. All of this happened on a Friday, and I fully expected that the execs planned to fire everyone on the spot. But they didn't. We were lucky, very lucky; and after the meeting, Jacob, Bobby and I walked back to our cubes on what felt like a cushion of air.

"Well, that was a close one," said Bobby.

"Yeah, I thought we were about to get canned."

Jacob shook his head, "No way. I wasn't worried."

"Why not?" I asked.

"We have a strong balance sheet and stuff; we're okay," he said, as if trying to convince himself.

"Well, these aren't usual times now, are they?"

"Let's not talk about it."

We turned the corner to arrive back at our cubes, and for a while we stood around Jacob's desk and chatted. We talked about our projects, talked about bars, and talked about the meetings, which led to talking about layoffs, the end of the world, and then eventually no talking at all. Silently we decided to play some mini basketball with a small hoop sticking out from a tall shelf. We took turns shooting three-point shots with a koosh ball. I tried shooting with my left hand but missed. Jacob shot from his chair, and Bobby dunked with an exaggerated spin move. Then he went up for a behind-the-back dunk, hit the bookshelf, and missed. He sighed as we all watched the ball roll under a large desk.

"So, any luck finding roommates?"

"Umm, err, well paying roommates are harder to find than you think," I said. They knew I had moved into a bad part of town, but they though I had done it by mistake.

"It's been almost three months," said Jacob skeptically.

"Can't expect much from a sketchy neighborhood and a bad economy," I said defensively.

"Why don't you just go to the street and pull off some homeless people," joked Bobby.

I couldn't believe he had just said that, and I wondered if someone how he had figured it out. I could feel myself blushing.

Bobby and Jacob burst out laughing. Homeless people. Roommates. Ridiculous. A good joke. I laughed along with them and decided to have fun with this.

"I've already done it. I live with homeless people now. How ever did you know?"

We laughed harder. Jacob slapped his desk.

"Yeah, you're a funny one, Bjonerud," chuckled Bobby.

"Yeah."

"You'll find people soon enough. Don't worry about it," said Jacob.

"Yeah."

"Next time you look for a place to live, let us know first."

"Will do," I said.

"We can show you some safer neighborhoods."

"Okay. Yeah, next time."

After work I made my way down to the parking garage. Zip zip swoosh swoosh zip swoosh zip. Poof. Fully transformed, I ran up the stairs and emerged onto the plaza square where I began my walk home. I waved my hands and kicked out my foot to send a group of diseased pigeons flying out of my way. Thirty minutes later I stepped onto my block. From a distance, I could see Cheryl sitting on the stoop smoking her cigarettes. A few houses down sat a large group of neighborhood elderly ladies. Sitting in faded beach chairs, they sat in a circle and took up so much of the sidewalk that I had to walk out into the street to maneuver around them. As I passed by, they stopped talking. I looked at them, and they looked at me, blinked their nonexistent eyelashes and smiled, revealing mouths full of missing teeth. I smiled back but kept moving, not really wanting to chat. I did appreciate them being there because they made people feel like someone was looking out for the block.

They watched everyone and took mental notes of everything. Unfortunately, on account of their age, most were handicapped and did little to threaten criminals and drug dealers. In fact, just the other day, Jimmy the Rapist had his bike stolen. He set it up next to the light post, stepped into the corner store, bought a pack of cigarettes, and came back outside. His purchase had only taken twenty seconds, but his bike was already gone without a trace. Well, not exactly without a trace. The ladies had all watched a man walk over and take it not more than a few yards from where they sat. Too weak and feeble to do anything, they didn't even yell. They just sat there and attempted to foil the crook with a particularly violent finger wagging and some disapproving stares. But, alas, all their efforts were futile. The bike crook got away, and Jimmy let out a pained roar of injustice before collapsing to the sidewalk in grief. It was a good quality bike with red and black colors, a rare find in this community. Almost in tears, he explained to me how he had just stolen it last week and swore that he would kill whoever took it from him. I told him that I'd keep my eyes open for it and would let him know if I saw anything. By the time I had finished volunteering my help to Jimmy, I had reached my stoop and found Cheryl relaxing with a cigarette.

"Hey, Cheryl."

"Hi, Hon."

"Feeling better?"

"A little, but I'm still miserable."

I didn't say anything and looked at the bags under her eyes. She was wearing her faded pink t-shirt and jean shorts today.

"Don't I look miserable? Don't I?"

"I guess you look a bit tired."

"Yesterday I was bleeding all down my legs. I probably need surgery."

"Well, then I'll call an ambulance," I said, getting all passive/aggressive.

"No, no, not now."

"Cheryl, cut the crap. If you're sick, you're goin' to the hospital."

"I'm better now."

"You can't get a job like this," I complained.

"Don't worry, I'll be good as new in a day or two."

"Did you contact H.R.?"

"Of course. I talked with Jean. She's so nice."

"So she understood?"

"Yeah, and she said I could start new employee training next Monday."

"Will you start next Monday?"

"Yup."

I leaned back against a tree on the sidewalk while Cheryl puffed away on her cigarette.

"So, what's the deal with this guy who needs a place?"

"Yeah, please don't be angry," she started puffing more heavily.

"Why would I be angry?" I said, already getting angry.

"Well, this guy came by today and said his name was John. He was carrying luggage full of clothes and said he was coming here to live."

"Well, you told him that was ridiculous, didn't you?"

But I could tell by her face that she had not.

"He already took his stuff upstairs. I didn't know what to tell him," she pleaded. I dropped my bag on the ground and launched my hands into the air, flailing them around my head as I spoke. Words alone could not express what I had to say.

"Really? Really? You didn't know what to say? Next time, be creative!"

"It's just his clothes. I'm sorry."

"You took his clothes in the house?"

"Matt, relax. He seems like a nice guy."

"Cheryl, if we keep him, we increase our chances of getting evicted."

"I know, I know."

"All the rules I set up are for *your* benefit. They reduce the risk of *you* getting found out and thrown out."

"Okay okay. Hang on a sec and listen."

I didn't listen and continued to lecture.

"If we get caught early, then you'll be back out on the street. I'll be on the street."

"But he's willing to pay rent!" she announced, smiling, as if this would solve all our problems.

"So what?"

"I figured he could help pay utilities and groceries. Maybe help with rent."

"How much is he willing to pay?"

"One hundred a week."

"A hundred a week? That's four hundred a month!"

"Great, isn't it? Think about how much easier everything will be."

I did think about it. I was paying three times what I had paid at my friend's condo in the suburbs and had to run a monthly deficit just to keep the water and electricity on. For once I wouldn't have to take money out of savings, and maybe I could put some away for a rainy day or something. And he would already have a job, which meant that we'd have three people in the house with jobs. A majority of job holders that could help put the pressure on Paul to get one of his own. This could be good, but I couldn't. I mean, I guessed I could, but I decided that I shouldn't go through with Cheryl's plan. This house was never designed to turn a profit.

"Cheryl, I can't."

"Why? Why the hell not?"

"Because this house is built on principle."

"But you won't be profiting. You'll be making some money to help cover the rent!"

"I don't care."

Cheryl's voice changed from soft and pleading to angry, and I could almost hear a growl beneath her voice.

"Maybe you don't need the money, but some of us do!"

And there it was. I couldn't believe I hadn't seen it before. They had invited him in to make money. They didn't care about this guy. All they wanted was the rent money, and they had probably already worked out a deal with him. Perhaps they planned to blackmail him, get more money, maybe just outright steal from him. How dare they use my house, which I gave them for free, to charge others. I was outraged, furious, and ready to explode. My arms tensed and my jaw clenched, but then I remembered.

I remembered that I had expected this since before I rented the house. Betrayal, theft, and general unpleasantness were all things I knew would be part of this experience. I knew human nature too well to not see this coming. I reminded myself that I had planned on this happening from the beginning even though I had temporarily forgotten it. Enduring stupid things like this was not only expected but necessary, absolutely necessary. What credit is it to me to love people who love me back? If this hadn't have happened, then they may have confused my good will towards them to be reflective of their good will towards me. But now I could finally show them that no matter what choices they made, they could not strip themselves of their own inalienable value, whether they recognized it or not. I was determined to transform this new development into something good.

Rolling up my sleeves, I prepared to navigate through this illogical situation in such a way that didn't violate my principles nor reward their stupidity. Rubbing my forehead, I paused a few seconds while I formulated a plan. Cheryl puffed away as she waited for my response. I could tell the silence made her uncomfortable by the way she rocked back and forth on the stoop.

"All right, I'll tell you what I'm going to do."

"What?"

"He'll get two weeks."

"That's sounds reasonable, hon," she said nodding.

This pleased her, and she relaxed her shoulders. Puffing less severely on her cigarette, she must have been relieved that everything was progressing as planned. She probably figured that if the two weeks went well, she could surely argue for an extension, perhaps a permanent one, but I wasn't finished yet.

"Rent free," I said.

"What?"

"You heard me."

"Are you crazy?"

"No."

"He'll pay! He'll pay! Damn it!" she roared.

"He's staying with us for two weeks rent free. That's it. That's final."

"It's not fair!"

"No. It is very fair."

"Paul's going to be damn pissed."

"Why? Why would he be mad? I'm letting his *good friend* stay here. He'll be thrilled."

Cheryl puffed harder on her cigarette to the point where smoke was almost coming out of her ears. She furrowed her brow as the wheels in her head turned to figure out how to profit from this new scenario.

"So, how long has Paul known this guy?" I asked.

"About a week."

"Interesting."

"Maybe two weeks," she corrected.

"Where is he?"

"Around the corner," she said. She sounded as if she didn't care anymore.

"He's just waiting around the corner?"

"Yeah."

"Well, go get him."

"Where are you goin'?"

"Up to change."

Upstairs I decided to peek inside the guest room to see what this guy had brought over. It was a decision I regretted. On the ground lay an industrial sized trash bag with ragged looking clothes overflowing out of it. Some of his things poured onto the ground, and this did nothing to reassure me. How could it? It was a trash bag that somehow was also a piece of luggage. What kind of self-respecting person travels with luggage trash bags? Didn't he have a job? Could he not afford a proper suitcase?

"Matt, he's here!" she called.

I made my way outside and found Cheryl smoking cigarettes, talking with a tall, lanky white man. A few scraggly long hairs protruded out of his head and four yellow teeth stuck out of his gums. He wore a dirty wife beater covered in sweat stains. His ripped jeans extended below his work boots. When he saw me, he extended his hand and approached. I couldn't help but notice his long nails had black dirt jammed underneath them.

"Thank you, thank you," he said as we shook hands.

"Thank me for what?"

"Your mom said you were going to take me in," said the man.

There "Mom" goes again, always making sure that my life is never dull.

"Whoa there, buddy. Let's slow down a second. First of all, my name's Matt."

"I'm John."

"Very good. Now tell me why you're a mess."

"Excuse me?"

"In! I mean, tell me why you're *in* this mess."

"Listen, bud, I've a solid job installin' carpets and can pay yuh decent rent."

I glanced disapprovingly over at Cheryl while John reached his dirty hands into his pocket. I thought he was going to produce some cash for the month right then and there, but he didn't. Instead he pulled out a crumbled up piece of notebook paper which he shoved in my face.

"What's this?"

"Proof that I paid rent at my other place."

"How did you get evicted?"

"I was a good tenant, but the sublet guy cheated the landlord. The next thing I knew, we both was evicted."

I looked over the paper as John spoke. Written in pencil was a list of barely legible dates with the word 'paid' scribbled next to them. The bottom had two different signatures on it. I tried to keep a straight face. This paper was supposed to build his credibility? He must have been joking. Between the trash bag luggage, his physical appearance, his eviction story, and his friendship with Paul, I felt that I knew enough about his credibility. I handed him back the paper and was extremely glad, no, overjoyed that I would never be collecting money from him. Cheryl smoked on the stoop and watched in suspense as we spoke.

"Thanks, I appreciate this, uh, evidence of your credibility," I said.

"I'm very trusthwory," said John, sticking out his chest and looking proud.

"Here's what I'm going to do."

John got real still and looked me square in the eyes.

"You have two weeks to find a place to live," I said.

"Huh?"

"During that time, you may stay here."

"Okay."

"Rent free."

"What?"

"You heard me."

"Two weeks, that's it? But I can pay yuh. I wanna stay longer."

"No."

"Please?"

"No."

"Why?"

"Landlord."

"Landlord?"

"Won't let me have extra roommates. Sorry."

"He can't tell yuh that."

I raised my eyebrows.

"Oh, yes he can. It's even written in the lease."

"He doesn't have ta know."

"I will know."

"Fine, fine. Two weeks is enough. It's enough time to show yuh that I'm a good guy."

"Nope. Two weeks and you're done."

"Okay, okay. Whatever, man."

"You may stay for fourteen days. On the fourteenth day, you must vacate the premises."

"Okay."

"We clear?"

"Clear."

"Good."

"Okay."

"And, umm, I guess, welcome to our home."

John left to go collect a few more things that I guessed couldn't fit in his trash bag. The sun was setting and the neighbors were all out and about. The bar across the street had several motorcycles parked outside, a few of them Harleys. A couple old men with long beards stood out on the bar's stoop and smoked their cigarettes as they watched the comings and goings of the neighborhood.

That night, Cheryl made Paul and me venison steaks, mashed potatoes, and string beans. Cheryl was an excellent cook, much better than I. She knew how to prepare steaks with just enough pink in the middle, and she added all the right spices and seasonings to make me want to lick the plate. Unfortunately, these steaks were the last of our real food, which was from a refreshed and final supply of a friend's donated deer meat. From then on, we would be eating only handouts and other people's leftovers. It was kind of like playing the lottery for dinner, but I figured that there were worse things in the world. Dinner was almost ready, but Paul was restless.

"Say, Matt, umm, you wouldn't wanna play cards, would ya?"

"Cards? What game?"

"Gin Rummy?"

"I don't remember the rules."

Paul took out some cards and began dealing them on the table.

"I'll show ya how."

I sat down, and we played Gin Rummy without the Gin or the Rum. We weren't allowed because Paul used to be an alcoholic and he didn't want to start drinking again. He wouldn't go into bars, not even with Cheryl. I was impressed by his self control, and it gave me hope that one day this would all be behind him. After a few training examples, Paul dealt the cards, and we played several hands. Paul won the first two games which surprised me as much as it pissed me off. This wasn't supposed to happen. He giggled gleefully after winning each round. I hate gleeful giggling, especially at my expense. I decided to focus with extreme concentration; and within a few rounds, I had the upper hand. I won the next several hands, and then it looked as if I might win the entire game. Paul didn't like this at all and was convinced that he was going to win the final three rounds and claim victory for the tournament. While dealing the next hand, Cheryl banged her stirring spoon on one of the pots.

"Dinner's ready, boys."

"Cheryl, he's beating me," Paul complained.

"You can finish him tomorrow, hon," said Cheryl.

"Nope. I refuse," I said.

"Cheryl, we're finishing it now. I'm about to win," yelled Paul.

"Nope. The game is over now. I win," I said.

"You don't win. We're playing until it's over," said Paul, shuffling the cards.

"No, I win."

"You don't win."

"Yes, I do win."

"No, you don't!"

"We don't have time to finish. I win," I argued.

"No."

"Boys! Boys! Stop." Cheryl started slapping us on the knuckles with her wooden spoon.

"Cheryl, stop!" shouted Paul.

"Dinner is getting cold!"

"Fine," I said.

Paul just grunted and cleaned off the cards. Cheryl placed our three plates in front of us. She would have set a place for John, but he wasn't back yet. Cheryl explained that he was a crack addict and that they had explained to him that drugs weren't allowed in the house. I appreciated their mediation in the matter, and it made me feel as though they took my threats about the landlord seriously.

The steaks were perfectly cooked and seasoned. The mashed potatoes tasted of buttery goodness, and we stuffed our faces accordingly. There was very little talking, partly because of card game bitterness and partly because we needed to eat quickly. "Deal or No Deal" had just started. I finished my steak in four bites as Cheryl crammed heaping spoonfuls of mashed potatoes into her mouth. Paul had already finished. Leaving our dirty plates on the table, we all scrambled into the family room to catch the show. This was a great TV program that involved money, hot girls, and suspense. Contestants were brought up and placed in front of 24 cases. Their job was to guess which case had the million dollars. It was interesting, but even more interesting was watching Cheryl watch the show.

She liked to advise the contestants through the television because she was convinced she knew the answers. Convinced. One time we were watching and she started yelling for case twenty-four, demanding that it be picked. A terrible decision, I knew, because it was clearly case seventeen. I had a feeling, a premonition as Cheryl called it. But, of course, neither of us were right for no other reason than because we were wrong. The million dollars was in case number eight. Go figure. Even though this happened over and over again, Cheryl never stopped advising the TV. It was a shame when she was wrong, which was every time; but in her defense, Cheryl said her clearest premonitions dealt with the lottery. She had visions where the winning numbers appeared out of thin air, right in her mind's eye. Yes, often she could see all the winning numbers in perfect order and in crystal clear fonts. Whenever this happened, she would run, physically run, out the door to buy a lottery ticket. Later, when her tickets lost, she acted completely mystified, as if she couldn't understand how that could have happened. Perplexed at her confusion, I tried to explain to her that the lottery was a tax on people who couldn't do math, specifically statistics. I told her many times but she preferred to listen to her premonitions. We finished watching "Deal or No Deal" and a few other shows after it, but John never came back. None of us were overly concerned, and Paul speculated that he might be spending the night at his sister's place which happened to be a few houses up from ours.

I know, I was outraged, too, when I found that out. However, his sister lived in a single room with eight illegal squatters, including her two children. She insisted that there was no room for John.

Over the next several days, Cheryl recovered her strength and John acclimated himself to the house. I thought he fit in fairly well, and we both got along, which for me was a big surprise. Sure, we didn't go out to the bars together, but we coexisted, occasionally chatting about the Orioles and relaxing on the stoop. We got along as best could be expected. Unfortunately, my patience was not contagious. Cheryl and Paul began to hate him the second he moved in, and they started looking for reasons to have him thrown out early.

"Paul, it was your idea to bring him into the house," I said, between sips of beer. I was amazed. I had just come back from the bar where I had bought a Cobra 40 ounce for two dollars, which even included tax. Anywhere else in the world people would have probably paid triple that price. Even though it tasted like dirt water, it was worth it, and I would get used to it because I couldn't afford any other brand.

"Well, I was wrong!" yelled Paul.

"I thought he was a good friend. Where will he go?"

"I don't care," he complained.

"What's your issue with him anyway? You spend your entire day on the corner."

"My WIFE shouldn't have to clean up after that slob!"

"Slob?"

"This mornin' Cheryl had to get up and clean his piss off the bathroom floor."

"Huh?"

"He pees all over the floor."

"That's gross. Cheryl shouldn't clean up after him," I said.

"Damn straight!"

"Paul, just make John do it. Talk to him."

"We should kick him out today! Nobody wants him here."

"I gave him my word."

I couldn't help but be amused at how Paul's money-making scheme had backfired. For me this vindication was sweet. He shook his head and carried his bike out the front door. A few minutes later, Cheryl came downstairs.

"John is so obnoxious. I can't stand that pig."

"So I heard," I said, enjoying the warm breeze from the window.

"What? Did Paul tell you how much of a mess he makes?"

"Yep."

"He got barbeque sauce all over the chair and the couch," she said, clearly frustrated with my lack of concern.

"I see."

"He got soggy noodles all over the kitchen counters and the floor."

"Why are you cleaning it? Make him do it."

"He won't do it."

"Cheryl, there's only eleven days left; then he's gone."

Cheryl sighed and put on her grumpy face.

"Can't you try to deal with him for a few more days?"

Cheryl grumbled, "I guess."

At work the next day, I spent my lunch hour printing rent ads that fit John's price range. I brought them home, spread them out on the table, and left a motivational note – *ten days left, good luck.*

Chapter 11: Repairs

A month ago I received an invitation to a wedding in St. Louis for a good friend of mine from Pittsburgh. I didn't like leaving my 50-year-old housemates home alone, but I would go because I figured it was important to experience as much of a regular life as possible. I enjoyed being around friends, and they helped me stay grounded. In general I made a point to try and stay home after work on the weekdays, but the weekends were an entirely different story. Usually I left the house altogether. I would stay with friends or family and hoped that this routine would help ensure that Paul and Cheryl would not become dependent on me.

Friday, I woke up in the heat of an unusually warm May morning. A printed-out flight itinerary awkwardly stuck out from my wallet. It was very crumpled, maybe too crumpled, and I wondered if it would scan properly. If it didn't, then I'd be stuck in the airport and probably delayed for hours. Surely they would let me reprint it, but I didn't know. I hadn't even gotten out of bed and already I had a problem to resolve. This didn't bode well for the rest of the day.

The plane to St. Louis was to depart at 5:00 PM, which meant I would have to leave work a few hours early to make the flight. Jumping up from my blankets, I dug out my undershirt from the clothes pile. I could hear loud snoring grunts echoing loudly from the other two bedrooms as I tiptoed down the hallway; and once inside the bathroom, I quietly shut the door and looked into the mirror. Shocked, my mouth dropped open. I wobbled and instinctively gripped the sink. Trying not to lose my balance, I tightened my grip but started to feel sick. My eyelids slowly closed shut while my heart beat faster by the second. Unfortunately these were not the frantic thoughts of a bad hair day. In the mirror's reflection, I looked behind myself at the horror. The horror!

I didn't want to turn around and began hoping that I was dreaming. I sighed and put some water on my face and then rested my forehead on the sink. At twenty-three-and-a-half years old, I was getting too old for this stuff. Turning around, I decided to inspect the heap of destruction that was once my shower. Kneeling down, I examined the pile of pipes, shower curtain rods, and metal parts lying in the tub. I opened up the palms of my hands and slowly sunk to the ground, I became very tense, but then relaxed, and dropped my head to my knees. Eyes closed, I remembered that I knew this would happen; this was what I had signed up for. Things like this were supposed to happen all the time, remember? It was all part of The Plan, but that didn't mean I didn't get to be angry.

I got up off the ground and continued inspecting. It looked as if the pipes had been broken off and were essentially snapped in half. The curtain supports had been torn from the ceiling, and there was some note left on top of the shower. Too enraged to bother reading it, I knew that nothing it could say would make this better. Nothing.

At least the shower tiles and the drywall looked untouched, but the bathroom carpet was soaked, completely soaked from the water that must have gone everywhere and could have possibly flooded into the downstairs. Water damage would be bad and could lead to structural issues which would mean that I'd have to inform the landlord.

The longer I stayed in the bathroom, the worse my imagination got. I stomped over to Paul and Cheryl's door. I would have answers. Answers, damn it! I pounded, kicked, and almost broke the door down. A few seconds later, Paul appeared groggy eyed and wore an oversized pair of blue boxer shorts. He scratched his stomach through his extra large, bright orange Orioles t-shirt and yawned.

I stood in the doorway and crossed my arms.

171

"Explain."

Paul smiled and then stopped. I was not smiling. My lip quivered with anger.

"John had a seizure."

Arms still crossed, I slowly repeated what he said.

"You think John had a seizure?"

Paul nodded confidently.

"Yes, a seizure, and he grabbed onto the shower curtains and fell down."

I doubted Paul's explanation and knew it was a lie. I had a friend with epilepsy and learned that when epileptics have seizures, they just collapse; they don't grab. Bite, yes; but grab, no. They can't because during a seizure, they have no control over their hands. But I no longer cared how the shower broke; and unable to find any logical motive, I figured it was probably an accident anyway. If it had been malicious, then the walls probably would have been broken and the mirror smashed. Now the priority was getting the shower fixed. I asked if John was okay, though I wasn't sure if I cared.

"He's sleeping now. He seemed fine afterwards," said Paul.

"Where did all the water go?"

"Cheryl cleaned it."

"Was there a lot?"

"Oh, yeah."

"When did it happen?"

"Late. I'm surprised yuh didn't hear it."

"You should be glad I didn't."

"It was the loudest bang I've ever heard," said Paul, almost chuckling.

"You need to get it fixed."

"I know a guy--

"By Sunday."

"This guy's really-- ."

"Just get it done."

172

"Okay, okay."

Somewhere between "Home Improvement" episodes and do-it-yourself plumbing books, I became ambitious with home repairs. The thought of Paul handling the repairs was a joke. A farce. By now I was supposed to be hundreds of miles away at the wedding in St. Louis, but my bad weather canceled my plane and couldn't be rescheduled. Though surprise visits were nothing new, they had expected me to be in St. Louis by now. They would never expect me to come home early, at least not this weekend. Of all the weekends, this was the one where they would be most likely to get into mischief. On the drive over, I was plagued with visions of finding them shooting up drugs in the living room with cigarettes in their mouths and 40-ounce beers duct taped to their hands. They would be drunk, high, and generally defiant, possibly violent. They would probably have had friends from the homeless camp over for a finding-and-taking-whatever-metal-was-in-the-house party. I expected to walk in and see everyone tearing pipes and appliances out of the walls. I didn't think I could bear it; and if I saw this behavior, I would have to shut the house down. I couldn't allow them to live here and hurt themselves. I wouldn't have it.

I barged through the front door of my house with bags of pipes, showerheads, and curtain rods resting awkwardly in my arms. The lights were off and the ceiling fan spun, occasionally emitting high pitched squeaking noises. Inside, the house felt warm. I walked over and checked the thermostat. It was off. I smiled. They were learning. I called out to make sure they weren't home.

"Hello! Helllllo?"

I took a step and accidentally snapped a pencil with my foot. Colored markers and pencils were spread all over the ground at my feet. A few heavily used candles, which were now burnt blobs of wax, sat next to some of the markers as if props in a séance. The next thing I saw made me scratch my head. Propped up against the TV stand was nothing other than the Wall of Want, which had been removed from where it was hung in the middle room. It seemed as though Cheryl had drawn a giant picture of Jesus, complete with shining halo, on the board in permanent magic marker. Once I got over an avalanche of unintended symbolism, I couldn't help but notice the accuracy of Cheryl's proportions. She had done a beautiful job with the drawing. Underneath some of the markers next to the board, I found a crumpled up church pamphlet that had the same image on it. Clearly she had used it as a model, but her drawing looked much better.

Our household was constantly getting condemned to hell by those pamphlets, but Cheryl stuck them all over our fridge nonetheless. I don't really know why Paul bothered bringing them home. And now, I guessed, Cheryl had decided to use them as drawing references. Either way, she had filled the entire Wall of Want with a giant drawing of Jesus, and I thought it was just great.

Relieved that everything looked somewhat normal, I dragged the plumbing parts upstairs and laid them on the floor before setting to work. I would become a master plumber who could fix anything. My mind filled with a vision of myself, a vision that showed me as a muscle bound genuine handyman complete with a beard, flannel shirt, and tool belt. A handyman with my own TV show! People would tune in around the world to watch me fix things, things that I had no prior experience fixing. Do projects that I had no idea how to do. I would show the world how to build a shower from scratch without any prior plumbing experience. But like my iron chef dreams, guitar ambitions, and tree house construction, this too was not meant to be. I failed within a matter of seconds, as I held up the pipes and saw that they were much too big and far too tall to fit the shower. I just stood there holding the pipes in shock at how my memory had betrayed me. Not a single pipe or clasp or screw was the right size or shape for this shower. Completely bewildered, I wondered how quickly a professional could get over to the house. I cringed at the thought of how much it would cost, but there was no other option. Cheryl was on the verge of an employment breakthrough and I wouldn't let a broken shower stand in her way.

"Whatcha' doin?"

Paul startled me, and I dropped the pipes on the floor with several loud clanging noises.

"Um, I, uh, well, I am trying to fix the shower."

"Stop. Skip's gonna fix it."

"Who's Skip?"

"He's a plumber."

"When's he gonna fix it?"

"He's already looked at it."

"Really?'

"Yeah."

"How long will it take?"

"Tomorrow afternoon."

I didn't really believe him, but he sounded so strangely confident, not that it mattered. The parts I bought were worthless. I could see that now. My plumbing ambitions had drowned, and I had to trust him. There was no way I could get a plumber until Monday or Tuesday and so I would trust him until Monday or Tuesday.

"How do you know him?"

"We're old friends"

"I hope you're better friends with him than John."

"Don't worry, we've been friends my whole life."

The stairs creaked as Cheryl made her way up to join the commotion.

"How much will it cost?"

"Umm, Skip said—

She poked her head through the door.

"Matt, promise me you won't pay for it."

"Cheryl, it has to be fixed."

"John has to pay for it," she begged.

"Fine. I don't care who pays for it as long as it gets fixed," I said, throwing my hands up.

I spent the rest of the weekend at my parents house trying to remember what normal life felt like. I was beginning to think I had gotten myself in over my head. But just like Pat said, Sunday afternoon I rubbed my eyes in disbelief. Unbelievable. The shower looked good as new, almost shining. If finding the shower destroyed was the most shocking moment of the year, then waking up and finding it completely repaired was the most shocking moment of my life. I turned it on and put my hand under the flowing water, which had never felt so refreshing or so relaxing. A spa, my house had a spa! And the water pressure was stronger than before. Running down the stairs, I shouted, "It's fixed! It's fixed!" I leaped down the last four stairs and ran out to the back porch to tell Cheryl and Paul in case they didn't know.

"Cheryl, Cheryl, it's fixed!" I shouted, jumping up and down.

"I know, I know, hon!"

"I can't believe it!"

"Why?"

"It doesn't matter…it's fixed!"

"Yeah, for now," said Cheryl, looking glum.

"Huh?"

"Last night, John tried to destroy it."

"Why would he do that?" I asked and stopped jumping. Then I thought about it for a second and I actually wasn't surprised. Things stopped making sense a long time ago, and there was no reason for that pattern to stop now. It was only natural that John would try to destroy the shower after this miraculous recovery.

"Yeah, there was a huge shouting argument. He almost punched Paul in the face."

176

"Why?" I asked.

"He wanted to fix it himself and doesn't want to pay for it," said Paul.

"How much is it?"

Sixty dollars," said Cheryl.

Sixty dollars? That's all?" I exclaimed, "That's reasonable."

"Well, Skip's charging us at the friend price," said Paul.

"Where is John now?" I asked with feigned anger. I found it very hard to be angry because I was just too happy. We had a fully repaired, fully functional shower with slightly improved water pressure.

"Don't worry, we've settled it," said Paul.

"He will have the money tonight. Skippy is coming to collect it tomorrow," said Cheryl.

"Good, good," I said, nodding my head.

We spent the rest of the afternoon on the stoop watching the comings and goings of the neighborhood. Cheryl brought out some cold glasses of sweet tea, and Mitchum and Jimmy the Rapist stopped over to hang out. John never came home. Paul assumed that he probably spent the money on crack and other assorted drugs.

Chapter 12: Beer and Knives

Sudden rapid knocking on the door startled me. Too tired even to make it upstairs, I had settled down for a nap in the living room and fallen into a deep sleep. It had been a long day, and it felt good to stretch out on the couch. Work had taken a lot out of me, and I was not in the mood for much else other than sleeping. Against my better judgment, I got up and opened the door. A gangly man stood clutching the handles of a bicycle. I did my best to restrain a frown. I had the urge to slam the door shut, but I resisted.

"Hi, is Paul home?"

"No."

"Where is he?"

"He's on the corner," I said.

Though the man seemed perfectly friendly, he did not look as though he intended to leave.

"Are you Skippy?" I asked.

"Yup. You must be Matt, right?"

We shook hands. Skippy had a torn oversized tank top, bleached jean shorts, and long blond hair. He looked like something out of a bad 70's exercise show and even wore a faded pink sweatband around his head.

"You did some nice work on the shower," I said.

"Thanks, man," said Skippy, " That stupid John guy wanted to rip it out again."

"I heard."

"Speaking of the jerk, he owes me money."

"Right. Well John didn't come home last night."

Skippy's jaw clenched and he looked like he might just explode right then and there.

"But don't worry, there's an ATM around the block. Come with me and I'll pay you."

Skippy and I chatted as we went up to a nearby bar with an ATM. After getting his money, Skippy biked away but said he'd return later to visit with everyone.

An hour later, John, who never came home last night, knocked at the door. Thankful for a solid nap, I was in a better mood and opened the door, though this time I was greeted with a gust of marijuana. Each of his bloodshot eyes blinked at different intervals, like a crazy person's or a cartoon character's. He mumbled something about coming back inside, but it wasn't going to be that easy. Not budging, I didn't open the door any wider because I was a tough guy, a negotiator.

"Do you have your repair money?" I asked.

"I got it, I got it."

"Show me."

Grumbling, John reached into his pocket and produced a wad of hundred dollar bills. I just stared at the wad of cash. I did not ask any more questions.

"John, what the hell."

"Wha?"

"I don't have change for $100 bills!"

"How about we grab a drink at the bar, on me?"

Not exactly sure what to make of this gesture, I responded, "Umm, okay."

At the bar, John treated me to a few beers. When the change came, he handed me $60, which was unbelievable. John then proceeded to tell me about how his family fell apart, how his brother was murdered across the street, and how he desperately wanted to live close by. Why he wanted to stay close by, I did not know. I asked, and he repeated his story, but that didn't help. Why would someone want to stay close by to where his brother was murdered? It made no sense, but he insisted that it was what he wanted. He said this many times, and I began to suspect that his brother was murdered by a drug dealer. A drug dealer that probably sold drugs to John. Drugs were powerful, addictive, and sometimes mind altering. Addicts made illogical decisions, stupid decisions like wanting-to-live-next-to-your-brother's-death-bed decisions. As he spoke, he became emotional and his cheeks flushed as tears started to run down his face. That was probably one of the few times I've ever seen a grown man cry, and it was certainly the first time I had ever seen a grown man cry in public. It was at this point that he asked my permission to become a permanent roommate. I didn't answer, and he filled the silence by repeating over and over again that he would pay for the room. I believed his story about his family, I really did, but I refused to let him stay. I could not house every homeless person in the city. The house wasn't big enough.

"You have seven days left," I said.

"C'mon."

"I'm sorry."

"It's the shower, isn't it."

"No."

"The shower was an accident."

"The shower is a non issue," I said, slamming my bottle on the bar, causing beer to spray out. "We made an agreement at the beginning. I printed out rental places last week. They're still on the kitchen table. I suggest you call them."

John looked increasingly frustrated and slammed his own beer down which was now empty. He stopped talking and walked out. The other people in the bar lowered their voices to whispers.

Outside I found John waiting for me, and then the unexpected happened. He pulled out a large knife from his belt. I was completely unprepared. Honestly, in broad daylight? In front of blue flashing light video cameras? Regardless, I was ready to run, no, sprint to safety. If only I had worn my sneakers. But I didn't. Instead, I was wearing my wallet sandals. Damn near impossible to run in, and I would surely fall on my face. So my only option was to stay and fight which was okay because I had seen exactly this situation in a Jackie Chan video. Well, not exactly *this* situation but similar. Seeing that I was ready to fight, John would become intimidated, and he would probably throw his knife directly at my face. It would rapidly spin through the air, making a metallic sound as it flew; but in perfect Jackie Chan form, I would catch the knife in my teeth. John would be stunned, completely freaked out, and he would run away knocking down trash cans as he went.

I flexed my arm muscles as a warning sign and showed no fear. But all this was pointless. I had misunderstood. John did not want to fight me, or run from me. All he wanted was for me to take the knife and leather sheath back to the house and put it in his room.

"Why?"

"Because I'm not gonna be back home 'til later. I don't want to carry it around."

"Umm, okay."

"Just leave it in my room."

"Sure, whatever."

The knife brought a little more realism to the situation. I wondered if it was a threat as I stuffed the knife inside my belt. Maybe he would hide it when he got home, perhaps accuse me of stealing it so that he could justifiably stab me with it. Maybe he *already* stabbed someone else. Of course! He needed my fingerprints. I regretted that I had already touched it.

I rounded the corner, trying to wipe the knife handle clean of my fingerprints when I spotted Skippy, Paul, Cheryl, and another guy hanging out on the stoop. The other guy looked to be in his early twenties. I didn't recognize him from the neighborhood.

"Hey, hon," said Cheryl, "I hear you met Skip here."

"Yes, I did."

"Well, let me introduce you to Skipp's nephew, Lil' Barry."

Lil' Barry and I shook hands. Sporting a black wife beater and saggy jeans, he eyed a cigarette butt lying on the ground. He picked it up, popped it in his mouth, and then lit it.

"Sum people are jus' so wasteful."

Cheryl took a puff of her own cigarette and eyed the knife in my hands.

"What'cha doin with that knife, hon?"

"I, uh, umm, well."

In half a second Barry whipped out his own knife. Pulled it right from his back pocket. An impressive feat, as he was still sitting down. He slashed the blue handled butterfly knife into the wind, stabbing the air as if it had made a particularly offensive comment about his mother.

"My knife is bigger than yours."

"Your knife is bigger than John's," I corrected.

"Uugh, that John is so obnoxious," scoffed Cheryl.

"Well, if he gets on your nerves, Cheryl, I'll take him down for ya," said Lil' Barry, still slashing.

"No knife fights in the house," I said, joining them on the stoop. I was such a party pooper. Today was Cheryl's *second* first day of her actual job. I was anxious to know how it went so I sat next to her. Maybe I would get a few early whispers of news. Neighbors smiled and waved as they walked by, and even Jimmy came over to say hello. The front of the house was getting crowded, and I noticed that we were the most popular stoop on the block. Distracted by all the commotion, I was unaware that Barry had fallen strangely silent in a type of hyper concentration. Then Lil' Barry, who had previously been very quiet, started making inane, nonsensical noises. First whistling through a gap in his teeth and then making high-pitched yelping sounds. His lips didn't move, yet he was

182

surprisingly loud, like a ventriloquist. I had never seen something like this done before. I shouldn't have made fun of him. He was probably ill, maybe mentally ill, but I couldn't tell for sure. Seeing my confusion, Cheryl pointed over at a couple of girls sitting on a bench. They were wearing mini skirts. I mouthed the word "oh" and nodded. But Barry's noises were piercing and started to give me a headache. Soon he abandoned his yelping and started grunting like a common farm animal. It was funny at first and almost amusing, but it got old fast, and then SMACK! I slapped the backside of his head.

"Ouch."

"Sorry."

"What did ya do that for?"

"Had to."

"Why?"

"It's for your own good."

"Huh?"

"There are better ways."

Cheryl, Paul, and Skippy all started laughing.

"Don't worry, Barry, I'll take ya to the hooker corner tonight," said Skippy.

Barry perked up and got all excited. "Really?"

"Yeah, I got paid today. I can get you a nice one."

"You boys," said Cheryl, laughing.

"Hooker corner?" I asked.

"It's one of the light rail stops."

"Oh, right, of course," I said, nodding as if I knew it well.

"Hookers everywhere. It's a good place to go when you have a dry spell," said Skip, who jumped back onto his bicycle.

Barry got his bike ready and prepared to roll out.

"It's good meetin ya. We'll be back later this week."

183

As Skip and Barry biked up the street, Barry made sure to yelp at the girls on the bench, but they looked away in disgust. We chuckled as we watched them go. After they left, Paul and Cheryl leaned on each other, passing their cigarette back and forth. She rested her head on his shoulder, and he put his arm around her back. I looked out at the neighborhood and let the breeze brush my face. Paul kissed Cheryl on the cheek, and the last cigarette ashes fell to the ground.

"I'm off to the corner. See you guys later," said Paul.

We watched Paul bike down the block. When he turned the corner, I jumped down from the stoop, and turned to face Cheryl.

"How was your second day at work?"

Cheryl hesitated, and I braced myself for the next excuse. Whatever the excuse, we would figure it out because no obstacle would be too big, no hurdle too high, and we would get through it. We had not come this far to give up. Cheryl smiled and removed the cigarette from her mouth.

"My first day went great! Though employment for us new hires is pending a security check."

"But you can still start your job?"

She nodded.

I gave Cheryl a very powerful and very loud high five.

"Cheryl, if you keep this job, do you know what this means?"

"It felt good."

"This means everything."

"Thanks, hon."

I felt something leap inside me. A smile ripped across my face. It was actually happening. Could it be true? I wasn't sure. But I was sure that if it wasn't true, she would have picked an easier lie to tell, one that would not be brought up again, a lie that wouldn't need to be remembered. From the very beginning, I had never shown anger, never shown frustration with any of her set backs, or Paul's faults, for that matter. All of my reactions to their job progress were positive or, at the very least, neutral. There was peace and harmony in our house and, therefore, no reason to lie about getting a job. No ultimatums had been issued and few- to- no threats levied. Maybe I just wanted to believe her so badly that it silenced my skepticism. But then I figured that if she had not gone to work, it would have been easier to come up with another excuse. If she hadn't gotten a job, it would have been easier to make up *any* lie except that one. Even lying that she was attacked by alley cats would have been better. However, lying about getting a job would mean that it would have to be remembered and expanded upon. She knew I would ask questions, hundreds, possibly thousands of questions which I would repeat on a weekly basis. In my mind, there was a good chance that she was telling the truth, but I needed to verify everything. All facts needed to be checked, and I would ask my questions again and again and again. Only the honest would make it out alive. I would ask the same ones with the intent of weaving a web of words designed to ensnare liars. In the process, I would catch her in her own lies or prove she was telling the truth.

"So tell me about it."

"It's gonna feel good gettin' a paycheck."

"When does the first one come?"

"Three weeks; but after that, it will be every two weeks."

"Do you like your co-workers?"

"I'm in a training session for a week. After it's done, we get spread out all over the hospital."

"Do you know which department you're in?"

"Not yet."

"Oh."

"By the time I finish training, I should be through all the clearances and ready to go."

"This is so great," I said beaming.

"I think so too."

"I'm happy for you."

"Me, too," she said, and I noticed she was beginning to tear up.

Chapter 13: Intervention

I guess you could say that my immediate family was pretty small. It consisted of myself, Eric, Dad, Mom and Kicker, the dog. My extended family did not add many numbers to our ranks and totaled somewhere around 12 people, including the dog. We tried to visit the various parts of the extended family about once a year. The logistics were negotiated between Mom and the other family members who were scattered from Las Vegas to Boston. These trips never had a set time of year and generally were classified as random. Sometimes they happened in the winter, and sometimes the summer; and most recently, in the spring for college graduations. However, the year was almost over, and we still had to see my cousins, uncle and aunt in Boston. Mom called me at work on a Tuesday. She informed me that tickets had been purchased for our annual New England visit. Our plane was to take off in less than four days. The way I saw things, I simply couldn't ask for a better family, I couldn't ask for better parents, and I couldn't ask for better grandparents; but I could have asked for better timing on this year's annual visit.

My uncle, who was a rocket scientist, had recently bought a vacation house that sat right on the water of Lake Winnipesauke in New Hampshire. The house had oak hardwood floors, a couple of fireplaces, and plenty of deck space. One of my favorite features of the house was how the master bathroom's huge mirror was situated in such a way that it reflected the entirety of the lake's glimmering blue waters. This created the illusion that one was overlooking the water while brushing one's teeth.

The lake was almost five miles long and had a thriving vacation community. It was heavily populated in the summers with boaters, swimmers, water-skiers, and fisherman. Tall, dark green pine trees that stuck out like dark spires in the morning mist thickly covered the shores.

The house was conveniently located less than two hours from Boston where my cousins Andrew and Ashley, Uncle Bob and Aunt Sharon lived. My cousins were in high school, and Andrew was getting ready to leave for his first year of college. After they bought the house, I heard that they came up every weekend during the summer. I had never been there and wondered how a family could travel to the same place every weekend for so many months, but I soon found out. The lake was huge and had many hiking trails to explore, restaurants to eat at, and water to swim in. They also had a motor boat that was prefect for tubing and waterskiing.

Dad and I met at the airport and caught our plane with ten minutes to spare which, in case you weren't aware, is the cutoff time for boarding. When we landed, Dad and I turned on our phones and simultaneously received text messages from Eric, my brother. He had missed his plane and wouldn't get in until the next morning. But this was normal. It wouldn't be a proper Bjonerud family vacation unless at least one person missed their flight and incurred hundreds of dollars of fees in the process.

A few weeks before, I had decided that it was time to finally fill Dad in on things. I did this over lunch after a round of golf. It had been almost six months, and things had gone better than I could have ever imagined. I knew there was no better time. So when the burgers came, I didn't touch mine and just waited. Dad immediately took a bite which was followed by several others. After setting a half eaten cheeseburger down, he looked up and saw that I hadn't touched my food. He asked. So I told him -- everything. He said that he knew I was up to something, and he figured that I'd tell him when I was ready. After our discussion, he suggested that I wait a week before I told Mom.

"What do you mean before *I* tell Mom?" I asked.

We argued briefly until finally he agreed to tell her, after suggesting maybe waiting two weeks. I think he had some board meeting he was preparing for and didn't want to have marital strife while he was trying to lead the charge at work. It would be best to spread those things out, he explained. And he didn't get any arguments from me. I agreed wholeheartedly. From my perspective, telling Mom was now *his* responsibility. So to make another long story short, he told Mom two weeks later which happened to be the day before we showed up to Lake Winnipesaukee.

I had expected Mom to explode with concerned rage, but she didn't. In fact, she was inhumanly calm considering all the dangers that I had thrown myself into. I later found out that she was worried that if she had responded harshly, then I might not bother coming home. Not only that, but I suspected that she could say very little against me. Cheryl had a job, we had coexisted for months, and I was happy and employed. My well- balanced life had bound her tongue.

Mom went up to the lake a few days ahead of the rest of us, and the night before we arrived, she decided to spill the beans about my little adventure. From what I hear, I guessed they hadn't seen it coming. She explained the whole story to them all at the dinner table. I heard rumors of open mouths, general shock, and lack of appreciation for my choice of strategy. I, of course, had no idea these conversations had ever happened. So when Dad and I showed up at the house for dinnertime, I was completely unaware of the politically charged environment.

After an extended period of warm greetings, we all sat down for a barbeque chicken dinner. Steamed vegetables, homemade coleslaw, corn on the cob, and platters of chicken were set about the table in between glasses of white wine and pitchers of water. Seated comfortably around the large dining room table, we all dug into our food, with the exception of Eric, who had missed his plane. I'm not entirely sure, but I think it was somewhere around the first twenty seconds of conversation that Aunt Sharon made the first move.

"So Matt, how's Baltimore?" She asked.

"Oh, it's pretty good."

"Do you like it?"

"Yeah, it's kinda exciting."

"How so?" asked Andrew.

"Umm, many ways, I guess." I said, not thinking much of the question. I stabbed a piece of broccoli with my fork.

"So, work's good?" asked Uncle Bob.

"Yeah, it's goin well."

"Anything else interesting going on in Baltimore?" asked Ashley.

"Yeah, a bunch of stuff."

"Like what?" they asked.

"Stuff."

"Matt, your mom told us what you're up to," said Andrew.

"Oh, did she?" I asked, immediately looking down at my plate.

"Yeah, we know about your roommates," said Ashley.

"Oh," I said, cutting my chicken rapidly.

"We do, and we think it's awesome," Andrew said smiling.

I looked up and noticed that everyone was looking at me. So I looked back down at my food. What a way to start the vacation. I felt like I was in the middle of a surprise interrogation. The lights in the room felt like they were getting brighter, and I started to perspire under the pressure. Then people started going back and forth asking all sorts of questions.

"Why are they homeless?" asked Bob.

"Life dealt them a few bad hands, I guess," I answered.

"Do they do drugs?" asked Sharon.

"Of course, they do," chimed in Mom.

"Mom!" I barked.

"What?"

"They do not. I've checked their arms and feet. They don't have puncture wounds, and I haven't seen them display behaviors of drug addicts."

"Have you tested them?" asked Mom.

"How could I do that? No, obviously I haven't. I'm not a doctor."

"Do you think they're dangerous?" asked Sharon.

"Yes. Desperate people are always dangerous," answered Dad.

"They're harmless," I responded. Where was Eric, my family ally, when I needed him? Arguing with Mom and Dad was one thing, but when combined with uncles and aunts, it was too much.

"What about the neighborhood? Is that dangerous?" asked Bob.

"I won't even drive there," said Mom.

"Yeah, it's kinda bad," I agreed, "but it's not bad to drive there. I try to avoid walking around after dark."

"They have actually gotten jobs, right?" asked Andrew.

"Yeah. Well, Cheryl has gotten a job. Paul still panhandles."

"Why?"

"He's waiting for his health benefits."

"This is outrageous. We work hard while people like this sit around on a corner and collect our taxes," Mom complained.

"Why are they homeless?" asked Andrew.

"Honey, unfortunately these days the government rewards laziness. They just fling welfare around until people have no incentive to work," Mom responded.

"You know they're taking advantage of you, don't you?" Sharon asked.

"I guess you could say that."

"Yes, of course, they are," she responded, "The only reason I bring it up is because I don't want to see you get hurt, honey."

"They're doing what he asked. Or at least, Cheryl is doing what he asked. She got a job, didn't she?" Ashley argued.

"Well, then, they should pay you for rent," said Dad.

"Okay. I'll let them know," I said sarcastically. "And so what if they take advantage? If taking advantage means sleeping with a roof over their heads and a warm shower, then I think I'm all right with that."

Andrew and Ashley nodded in agreement. I drank a sip of wine and triumphantly put some more chicken on my plate.

"Why are you doing this?" asked Bob.

"Because he's trying to help people," answered Andrew.

"Our society has programs and services to help these people. That's why we pay taxes," said Mom.

"Exactly. They have things like soup kitchens and section-8 housing," said Bob.

"That's right," Dad agreed. "Bob, tell him about your rental house."

"You have a rental house?" I asked, looking over at Bob.

"Yes ,we do. And we have section-8 classification. It's one of the few functioning government programs that provides subsidized housing for the less fortunate. It keeps them from becoming homeless."

"But those programs can't help everyone. People need to help, too," argued Andrew.

"And what about the people who can't work?" Ashley asked.

"Immigrants don't have any trouble finding work," answered Mom.

I didn't say anything and just pushed my food around my plate. I wasn't really sure what people wanted me to say. Nothing discussed was going to make me change my mind. But I chalked this up to a double helping of parental persistence.

My mom continued, "Matt, most, maybe all of the homeless are convicts, murderers, thieves, liars, cheats, drug addicts."

"Don't forget the rapists and alcoholics," I added sarcastically.

"Oh, heavens, yes, the rapists and alcoholics, too. They are dangerous, and these are just stupid risks. Just reckless. There are other ways of dealing with these problems."

"Like what?" I asked.

"Like we said. Soup kitchens, shelters, caseworkers, psychiatrists. Trained professionals who have experience dealing with these types of problems," said Bob.

"It's why we pay taxes," Sharon reminded us.

"So if we have a way of dealing with these people, why isn't it working? That's what I want to know. Why doesn't it work?" I said.

"They all can work; and if they got up off the corner, they could find it," Mom continued.

"There are plenty of terminally ill children that need help. Plenty of hospitals that need volunteers," said Dad.

"And plenty of seagulls stuck in oils spills," added Ashley.

"Yes. Brilliant point, Ash. There are many good causes out there in the world, like oil covered seagulls; and if anyone wants to accomplish anything, then regular people need to help out, too."

"So go volunteer at a hospital or something," pleaded Mom, "Think of the children."

"Mom, everyone is always thinking of the children. Most people want to help the children, and that's great. By all means, you go help the children," I answered.

"Why spend your time with Paul and Cheryl?" asked Andrew.

"Because they deserve it."

"How could they deserve it, Matt? Respect is something that must be earned," complained Dad, throwing down his fork.

"They have earned it."

"How?" Dad asked.

"By being human."

After dinner, Andrew and Ashley took me out to get some ice cream at one of the many ice cream stands around the lake. Apparently they have this strange flavor called black raspberry. I've heard of red raspberry, blueberry, and blackberry but never black raspberry. It was the most confusing name for an ice cream that I had ever seen. Apparently it's a well- known flavor in New England, though I still think it could all be an elaborate joke.

After we got our ice creams, we all went walking around the harbor. It was late at night by now, and the lake clearly reflected the full moon above us. Andrew and Ashley peppered me with questions about Paul, Cheryl, the house, the landlord, work, etc. By the end of the weekend, I didn't want to leave and had gotten plenty of rest to deal with what was coming.

The months passed quickly, and the weather got hotter and more humid. Air conditioning blasted out of the vents while the ceiling fans spun rapidly, squeaking loudly. The bills piled up and threw me way off of my carefully mapped out budget. My savings were getting killed.

Under constant attack, they had no way to replenish themselves. And in the middle of the fiscal year, there was no hope for bonuses, raises, or anything of the sort. I had no time for a part-time job, and I wouldn't ask for loans, nor would I ask the churches for handouts. By keeping the money mine, I would not have to answer to anyone nor would I have to meet my donors' expectations. But I would have to face the facts. If this kept up, then soon I wouldn't be able to afford to keep the lights on. I hated to admit that fate might take an ironic turn forcing us all back into Paul and Cheryl's tent.

Outside on the porch, my arms burned as I slowly raised a heavy dumbbell above my head. I lifted it over and over again as sweat trickled down my face. My arms completed five more reps before I dropped the weights to the ground. Mosquitoes swarmed and bit at my face and legs. The blaring of sirens and the rumbling of motorcycles was so common that I didn't even hear them anymore. A pit bull barked in the distance as a downtrodden man kicked an old vegetable can onto the road where it rattled and rolled under a parked car. He dragged his feet along the sidewalk, and I could hear him sliding over small unevenly sized pebbles as he passed by our back fence. Just as he walked into our alleyway, the back door slammed opened, and Cheryl came out onto the porch.

"Are you lifting in the dark?" she asked, flipping the light switch on.

"It was light out when I started," I said. "The porch light attracts mosquitoes so I kept it off."

"I figured."

Cheryl triumphantly held up a can of bug spray. She was such a mom. While I sprayed myself down, she picked up my jump rope and started skipping. I stopped spraying myself down and just watched with an open jaw. She knew that she defied my expectations, which I based on the size of her gut. With every successful skip, her smug smile grew wider to the point where it looked painful. Watching her jump over and over again, I became more and more amazed. Finally, reality set in, along with the laws of gravity; and after her lungs gave out, she collapsed into a cheap plastic lawn chair. Sweat poured down her faded pink tank top. Before I could compliment her on her jumping skills, I heard a muted thud inside the house, followed seconds later by Paul barging through the door wearing only a pair of shorts. He did not wear a shirt. The baggy denim shorts clung to his waist with the help of a string belt which was not a special type of belt but rather a string masquerading as a belt. He was so thin that his ribs and other bones were clearly visible through his skin. Also, he had a cigarette in his mouth. A lit cigarette. I was not pleased.

"Paul, what the hell are you doing?" Cheryl asked.

He looked confused and asked, "I, umm, err wha?"

"Were you smoking in the house?"

"No, no, no, nope."

"Liar."

"Okay, okay, I did, but only for a second."

"Why? You know it's a rule."

"Lost my lighter, Cheryl."

"So?"

"I needed to light this on the stove."

He looked at me, but I just folded my arms and looked angry. He decided to try and change the subject.

"So, can yuh do pushups?"

"Yeah, sure," I said, forgetting my anger.

"Can you do more than this?"

"Than what?"

Paul, who was still smoking, dropped down and lay on his stomach. Then he propped himself up with his hands and began doing pushups. While he knocked out rapid sets of pushups, I sat down in a chair next to Cheryl, put my feet up, and counted almost forty of them.

"Not bad," I said, impressed.

"When I was your age, I had massive arms. I did 80 of these a day."

"What happened to you?"

"Stuff," said Paul, taking a big puff of his cigarette.

"Oh."

I did not smoke, but I decided that if I ever did smoke, I would never use Paul's brand of cigarettes. Ever.

Between impromptu pushup competitions and board games, I was able to enjoy life with them. I enjoyed their company, and I did my best to split my time and conversations between job strategizing and agenda-less hang out time. But I was still not satisfied. I had to go further to find more ways to hang out with them. I always had to go further, a character trait that usually ended with me breaking some kind of rule, which in this case was an unwritten, sacred rule that probably should never have been broken.

Back at work, I sat in my cube and pounded out numbers on my calculator as I put the final touches onto one of my operational assessments. In the midst of uploading the report into our computer systems, my phone rang. Seeing that it was a call from the executive floor, I picked it up instantly.

"Hello...What? Someone cancelled?...You have four tickets? Umm, no, I really should stay home, I probably can't--Uh..huh...uhh..huh...uhhh..huh...., err, you make a good point. Free. Yeah, I'll take 'em." That night I arrived home beaming.

"Cheryl! Paul!" I shouted, coming through the door.

Cheryl was reclining on the couch eating a bag of chips.

"What's up, hon?"

"I got us some baseball tickets," I said, jumping up on the couch.

"Matt, get your feet off the couch."

"I got baseball tickets!" I said getting off the couch. "How?"

"I got 'em through the Firm. Someone cancelled last minute so I got 'em. Do you and Paul wanna go?"

"Oh, not tonight. I don't like baseball, but get me a Ravens' ticket, and I'll be there anytime, any day."

I was a little disappointed. I thought this would make her happy.

"Oh, okay. Well, do you think Paul would want to go?"

Cheryl nodded rapidly, "Yup, yup, he'd go."

"He's on the corner?" I guessed.

"Yup, tryin to make sum money."

"He needs to go get a job. Have you talked to him about getting something with Mitchum at the factory?"

"I did, but he won't go."

"Why?"

"I don't know what goes on in his head. He's more stubborn than a mule."

"What about Lil' Barry and Skip? Have you seen them?"

"Nope. Just call 'em. They'll go."

Cheryl handed me a piece of scrap paper with Barry's number on it. I stuffed it with the tickets into my cargo pockets and made my way out the door. Then I walked the ten blocks to the corner. On my way, I passed the basketball court adjacent to the local school and gripped my fake wallet tightly. The locals were playing pickup games, and the place was overrun by large, intimidating locals. Between the players and spectators, there were almost fifty of them, all wearing saggy jeans, bandanas, wife beaters and very expensive sneakers. Rap music blasted from a large eighties era boom box. I constantly worried about getting mugged, especially around large groups of locals, yet I chose not to cross the street and stayed on the side closest to the crowded school basketball court. Not only was I a minority, but without any tattoos or piercings, I was somewhat clean-cut. Many of them looked at me but then turned their attention back to the games, and I relaxed my grip on the wallet. Months before, I would have been too scared to even think about attempting this. Instead I would have walked around the block entirely, but no longer. Familiarity with the area had made up for my lack of courage, and I was finally able to maneuver about with an increasing degree of freedom.

A few blocks later, the corner came into view. Paul's distinct hobble was unmistakable as he walked back and forth between cars stopped at the lights.

"Hey, Paul!"

Hunched over and bent down, I watched Paul pick up pennies from the street curb. Cars whirled past him, missing him only by inches, and he retrieved a few more pennies before standing upright.

"What the hell are you doing?"

He held one of them up and smiled, "Pennies."

"Those cars were inches from killing you."

Casually he said, "They missed, didn't they?"

Deciding to drop it, I moved on.

"I got tickets to the game tonight. You wanna go?"

His face softened, and he stood up slightly.

"Tonight?"

"Yeah, but you kinda have to change into something a little nicer."

He scratched his beard and looked at the ground.

"Gee, I haven't been to a game in ten, maybe twelve years."

"So you'll go?"

Paul smiled and nodded. We agreed to meet back at the house in an hour.

"I'm gonna go call Skip and Barry."

"Good."

"You have a phone?" I asked.

Paul shrugged, "No more minutes, but there's a pay phone down the block."

Calling from the pay phone, I listened as Lil' Barry excitedly accepted the tickets to the game. He and Skip said they were on their way.

An hour later, I was back in the living room watching TV. Cheryl sat at the kitchen table diligently making penny towers and packaging them into rolls. It was getting dark out, and we turned on a few lamps. It felt cool out so I turned down the fan and opened the window. Even at the slowest speed, the fan still squeaked every other revolution. I was careful when I walked around the dining room because Cheryl had stacks and stacks of pennies all over the kitchen table. The slightest thud or hard step could send them all crashing down. Upstairs, I heard the muffled sounds of the opening and shutting of doors as Paul prepared himself for civilization. I turned on the TV and tried to relax while I waited for him to get ready. A few minutes later, Paul started shouting for Cheryl, which startled her and caused her to knock over some penny piles.

"That man'll be the death of me," she muttered, getting out of her seat.

I just chuckled to myself and slouched down deep in the comfy dish chair.

Hearing the shower faucet squeak and the water run, I sat bolt upright.

"Cheryl, I can't believe I'm asking this, but…

"Praise the Lord! I think he is," said Cheryl, clasping her hands together.

"Wow," I said unable to remember the last time I had heard of Paul taking a shower.

"The other night I rolled into his arm pit and woke up hacking. It smelled so bad I thought I was gonna suffocate to death," she said, pinching her nose.

"TMI, Cheryl. TMI," I said, plugging my ears.

Cheryl went upstairs to help him with his bath, which was one of the first baths he had taken in months. Generally he looked terrible, but he liked it that way. He purposefully designed his appearance so he would look needier and even made a point to accentuate his limp, wear ragged clothing, and grow out his beard, all in the name of panhandling. Simply put, people gave him more money if he looked dirty and ragged. Much to my dismay, he never stepped out of character even in the comfort of his own home. But I didn't care about his appearance so much as I couldn't stand his smell which reeked of dried sweat, dirty feet, and rotten eggs. I could smell him even when he was up in his room and I was down in the kitchen. We tried to convince him that people couldn't smell him from their cars, but he still didn't listen. At least Cheryl took showers almost twice a day and she smelled like flowers and lavender, but that didn't come close to neutralizing Paul's odor.

After another twenty minutes or so, I heard the water twist off. Then I heard some stomping around, some grumbling, the slamming of drawers, the closing of closet doors and then a very loud smooch. The first to come down the stairs, Cheryl wore a goofy grin on her face, and I could have sworn that her eyes were literally twinkling.

"Paul's all excited about tonight," she said.

I smiled, "So am I."

I turned off the TV and tied up the laces on my sneakers. Another minute passed, and Paul stomped downstairs. Doing a double take, I slowly stood up from the couch and beheld Paul standing in front of me. He was decked out in a collared shirt, khaki shorts, and brand new loafers. He looked completely different, and I could hardly recognize him. He almost looked stately, like one of executives at the Firm.

"Paul?" I gasped, "You shaved your beard."

He nodded and felt his face. I took a step closer and inhaled.

"You don't smell....quite so badly."

He smiled and raised his arm, put his nose next to himself, and inhaled deeply.

"See, he can dress himself up if he needs to," said Cheryl, practically beaming. She stood behind him and ran her hands through his damp grey hair. She leaned around and planted a kiss on his cheek.

"Aright boys, you better git a move on."

After only two blocks into our trek to the stadium, we ran into Lil' Barry and Skippy. They were sweating and out of breath, but were ready to go. By their deep breaths, I guessed that they must have run all the way from the light rail stop. I was glad that we had intercepted them.

Inside the stadium, we followed crowds up the concrete ramp ways. Then we climbed flights and flights of stairs until finally we reached the nosebleed sections which provided a magnificent view of the city. From our vantage point, we could see all of Baltimore rising up behind the emerald green grass of the baseball field. The water of the Inner Harbor glimmered like an open sea, and the deep red sunset flashed brightly off the windows of the surrounding skyscrapers. Below we could see the players assembling onto the field.

"They look like ants from here," said Barry, awestruck.

"We're pretty high up, Barry," said Skip.

I was glad that they were distracted by the view because I was completely lost and had no idea where our seats were. Perceiving our confusion, an attendant came over to help us figure things out.

"Sir, I may be able to help you find your seats."

"Thanks. I've never been good with directions."

202

"I can see that. You are in the completely wrong section."

"Oh, is it on the other side?"

"This is not even your level," sighed the attendant as if he had been dealing with incompetent fans all day.

"Whoops," I said.

The attendant pointed to the field.

"You're down there right behind the dugout."

"What?"

"Sir, please make your way over to the elevator and someone will show you to your seats."

"Thanks, will do."

We made our way to the elevator.

"Barry, you ever been to these seats before?"

"Naah, I ain't never even been to a baseball game before."

I looked at him funny.

"Really?"

He paused and then said, "Yeah. Thanks for takin me."

We made our way down to our section and found that some other people had taken our seats, but another attendant shooed them away for us and then dusted the seats off in dramatic fashion. Lil' Barry immediately took out his cell phone and started taking pictures of everything from the players and the people to the stadium and the city skyline. I could hear Skippy and Paul reminiscing about how, when they were younger, they used to come to these games together. They told stories of how they would sit in the nosebleed sections, drink beer, and smoke weed.

"Smoke weed?" I asked.

"Well, the restrictions were a lot less strict in our day."

Lil' Barry and I laughed and we continued watching the game.

"Skip told Cheryl that you were thinkin' about getting your GED."

"Yup, thinkin' about it," said Barry.

"You know, I can help if you want. I can tutor you at the house."

Barry looked at me and raised his eyebrows.

"Really?"

"Sure. Just come after six any day next week, and we'll start."

He smiled.

"Cool."

By now it was the top of the second inning. We were so close that I could see the stitching on the baseball. The Orioles were fielding and had already caught one out. The other team had runners on first and second base. The batter stood waving his bat high in the air. His arms were huge, almost bigger than Mitchum's. The pitch came in low, and the batter swung but missed. The pitcher threw a high fastball, and the batter swung and hit a grounder straight to the shortstop, who caught the ball and tagged the runner going to third. Before anyone could blink, he tossed the ball with his glove to the second baseman to make a double play, and the crowd erupted out of their seats cheering. Normally double plays don't get such a hearty cheering, but the Orioles were down by five runs, and I guess the crowd needed a reason to cheer.

I looked around at the people sitting next to us. We were only a couple rows from the backstop of the field, and I knew these were expensive seats. These were the seats that the players' wives sat in. These were the seats that corporate guests, bank presidents, politicians, and other influential community leaders sat in. There was no telling who was sitting around us tonight. They looked wealthy and powerful, but I couldn't be sure. These were some of my Firm's prime seats. I hoped no one would recognize me; otherwise, I may have to explain my motley crew, or rumor may even spread back to the Firm. I couldn't help but think that this was not the proper business use. Maybe I should have asked, but I didn't.

Sometime around the fifth inning, one of the lemonade guys came over shouting "Get your ice cold lemonade! Ice cold here!"

"I'm gonna get one of those," said Barry.

The lemonade man came running over when he saw Lil' Barry flagging him down. The man dislodged a giant bucket of cold, refreshing, sweet lemonade and passed it to Barry.

"How much?" he asked, reaching for his wallet.

"Four dollars," said the man.

"Four dollars!" yelled Barry, outraged.

"Yup," confirmed the man.

"Four dollars! Four Dollars! I could buy two 40s for four dollars!"

The lemonade man just stood there a bit confused. He held out his hand.

"Oh, hell, no, I ain't payin that. This blows!"

"Barry, be quiet," I said, taking the drink out of his hands and giving it back to the attendant.

"Sir, I think we're fine right now."

Skippy laughed and handed Barry a small used plastic cup for the water fountain.

"There's a water fountain up there, if you want."

Later that night, Paul had gone to bed early and left Cheryl and me watching television. It was almost midnight, far past my usual bed time, but I was enchanted with Cheryl's work stories. She told me of her co-workers, her manager, and her training. I listened carefully for any sign of discontent but heard none. The only way this job would last was if she genuinely liked it. I was pleased to hear that everything was going so well because it gave me hope that this could be a long term job.

"It sounds like you're really enjoying everything."

"I am."

"Those managers can be a bit tough, but just keep your head up."

I sat deep in the dish chair as Cheryl sat on the edge of the couch. She seemed to get bubbly and more joyful when she told work stories. I think it made her feel normal again.

"Do you find the walk to be very long?"

"Matt, it's only a few blocks. I would hope that I could make that walk."

I laughed, "Yeah, I guess."

She spoke over the sounds of screeching tires, yelling, and bottles being smashed on the curb, but they were such common neighborhood noises that we didn't even notice them anymore. Tired, I got up out of my chair. All of her stories gave me a pretty good picture of her normal work day. After a brief stretch and yawn, I asked one last question before heading for bed.

"Which co-workers do you eat lunch with?"

Cheryl paused and she looked away from my face.

"Cheryl?" I asked.

"I don't eat lunch."

"Why?"

"'Cause I haven't gotten my first paycheck yet; I can't pay for it."

"So what do you do? Just sit there and not eat?"

"No. I sit outside and take an extended smoke break."

"What?"

"Yeah."

"But I've run out of money for cigs so now I've got to roll 'em myself."

"Doesn't Paul bring in enough?"

"He won't share now that I have a job."

"But you haven't gotten your paycheck yet."

"I know, I know."

"This is dumb," I said.

"Well, it's not the lunch that bothers me. The real issue is when all the girls chip in for coffee and donuts," she said.

"Can't you eat their donuts?"

"I did the first week, but I don't want to be that person in the office who mooches off everyone."

"Does that happen often?"

"Every other week and sometimes for birthdays."

My office did similar programs where we alternated chipping in for birthday cakes and various potluck lunches. Anyone who didn't pay risked becoming the black sheep of the office, and I suspected that it was even worse for someone who is trying to make friends. Pitching in for coffee and donuts is an essential part of making friends and fitting in. It's where all the non-work conversations happen. Horrified, I pictured poor Cheryl freeloading during office snack time and disappearing during lunchtime. People probably said mean things when they noticed she wasn't there. They probably took offense and figured that she thought herself to be too good to eat with them. The last thing I wanted was for the office to be gossiping about Cheryl, the thought of which infuriated me. I sat up in my chair and put on my shoes.

"Cheryl, I'm so sorry. I had no idea."

"Hon, it's okay, it's okay."

"No, it's not okay."

Cheryl was standing up, trying to ease my concern.

"Where are you going? It's late."

"You're going to have lunch tomorrow."

"Huh?"

"Tomorrow you're going to chip in for next week's coffee and donuts, too."

I slapped ten dollars in her hand and bolted out the door. Cheryl stood and stared at the crumpled ten dollars in her hand. She opened the door to stop me, but I was

207

already gone. I had taken off running because it was stupid to walk around so late at night. I figured it was safer to run all the way to downtown as if I were running from the cops or something.

An hour later, I returned with a 7 Eleven bag full of sandwiches, drinks and chips, enough for a week's supply of lunches. Cheryl would be popular, damn it. People would see her for who she is-- a good and generous person who was fun to know. She would make friends and sit and eat with them at lunch. They would wonder where she got such great lunches and such delicious sandwiches. Noticing that her lunches were better than everyone else's, she would share them with the office, and everyone would be happy. Harmony would reign in the workplace, and she would befriend good people who would be excellent role models. I was sure of it.

Chapter 14: Security Flag

I knew that one way or another, my window of success would probably soon close, and so I decided to use the opportunity to tie up a loose end before things took a turn for the worse. I dialed the number and imagined a dusty telephone ringing on a large wooden desk.

"Hello, St. Vincent's."

"Is this Father Lorenzo?" I asked.

"It is."

"Father, might you be available for dinner?"

"I think I'm always able to make dinner."

"Great."

"Where will it be?"

"My place."

I had already picked up some bread, pasta, and salad in anticipation of the dinner. Cheryl was confident that she could make a feast from the leftovers that Paul had collected the previous week. The good people of Baltimore could not have been more generous with food handouts. Every day Paul came home with Cheesecake Factory, Uno Restaurant, and McCormick and Schmick's leftovers. They were always very good and ranged from appetizers to desserts to main courses. Armed with brand name leftovers, fresh salad, and pasta, Cheryl intended on outdoing herself. A talented cook, she had already impressed me with her cooking abilities the night we had venison steaks; however, cooking steaks was nothing compared to what she would attempt for the dinner that night.

Rushing out of work, I decided to pick up an extra bag of salad on the way home. Dark storm clouds rolled in, and the warm winds began to pick up. I burst into a kind of sprint walk, salad bags in tow, and made it all the way home before the heavy rains started. The wind blew leaves and trashy fliers in my face as I fumbled with the front door knob. Finally getting it unlocked, I came through the door, almost dropping the groceries in shock of what I saw.

"How? --- What? – Who?"

Cheryl popped her head out from the kitchen beaming but exhausted.

"You did this?" I asked.

On the kitchen table and nearby cabinets were mountains of food and candles. Before me I saw a huge spread of bruschetta, cheese wedges, grapes, sliced wheat bread, a huge pot of pasta, chunky homemade tomato sauce, meatballs, spread dip, crackers, pitchers of juice and water, and many other delectable things. Across from the table on a mid level shelf was a fresh salad and assorted dressings. The glow of lit candles danced on the silverware, and a shiny platter holding cheese, crackers, and grapes was elegantly arranged on the coffee table. A pot of water was already boiling for after dinner tea.

"Cheryl, how did you do this? Where did the meatballs come from? Where did the sauce come from? Bruschetta?"

I was really confused, shocked, and happily, unbelievably impressed.

"We had tomatoes and sauce, and we had some left over hamburgers that I used. Then I found some extra deer meat in the back freezer."

"Where did the candles come from?"

"I found those in some old boxes in the cellar."

"Can I try some bruschetta?"

"Sure. The bread is a little soggy, but it was the best we had."

I selected a piece. The platter was perfectly arranged, and I felt bad leaving a gaping white hole in the food pattern but ate it anyway.

"This is good and tasty. Cheryl, I could eat these all night."

I continued to munch, and Cheryl looked pleased.

"I hope Father Lorenzo gets here fast, or else I'm going to eat them all," I said, popping another one in my mouth.

"Don't you dare. I spent the whole day on this."

"The whole day?"

"It's one of my off days, remember? We discussed this. I have rolling weekends," she said, putting her hands on her hips.

"Oh, right, we did discuss it," I said, nodding and still chewing.

"Good. I'm gonna take me a shower and get ready for this dinner."

"Where's Paul?" I asked.

"Who knows," said Cheryl, slapping her hands against her sides. "Now go wait for Father Lorenzo. We don't want him to miss the house."

I had to wait outside, a consequence of hiding my iPhone at work. This was yet another measure necessary to project my external image of neediness and poverty. Unfortunately, this afforded me no way to communicate with the outside world except, of course, in person -- an ancient tradition. I was reduced to sitting on the stoop and hoping beyond hope that it would not start raining, even as occasional drops peppered the streets. I felt the strong warm breeze ruffle my hair and looked up at the darkening clouds as they completely blocked the sun. The floodgates had not yet opened, but it was getting darker and few people remained outside, except for Jimmy the Rapist who I saw coming towards me waving his hand. He was so skinny that I worried he might get blown away with a strong gust of wind. Giving me a fist pound, he sat down on the stoop next to me.

"It feels so good outside."

"I know. I like breezes," I said.

He then excitedly told me about the carnival coming to town. Apparently he made good money assembling and disassembling carnival rides.

"Sometimes I can make up to $200 a day doing that stuff."

"Cool," I said, my eyes still searching the streets for Father Lorenzo.

"Say, be sure to thank your mom for me when you see her."

"For what?"

"For my laundry."

"Your laundry?"

"Yeah. My washing machine broke so your mom has been doing my laundry, and I just wanted to thank her."

"I'll be sure to pass the message along."

I shook my head, unable to understand how Cheryl thought it might be a good idea to wash a rapist's clothes in the house. A house that belonged to a cop. His clothes probably had criminal evidence all over them. I didn't bother to imagine what the cop would say when he found out that evidence was being destroyed in his house on a weekly basis. After this conversation, I decided never to do any more laundry at the house. Ever. There was no way I could believe that my clothes could get cleaner here, not with washing machines lined with rapist evidence.

"Your house has got some good smells coming out of it," said Jimmy, rubbing his stomach.

"That's what happens when Paul goes to the corner."

"No, it smells like food."

"Oh, right, yeah. Cheryl outdid herself tonight."

"What did she make? Smells like Italian."

I saw a small grey car pull over on the side of the street and watched as a very large man struggled to get his stomach out the door. I waved him over to the stoop. It had just started to sprinkle a bit harder, and I could tell the downpour was not far off.

"You know that guy?" Jimmy asked.

"Yeah. He's our local parish priest. He's comin' over for dinner tonight."

"There isn't any extra room, is there?"

Normally I would have been happy to have Jimmy the Rapist, ex-con, over for dinner but not on this particular night, the worst of all nights. I just couldn't figure how the conversation would go. Jimmy believed that I was Cheryl and Paul's son. Father Lorenzo knew the truth and had come to discuss progress. The discovery of each of these two stories would certainly embarrass Cheryl and Paul and quickly become the talk of the town. Our situation would be compromised, the landlord would surely be informed, and evictions, court dates, and jail were sure to follow. There was no way Jimmy could come to dinner tonight.

"Jimmy."

"Yeah?"

"How about we have you over for dinner another week. Would that be okay?"

"Oh, okay. Just keep me in mind," he said, looking somewhat hurt.

"Sure, sure. Cheryl's been talking about doing a barbeque at some point. So we'll definitely let ya know."

Jimmy gave me another fist pound and made his way back up the block. He left and waved to Father Lorenzo as they passed each other on the sidewalk.

Two and a half hours later, I cleared the plates off the table. Cheryl and Father Lorenzo were going back and forth swapping life stories, and everyone had already eaten seconds except for me who had just finished thirds. Things had gone perfectly except that Paul's seat remained empty. We found out later that he had gotten stuck in the rain and didn't get back until early in the morning. Cheryl poured some boiling water for tea into our large green coffee mugs. "Father, you want a cigarette?" asked Cheryl.

"No, thank you. I have a pipe back at home. Love pipe smoke."

"Well, I need to take a cig break. I'll be right back."

Cheryl picked up her lighter and box of cigarettes before making her way to the back porch, leaving me and Father Lorenzo at the table.

Father Lorenzo stroked his beard and looked around. His stare fell on the wall of want.

"So what's on your mind?" I asked.

"This hospital job is a real turning point," he began.

I sat up straighter and leaned in just a bit. He had not spoken or mentioned anything of our situation at all. No questions on how we were doing; no questions on what had happened. In fact, he acted as if he were in the company of regular friends and as if nothing unusual or out of the ordinary was going on. We had all gone around and told stories, funny stories, life lesson stories, and sad stories, but no stories about homelessness. We did briefly discuss the plight of the poor in Baltimore and touched on general trends that he had seen over the past forty years but only on a macro level. There was no expression of surprise at how good the food tasted or how neat the house appeared. And certainly no comment on the fact that we still had running water and electrical wiring.

But finally he was going to speak on the elephant in the room. Maybe, hopefully, impart some words of wisdom, like what I needed to do next, because I didn't know. I had no idea what I was doing and no clue where to go from here. Guidance, I needed guidance! I knew we had to go somewhere, but where? Time was running out, summer would end sooner than later, and it would turn cold again, deadly cold. I would not be renewing the lease. I would not be finding another house for us to live in. I made it crystal clear to Paul and Cheryl that we had only one shot and we had to make it count.

"If she can get into that system, she will be set for life," Father Lorenzo said, almost solemnly.

"I know."

"They provide good pay; and more importantly, they provide benefits."

"Yeah," I agreed.

"Even if she doesn't like her job, there are plenty of places where she could transfer."

"I know."

"If she can keep that job, then her life will change forever."

"Change forever. Got it."

Later that night after Father Lorenzo had left, I sat in the dish chair, half watching television. It had been a big day, and Father Lorenzo's words echoed in my mind, *if Cheryl can keep this job, her life would change forever.* The house was dark, lit only by the television. The volume was barely on, but I just stared into the screen, trying to wrap my mind around the significance of those words. I wondered how I could help her not just keep the job but excel at it. She needed to knock their socks off with the quality of her results, her dependability, and work ethic. I needed her manager to appreciate --

"Hey, hon. Hon?"

I gasped and flinched, startled by the tap on my shoulder. Lost in thought, I didn't hear her coming. I thought she had already gone to bed.

"Oh, hey, Cheryl."

Her face looked a bit puffy as if she had been crying upstairs. She spoke softly and her voice almost shook.

"Hon, what do you think?" She was carrying several hangers with many different types of shirts and her three sets of pink and purple scrubs. Outside the rain had died down, but there was still the occasional rumbled of thunder.

"I gotta find a way to stretch this out longer," she said.

"What do you mean?"

"I can't look like I have only three things to wear. Everyone'll make fun."

"Oh, okay. Show me what you're thinking."

I paused to open the windows to let the fresh air in. I loved the way the air smelled after a thunderstorm. It was always so relaxing and had a way of calming me down. Cheryl laid out the combinations on the couch. Her flipping on the bright lights caused me to squint at first, but then my eyes adjusted. Describing the pros and cons of each outfit, she switched the three shirt-and-pant combinations around into several different looking outfits. Somewhere in between the fifth and sixth combination, I was caught by the irony of this situation and was amused that I, of all people, was being asked for fashion advice. By the way I dressed, I should have been the last person asked. But then I thought about it for a second and realized that I was the only one she could ask. She needed to change the appearance of her wealth and success depending on whether she was hanging out with the neighbors or hanging out with her co-workers, just like me.

"Those look great, Cheryl."

"Really? Ya think?"

"Sure do," I nodded.

"Good. As soon as I get my first paycheck, I can buy new ones."

"Yeah. No one will know the difference. Just keep 'em clean."

"Hon, you know me, I'm a neat freak," she said as she carefully folded up her clothes.

"Where did you get those other shirts?"

"Paul got 'em."

"How?"

"Streets. Someone just handed it to him."

One thing that never ceased to surprise me was the generosity of complete strangers. People had been unexpectedly kind and supportive throughout our whole experience. On the street, adults and children alike leaned out of their cars to hand Paul clothes and food on a daily basis. The neighbors gave Cheryl their extra scrubs, and in some cases, their friendship. Even more surprising was that Eric, my brother who asked random girls to buy him pitchers of beers at bars to save money, sent a large portion of his job's signing bonus to help pay the utility bills and rent. A complete surprise. Unaccustomed to this type of donation from my brother, I originally thought it might be a type of inter-family-predatory-high-interest-rate loan. But it was, in fact, a gift in its truest sense.

Originally, before I had even found the house, I went to churches to pitch the idea and ask them to support the effort. Some said no and some said yes; but in the end, I decided not to pursue any of those funding options. Once money was accepted from either a church or an individual, I felt like I would have to justify myself to them. It added a whole new dimension of responsibility. Even if they said there were no obligations, it didn't matter. I had asked for y to accomplish x, and whoever funded me deserved to have a say in how their contributions were used. But I didn't want to answer to anyone. I wanted to answer to Paul, Cheryl, and God alone for my actions. To ask for money meant that I would muddy the waters by inviting another type of politics into the equation. I wanted Cheryl and Paul to be clear on why I had chosen them to live with me. It wasn't so that I could get rent subsidies from the church or food subsidies from the shelter but simply to remind them of their inherent value and their potential as human beings.

217

However, I had no problem accepting unsolicited gifts. I felt like they were gifts generated from what I had already done and therefore did not have strings attached. Typically, I received them from people who had heard of Cheryl and Paul's struggles and wanted to help out. Not only did I see this as a way for others to participate, but I accepted these gifts because I needed help. I didn't have the means to accomplish everything with my own money; and in order to serve Paul and Cheryl best, I found myself accepting help over and over again.

On the top floor of our office skyscraper in the corporate offices, Kristen Whitworth filed her nails as she waited for me. She sat at her solid cherry wood desk with her blonde hair draped elegantly over her shoulders. Leaning back against her black leather chair, she twirled her hair through two fingers and put her feet up on her desk which happened to be covered with office trinkets. Miniature carvings of brightly painted animals, silver framed family pictures, vases filled with pink flowers, a dish of red candies, and a carving of a miniature pink purse holding her business cards lay strewn about her desk. I startled her when I came through the door, and her extremely high Jessica Simpson brand stiletto heels knocked over her strawberry scented candle.

"There you are!" she said, putting her feet on the ground and sitting up in her chair.

"You asked me to come up," I responded, eyeing the trinkets on her desk, specifically the miniature wooden carving of a pink purse holding her business cards.

"I did."

"Well, I'm here."

"Matt, I'm so, so, proud of you."

By her tone and expression, I quickly realized that she was probably not talking about my last operational efficiency report. She had put the pieces together and figured everything out.

"Oh, umm, thanks."

"I can't believe you kept this from me. Why didn't you say anything?"

"I don't know. It never really came up, I guess."

"Well, listen, I just can't get over it. And last week I put together a clothing drive for your 'housemates.'"

"Really?"

And with her hand she directed my attention in the back corner of her office.

"Yes, and look what we've collected already!"

Four large boxes were stacked on the floor behind me. They were rather large, and the top boxes were opened and overflowing with clothes, soap, purses, and shoes. I couldn't believe it. I knelt down and started going through them. It appeared as if a good portion of the office had participated.

"Kristen, some of these are brand new," I exclaimed, holding up a blouse still bearing a price tag.

She couldn't stop smiling.

"I know," she said.

It felt like Christmas morning, and I spent significant time rummaging around in the boxes. I found all sorts of pants, skirts, blouses, shirts, soap, perfumes, purses, wallets and even an envelope containing $25 from a co-worker. After sorting through everything, I returned back to my desk. I couldn't believe the positive response from my colleagues. I had never anticipated this and I felt ashamed for having kept it a secret for so long. In addition to generosity from work, someone outside the Firm, whom I had never met, sent me a government stimulus check and asked me to use it on running the house. I took each act of support as a sign that the community believed in Paul and Cheryl as much as I did.

About an hour before I was going to head home, I got another phone call which I expected to be that of another well wisher. But it was a very different type of call.

"Matt, is that you?"

"Yes, Cheryl. I'm at work. You're only supposed to use this line in case of an emergency!"

"I know, I know. Sorry to bother yuh, but I have a problem."

"What's the problem?"

"Paul's out, and I need some help."

"Help with what, Cheryl?"

"I need some tampons."

"Holy hell, Cheryl!"

"They're at CVS. I'll pay yuh when you come home, but I just can't move right now. I'm having cramps and stuff."

"Cheryl, enough, enough! I'll do it."

"Get big ones."

"Please stop. I'll figure it out."

"Thanks, dear. I appreciate this."

I sighed. I hadn't grown up with sisters and was unaccustomed to these types of requests. I had no idea what I was doing. Standing in the CVS women's aisle, I wondered why on earth the world needed so many different brands of pads. She sounded like she needed something specific. A pad is a pad, isn't it? What's the difference between Maxi and Always? I picked up boxes, read the labels, and then put them back. I did this several times. There were so many women's products, I wondered how any female made it back before the creation of CVS. It was all very stressful and I received many stares from customers and store staff alike. After several calls to some perplexed girls, I finally figured out what I needed to buy and brought it back to a very relieved Cheryl.

I also surprised Cheryl and Paul with boxes upon boxes of clothes and other gifts. Paul was mildly interested and barely paid it any attention, but Cheryl, on the other hand, had never been more excited. I had not seen her that happy in a long time. She ripped open the cardboard boxes and went through every article of clothing. Taking some of the new clothes, she put on a summer dress and high heels which she found in the box. Then she strutted around the house saying, "Don't I look good?" The flowery dress fit her perfectly, and the high heels did not look half bad either. I nodded and agreed that she had never looked better. Then she dove back into the pile of boxes; and amidst the tangled clothes, bath soaps, and assorted shoes, she discovered a small little black box. She held it and looked up at me and then started gushing tears.

"What? Is something wrong?" I asked.

The box appeared to be some kind of perfume. She looked at me and asked, "Do you know how long it's been since I've worn perfume?"

Her voice shook as she spoke. Carefully, she opened the box and took the perfume bottle in both her hands as if it were sacred. She admired it for a full fifteen seconds and then rapidly squeezed it, spraying it all over herself. I was confident that she used much more than the prescribed amount. Now smelling like roses, she wiped away her tears, but the scent was overpowering, and I thought I might suffocate right there in the living room. I opened the windows and the front door to try and air out the house, much like I would do when Paul came home.

The next day I came home to find things had started to change. Streams of dark blue eyeliner ran down her cheeks, and bright red lipstick smudges covered her chin. Her face hung in her hands, but she did smell like roses, fields and fields of roses.

"Cheryl, what's wrong?" I asked as I set my blue duffle bag on the sidewalk.

"They sent me home."

My heart sank.

"Why?"

"They said that my name was flagged in the police database."

"What for?"

"They don't know, but they're giving me a week to figure it out."

I paused and raised an eyebrow.

"You don't have any idea what it could be?"

Cheryl sat back and thought for a second and then answered, "No."

I turned on the step below Cheryl and sat down. I faced out towards the neighborhood and knew she was not telling me everything. Across the street, a few young children dressed in clothes that were way too big for them and played catch with a large wad of blue tape. One kid ran out for a long pass but missed, and the blue tape ball bounced off a car windshield. Always fearing this day would come, I knew exactly why the police had flagged her in their system. I knew exactly why they had sent her home. Closing my eyes, I rested my head on my folded arms. I had hoped that all of this might just blow over.

Two days ago, my phone lit up with a blocked number, but I knew who it was. Abruptly I jumped out of my chair and went running down the office halls. This call needed to be private and it needed to be now. There were only seconds before it would go to voicemail. It rang two more times and then I answered the call right before bursting out of the swivel door into the outside cobbled plaza. Pigeons scattered everywhere.

"Hello."

"This is Scott."

His voice sounded young.

"Scott, it's good to talk to you. I just---

"Do not ever send me an email on my work address again. Do I make myself clear?"

"Yes. I'm sorry," I said.

"How do you know my mother?"

"Listen, I've been living with your mother and father in a house near the stadium. I just wanted you to know that they're doing okay."

As it turns out, Scott was a young politician who had recently won office within Pennsylvania state politics. I thought it was ironic that he had run his campaign on family values. Cheryl talked about him all the time and was incredibly proud of him and all of his accomplishments. She thought the world of him.

"Do not call Paul my father. That man is not my father."

"Okay"

"What is this program? A halfway house?"

"No."

"Then who do you work for?"

"No one."

"So whose house is it?"

"It's my house."

"How did you meet my mom and Paul?"

"They were panhandling on the side of the street so I invited them to live with me."

Scott paused.

"You there?" I asked.

"Why are you doing this?"

"Because God loves them, and I don't think they realize that."

"Well, that's nice of you. Yes, very nice."

"They're good people," I said.

"I hope you take precautions. They are very dangerous people."

"Dangerous?"

"They're both on the local county's most wanted list. I saw their pictures on TV the other night."

I just sat and stared ahead at the pigeons gliding around the square. I knew that Paul and Cheryl's family

223

were nearby and I realized that if they wanted, they could be extremely helpful in supporting Paul and Cheryl.

"What are their charges?"

"Among a slew of other things, grand theft auto."

"Oh, boy," I said, sitting down on a bench. I slapped a hand on my head. It was comical to think of mild mannered Cheryl, complete with kitchen apron, stealing someone's car in cold blood. What did she do? Hold the owner up with a rolling pin?

"There's something else you should know, too."

"What's that?"

"They both have been addicted to heroin. We did everything we could to help them. I spent tens of thousands of dollars on legal fees and rehab."

"And it didn't work?"

"Towards the end, Mom begged us to stop helping. She said that she liked the drugs too much and she didn't want to see us waste any more time or money on her."

"She said she wanted the drugs more than the help?"

"Yes."

I decided to change the subject.

"She just got a job at the hospital in the medical records department. It pays benefits and enough money to allow them to become self sufficient."

"I'll believe it after six months of paychecks."

"Well, I just figured you should know. She's trying."

"She's a good woman. Caring, compassionate, and she's a good mom," said Scott. His voice was cracking.

"I know," I said.

"She could have the world, but instead she hangs out with that deadbeat."

"She can make it out of this. You'll see."

"Do you know, they used to live out of a van? That's no way to raise three small children."

"I heard."

"The kids are finally happy. They haven't missed a day of school since they've been with me. They have friends now, and they're even going on a camping trip this weekend. Don't mess this up."

"I'm happy for them. I'll keep you posted on any job developments."

Suddenly, the initial uplifting tone of the conversation changed. Again, the phone went silent.

"Hello?"

"Don't take this the wrong way, but do not ever contact me again. I severed connections with her over seven months ago. I can't risk having the kids get unsettled again. They don't handle it well."

"I understand." I said just before the phone went dead.

Cheryl pulled out a cigarette and began smoking. She had stopped crying and wiped most of the makeup off her face. I had always hoped to use her family as a support network, but only after she got back on her feet, of course. Unfortunately, they had been an integral part of my plan for continued support, and now it seemed as if they wanted nothing to do with this. But I wasn't giving up on her family yet, and I hoped that with enough accomplishments, I could convince their families to take them back in. I believed that if Paul and Cheryl got steady jobs, then they could convince themselves and the world that they were capable of standing on their own two feet. Their family had good reason to cut them off; but without family support, long-term success looked unlikely.

"Well, what's your plan?" I demanded.

"I don't know. What do you think?" asked Cheryl, puffing on her cigarette. She looked scared and on the verge of tears again.

"That's not good enough," I said, pounding my knee. "Cheryl, we've come so far. Nothing good ever comes easily. Now more than ever you must find the strength to push back."

" Okay, okay, you're right, hon."

"Cheryl, this needs to be you. I can't push for you."

"All right, I'll schedule a meeting with my lawyer tomorrow. He should be able to look up the charges."

"You have a lawyer?"

"Matt, I haven't always been homeless!"

"Right, right... Will he charge you any money?"

"No, no. It should be pro bono. He knows about my situation," Cheryl said reassuringly.

"Okay, good."

"I am just so nervous about what it is," she said, her eyes darting back and forth.

"Yeah, I bet."

"I don't want to go to jail, I just don't wanna."

"Jail?"

"It's one of the most awful places. I'm not that kinda girl. I don't belong there."

"It's probably just a misunderstanding. A giant misunderstanding. I doubt jail will be involved," I said, trying to calm her down. She was starting to breathe very heavily.

The next day Cheryl talked to the lawyer who looked up her charges and found that she was wanted for Grand Theft Auto. Upon further review, the lawyer found that Cheryl's last landlord filed the charges which perplexed her because her last landlord was an elderly woman with several physical and mental handicaps.

"Cheryl, if that's the van you and Paul lived out of, you need to return it."

"No, no. That was a different car."

"Well, I guess it doesn't matter. We still have to do something."

"I know."

Cheryl faced the ground staring deep into the sidewalk. I wasn't sure what it was, but something about knowingly harboring wanted felons in a cop's house made me a bit uneasy. I never thought renting from a cop could be so damn stressful. Cheryl's ignorance of her charges didn't help anything. Her very son, who hadn't talked to her in seven months, knew that she was on the most wanted criminals list for the local county. Between the suspected lies and the conversation with Cheryl's son, I began to question everything. I questioned things that she told me then, and I questioned things that she'd told me before. It was so confusing to tell the difference between truth and lies. She had told me true things about her son, that's how I found him, but she clearly lied about knowing her charges. If her son knew, she knew. Trust was one of the most important things that I had with them; and if I lost that, what then could I do? In the midst of all these dark thoughts, Cheryl spoke.

"I know what I gotta do."

"What's that?" I asked, still very distracted.

"I'm gonna turn myself in."

"You're going to do what?" I blurted out.

"It's the only way."

"Yeah, but Cheryl, if you go there…

"I know. But it's either this or keep running."

Her face turned red, and she started to tear up.

"And I'm tired of running."

I realized that this was a turning point. For the first time since the beginning of the house, she was about to take on some risk of her own. I considered this a huge victory; and instantly, all the uncertainties that plagued my mind were swept away. This was a sacrifice that she wouldn't be making unless she understood that there was no future in running. She understood that there was light at the end of the tunnel. I couldn't have been more proud.

"You can't let them keep me there long," said Cheryl, wiping her face.

"In prison?"

"I'm not a prison girl. Please don't forget about me there."

"Cheryl, I'll never forget about you."

She smiled as tears streamed down her cheeks and fell onto the ground.

"Those places are overcrowded, and horrible stuff can happen to you behind those bars."

"How do you know?"

"Paul's gone there several times."

"I should have guessed."

"Yeah, it's a long story. They all are," she mumbled.

"I promise I will make sure that you're treated properly. If you go at all, you won't stay there long."

"Thanks, hon," she said in between sniffles. Then she started crying again. Anytime someone cried, I felt awkward. It didn't matter if they were crying either from joy or sorrow. I simply didn't know what to do with myself so I just rested my hand on her shoulder in a weak attempt to comfort her. I could not have been more proud. Her choice to turn herself in showed me clearly that she knew what was at stake. She was willing to pay the price to fight for her future, to fight for her life.

Chapter 15: Landlord Woes

The next day I came home and found a small paper note on the kitchen table.

Matt, I have gone down to the Maryland courthouse, they will probably throw me in a holding cell, in prison. If I don't come home please tell Paul what happened. Also, whenever you can, come visit me.
-Cheryl

She made up her mind to go down to the courthouse, but she returned later that night. When she came back, she told me what had happened. She went down and timidly stepped into the public defender's office. She explained calmly how she had moved from living in a van to under the bridge, to a house in West Baltimore with a 23-year-old consultant. She spoke of her job search efforts, about the security flag, and about how much this meant to her. She then closed by saying that this was one big misunderstanding and that her son was a state politician and that he would be very disappointed to hear that this was going on. Back at home, I listened with perked up ears and an open mouth.

"You told him all that?"

"Yup, I did."

"I can't even imagine his reaction. What did he say?"

"He didn't really believe me."

"Then how did you get to come back home?"

"Well."

"I mean, I thought they would throw you into a holding cell."

"Well, they would have, except that they reviewed the police report."

"And?"

"It wasn't completed properly, and when they investigated it --

"Yeah?"

-- they found that the car didn't even belong to the woman who filed the report."

"What?"

She giggled, "So they now have a warrant out for her arrest."

It wasn't funny, but I laughed anyway. Too much tension had been released for me not to laugh.

"They also wanted me to testify when they find her."

"Where is she?"

"She's horribly handicapped and in a nursing home. That's why I was driving her car for her in the first place."

"So the State is going to sue this crippled woman?"

"Yeah. She's so old, too. I can't imagine getting her *physically* to the court room."

The image of the police dragging some old grandma kicking and screaming out of a retirement home just so a lawyer could build his reputation had us in stitches.

"I am proud of you for doing this."

"Me, too."

We celebrated across the street at Carl's bar where we ordered two large cheeseburgers and a couple of beers. My confidence and hope of Cheryl succeeding at her job had been restored.

The next couple of weeks went by without a hitch. Cheryl got everything cleared up at work. She finished her rotations and was placed in the medical records department. To better understand her responsibilities, she spent the next several weeks shadowing experienced employees. Every night I came home to stories about co-workers, crazy patients, and power hungry managers. Though there were tough days, she enjoyed her job. Less stressed and happier than ever, Cheryl developed a spring in her step and could never seem to stop smiling.

Our attention turned towards real estate ads and nearby for-rent signs. I had Cheryl save all of her money and told her to find a way to keep it from Paul. Well, actually, that was her idea, but I agreed wholeheartedly. Her father, whom she spoke to every other day, wanted to make sure that Paul never saw a dime of her money either. When I asked why her dad didn't offer a room to her, she explained that he had heart problems and had enough issues of his own. Not only that, but his house had no spare room, and his income was too small to support her, though he could certainly and gladly help hide her money from Paul whom he blamed for everything bad in the world. Cheryl's dad insisted on picking up her checks and keeping them safe, but I wanted her to get a bank account. She refused, citing thousands of dollars of outstanding medical debts. She feared her creditors would come after her. I looked into it and found that it *was* possible for creditors to come after her account; however, that was unlikely.

A bank downtown offered to provide basic financial literacy classes and encouraged me to try and sign her up. They sent home books and pamphlets, which she read, but was still too scared to open an account. She preferred cash because it was something she could touch, see, and smell. She could easily keep it safe from creditors though I still pestered her on a regular basis. Despite all of this, she was persistent, and so the financial literacy books, for the most part, sat unused on the bookshelf.

Vacations were few and far between, but every now and then I carved out some time to get away. I had gotten tickets to a Dave Matthews concert in Virginia Beach, and there was no way I was going to miss this show. The trip would take about four days, over which time I would leave Paul and Cheryl completely alone in the house. Before I left, I reiterated my many warnings and reminded them to keep a low profile. I did everything I could to communicate how important it was that they continue to smoke outside on the back porch; to stay out of view from the street.

Of course, it made me nervous to be so far away, but we had lived together for seven months without incident. Surely a few days wouldn't be so bad.

And yet, only 24 hours after my departure from West Baltimore, the house came as close as it ever had to being shut down.

The drive to the concert was seven hours from Baltimore, so I arranged to stay at a little house on the Maryland shore owned by my buddy Hutch, who frequently took me out hunting.

Duck decoys rested on the mantle, and camouflage pants and jackets lay on the couches. All the blankets in the house bore images of geese and deer. The fridge was completely stuffed with frozen duck, goose, deer, and turkey meat, guts still dripping with blood. The freezer attached to the fridge was packed, and I understood that there was another large separate freezer on order.

Hutch loved everything about the hunt from the preparation of the weapons to the thrill of the fatal shot, to the displaying of trophies and turkey feathers on his wall. If he had his way, I was pretty sure he'd go hunting twenty-four hours a day. But since it was illegal to hunt at night, it was a good thing he also liked Nintendo Wii. After about 30 minutes of the game, my character got slashed in the neck by a zombie and fell down dead. I decided it was a good time for a break and noticed someone had left me a voicemail. As I listened to it, my muscles tensed. It couldn't have been more than five seconds long, but it was enough to drain the blood from my face. Hutch laid his controller down and paused the game.

"What is it?" he asked.

"It's the landlord," I said, pacing around the room.

"What did he say?"

"I think he knows!"

I walked into the dark kitchen to think about how I would respond. My landlord, Dick, had left a very simple voicemail, but it was enough to bring me to the edge of despair. All he said was, "I have a few questions for you. Call me." I wanted to get this done tonight before Dick took matters into his own hands, but I had no idea what had happened. More importantly, I could not figure out how he found out at such a late hour in the night. It had to have been the neighbors. They must have said something. But what could have happened to cause them to inform him so late at night? Maybe it wasn't the neighbors. What if it was something else? Something worse. I braced myself and hit the call back button. Dick picked up in a flash and without warning launched into a full scale police interrogation.

"Where are you?" he barked.

"Um, Hi, Dick. How are you?"

"That depends. Just please answer my question. Where are you?"

"I'm on my way to Virginia Beach."

"Why?"

"I'm, uhh, going to a Dave Matthews concert."

"Really."

"Umm, okay, it's 11 o'clock at night, you know," I said, trying to cut to the chase, "Is something wrong?"

"You tell me."

"Excuse me?"

"Why don't you tell me why there's a giant piece of Baltimore crack-head shit sitting in my living room!"

I covered the phone and gasped. I pulled it away from my ear and pounded my head with my fist. How could this be happening? A nightmare. Trying to hide the desperation in my voice, I took some deep breaths before speaking.

"Uhh, err… I see you met Paul. I can explain."

"You better damn well explain. If I find out that you've moved out, I'm gonna--

"Okay, calm down, calm down. I definitely have not moved out."

"Then what are *they* doing in my house!"

"You know the neighborhood. It's important that someone watch the house while I'm gone."

"So they're watching the house?"

"Yes."

I knew this sounded crazy, but it *was* true. I hated to lie, and I purposely chose the words to my answers very carefully. In this instance, they were watching the house at my request. The neighborhood was a bit sketchy so it would make sense to want someone responsible to watch the house. What didn't make sense was that Paul looked more dangerous than anyone else in the neighborhood and should be the last person qualified to house sit.

"Where did you meet them?" asked Dick skeptically.

"I met them around Baltimore."

"How long have you known them?"

"For a while. They've been helping me understand the area a bit better."

The interrogation continued. Dick sounded increasingly frustrated as I rapidly shot back answers to all his questions.

"What do they do?"

"Well, Cheryl has a job at the University of Maryland medical center, but Paul is in between jobs right now. He fell out of a building and is kind of disabled. He should be getting disability soon, though."

"Listen, we need to set some new rules. I see crack heads every day, and they look no different than that shit-head. If you ever need to leave town again, you will call me and I will watch the house for you. I don't ever want them in my house again."

"Okay."

"Do I make myself clear?"

"Crystal."

When I returned home, I found Cheryl and Paul in the house. I sat and talked with them for about an hour. We discussed the concert, the weekend, the weather, and yet, somehow no one thought to mention that the house almost shut down. No one thought to let me know that we all almost got thrown in jail, or at the very least, evicted. Maybe they didn't think it was important that the *one person* who we spent months hiding from happened to show up at the front door. Discussing the weather was just too damn important. Angry, I announced that I knew everything. They were surprised. Surprised that I knew but said that I shouldn't worry about it. Cheryl assured me that everything went fine until Dick saw Paul.

Then she proudly explained how she smoothed things over by telling the following epic lie. She told him that she and my mom were good friends from their church and went on to say that their families had been friends for years, and how my mom had asked Cheryl and Paul to watch the house while I was out of town. Apparently, my mom was a little concerned about the neighborhood and wanted to make sure the house was watched in my absence. She knew that Cheryl and Paul were in the area and figured they would be able to keep an eye on things while I was away. This is not even everything that she said. She spoke for literally several minutes on how she and my mom had become such good friends. She made up several details to create a very intricate, believable story. Her ability to lie scared me. I knew that if she could convincingly lie to the landlord, then she could convincingly lie to me.

This lying was unacceptable. I could not tolerate it. I felt dirty knowing that I had participated in this deception, and I needed a shower. Immediately. I got a change of clothes, my towel, soap, shampoo and ran into the bathroom. After the shower, I decided to make things right. I told Cheryl that I planned to tell Dick everything. She began sobbing, and rivers of tears and makeup ran down her cheeks. Now that Dick had asked, I felt he deserved to know, especially now that he had seen them. She cried and begged me not to, but I said it was the only way to make things right. Paul gathered up his things and prepared to move, and Cheryl sulked around the house the rest of the night. The next day I called Dick. Twice. But he didn't pick up so I left a voicemail. I explained that I had much more to tell about how I knew Paul and Cheryl and asked him to return the call as soon as possible. But Dick never called back. Every day for the next two weeks, we waited in suspense, but he never returned the call. Perplexed, I decided to leverage this impending doom to create a sense of urgency. I used it to remind Paul and Cheryl that every day was a gift and that any day we could all be evicted. There was no time to waste, and we needed to arrange for their independence as quickly as possible.

Chapter 16: The Feast

Bounding upstairs, I threw the door open and found that my room was just as I had left it. White desk against the wall, books and papers scattered on top, and a pile of clothes in the corner. My green blanket, which had a giant moose head superimposed on it, was still crumpled in the middle of the floor. On another side of the room stood a long, frameless rectangular mirror that leaned against the wall. Pausing for a moment, I remembered that this mirror had actually played a significant role in this adventure. I had discovered it in the back of a closet after I had settled into the house. It was so covered in dust that it had trouble reflecting anything at all. I tried wiping it off with an old shirt, but the dust and grime tenaciously stuck to the mirror. I realized that cleaning it properly would have required stuff like Windex which was far more effort than I was willing to make. Though I didn't really care because the mirror was more symbolic than useful. I called it my decision mirror, so named because anytime I needed to make a big choice or strategy, I would sit in front of the mirror. Even though I only saw a blur of myself through the dust, it reminded me that no matter what anyone said at home, at work, or in the community, I was the only one responsible for my actions and inactions.

I was digging through my pile of clothes looking for my cargo shorts, I heard Cheryl calling me.

"Eh, Hon," she yelled from downstairs.

"Yeah," I called back.

"Whatcha' doing?"

"Changing."

"Lil' Barry and Skip are comin' over."

"When?"

"Soon."

"Why?"

"Barry broke his bike or somethin."

"So?"

"Paul's gonna help em fix it."

Hopping around with one foot stuck in my suit pants, I shouted, " Okay, I'll be down soon!"

A few minutes later, I grabbed a fruit rollup from the kitchen and joined Cheryl outside. The open front door let in cool breezes as well as a few gnats. I hated gnats, but they didn't bite as bad as mosquitoes. Mosquito bites were the worst so maybe I should have shut the door. But no, the air conditioning was off. We needed the breeze, and bites were a small price to pay for lower bills.

Outside, the neighbors sat out on their stoops, including the Irishman whom we waved to from across the way. He leaned heavily on his iron banister, teetering back and forth. For a moment it looked as if he might collapse on the stairs. Then suddenly, he lost his balance and down he went but inches from face planting right on the sidewalk. His hand wobbled through the air and miraculously caught the banister just in time. Slowly he pulled himself up to his feet and looked around to see if anyone had witnessed his little stumble. He must have caught a glimpse of something because his eyes bulged out, and then he started shaking, as if he were afraid. I looked up the street but couldn't see anything. I suspected that he must be hallucinating from too much alcohol. Just another scene from the daily comings and goings of the drunken Irishman.

The drunken Irishman was so called for two reasons: he was Irish, and he was drunk, always drunk, even at 10:00 in the morning. Often yelling racial slurs with a thick Irish accent, he was a neighborhood icon.

Speaking of neighborhood icons, I glanced up the sidewalk and spotted what was causing the Irishman so much grief. Emerging from behind some tall bushes a few houses away, Margery was making her way down the street with Spike at her side. Well, not exactly at her side, more out in front, dragging her behind him as if she were a lightweight rag doll. Luckily, she carried her wooden club which helped anchor her to the ground. It dragged behind her, kicking up little pebbles wherever she went. Though she was struggling to take control of Spike, she held her head up high. She was very proud, or at least very proud looking. Upon seeing the ferocious animal, the Irishman stumbled back inside his house, slammed the door, and locked the bolts, leaving me and Cheryl alone for the dreaded dog walking. I used this new privacy as an opportunity to ask Cheryl about work.

"How was work today?" I asked.

Cheryl nodded, "It's good. It can be kinda confusin' though."

"Oh?"

"There's so many things to remember."

"Really?"

"And they use different systems than I'm used to."

"Can you handle it?"

"Yeah, I think so."

"Doesn't anyone help you?"

"They do."

"Like who?"

"Carolyn"

"Who?"

"She's my helper. She's very patient."

"That's good."

Mitchum came around the corner wearing a large white shirt that came right down to his knees. He also had some torn blue jeans which, covered in dirt and stains, looked as if he had stored them on the floor of an unkempt horse barn. They were covered in oil stains, and I suspected that he might have also used them as mechanic rags while fixing his girlfriend's truck. Despite his shirt and jeans, his sneakers were white as snow. In fact, everyone in this neighborhood always had clean shoes, shoes that looked as if they had just come out of the box. Mitchum's shirt, which was soaked in sweat, stuck to his large belly. Dark, crusty scabs formed over the backs of his hands.

"You think it's hot out here, wait till you go in that factory."

"They don't have A/C in there?"

"Hell, no, boy."

He wiped his brow, trying to intercept the beads of sweat before they ran into his cataract-covered eyes.

"It's hard to breathe there."

"Don't they have fans?"

"Wha? Fans? They have fans everywhere, but they don't do nothin. All them fans do is blow hot air around. Hot air in my face, hot air everywhere."

Cheryl came out and handed him a frosty glass of water just as Lil' Barry and Skippy came coasting down the street towards us. They skidded to a halt in front of the stoop creating black skid marks all over the concrete. Cheryl frowned. I knew she spent hours sweeping the sidewalk, keeping it neat and tidy. We all noticed that Lil' Barry didn't look so good. Not at all. Cheryl put her hand over her mouth while Mitchum just stared. He looked up at us, and both Cheryl and Mitchum looked away, but I didn't.

"Lil' Barry, what the hell happened?" I asked.

Skippy laughed.

"Barry, you want to me to tell 'em?"

Barry wore a sweat soaked wife beater which clearly displayed the dried black scabs covering his arms.

"It looks like you contracted the plague," I said, pointing to his arms.

"Oh, yeah."

"Oh yeah what?"

"I fell."

240

"You fell?"

"Off my bike."

"Where?"

Looking glum, he chained his bike to the stoop and did his best not to meet any of our eyes, clearly embarrassed.

"Listen, listen," said Skippy, trying to restrain his laughter.

We all leaned forward with anticipation.

"We were biking down the stadium bridge."

"Uh huh."

"Cruisin' at a steady clip, when all of a sudden Barry here slams into one of the safety posts."

"A safety post?"

"Yeah."

"Wait, what kind of safety post?"

"They're the ones that keep cars from driving on the sidewalk."

"The waist high ones?"

"Yeah, yeah!"

"Aren't they painted in a bright yellow color?"

"Yeah, striped so they stand out even more."

"Got it."

"So, so Barry hits it dead on and goes flying."

Seeing as he was okay and it was hard not to find this funny, I just started laughing big, full belly laughs. Then everyone joined in except Barry, of course.

"Where did he land?"

"Flew about ten feet and landed on his head."

"Oh, Barry, you should be more careful!" scolded Cheryl.

"I know," he acknowledged. He sat with his head resting in his hands.

Skippy continued through his own laughter, "Scraped up his back, head, arms and everything."

"Your head?"

241

"Yup, yup," said Barry, rubbing his head.

Sure enough, there was a large lump and dried blood where the hair had torn away.

"Gross."

"Did you go to the hospital?" I asked.

"Ah, no, no. I was pretty drunk so I didn't feel that much pain."

Cheryl just shook her head. She decided it was time to play the *I told you so* game.

"Barry, we've talked about this drinking and driving."

"I know, I know," said Barry, rolling his eyes. "We've been through this a thousand times! Haven't I told you enough?"

"I said I know! And I'm sick and ti--

Barry just stopped speaking mid sentence. Some girls were walking past the far end of the block. They wore skin tight clothing and actually didn't look half bad. Like a bloodhound tracking a fox, Barry's head turned in their direction and froze. Craning his neck and staring, he did everything but stand up and point to get their attention. Then he tilted his head back and started making his stupid ear-piercing mating calls again.

"Barry, at least put a shirt on before you do that," said Skippy.

He momentarily paused, "Why?"

"Because it looks like you have the one of the worst STD's known to man," I said.

Cheryl chuckled as Lil' Barry turned bright red.

Skip looked around and asked, "Where's Paul? He needs to help us fix Barry's bike from the crash."

The wheel had been partially bent and the gears were in disarray. Though it was still functional, it wouldn't be so for long.

"Paul'll be here soon. Do you guys want anything to eat?"

Barry and I nodded aggressively. We were starving.

Cheryl went inside, and soon the clanging of pots and pans echoed out of the kitchen. Skip took the bikes through the house to the back porch. There was little fear of having them stolen back there. Yes, the neighborhood was the kind where crimes happened often, even in broad daylight. Hoodlums would just appear and take your bike. Sometimes they would be so bold as to actually fight you for it, despite the protests of the elderly neighborhood watch group. Though I always thought it was a bit ironic because I knew that no one around here ever bought bikes from the store in the first place. Paul and Cheryl both had bikes, which they swapped out for other bikes every other week. Why they bothered fixing them was beyond me when they could just steal another one. Skip and Barry showed up with different bikes all the time, but, I didn't ask those types of questions.

A little bit later, Paul came home with a large bag of assorted food leftovers and other handouts. We all helped him unload muffins, bread, summer sausage, crackers, etc onto the counter, Paul gave Cheryl a quick peck on the cheek before disappearing out back to help Skippy with the repairs. Lil' Barry and I went out front. We hung out on the stoop, watched the comings and goings of the neighborhood, and chuckled at Mitchum's angry phone calls to Lequita.

"So, what did you do today?"

"Nothin. Just helped Skip with whatever he's doin."

"No job? "

"Nah, don't need one."

"You don't need one?"

"Yeah."

"Well, how do you live?" I asked.

"I get a check from the government."

"How often?"

"Every month for $600."

"Really? Why?"

"It's because my mom passed away, I got bipolar some learning disabilities, and a few other things. So I get a check."

Mitchum disappeared behind the block to continue yelling into his phone. Not that it mattered. We could still hear him shouting from around the corner anyway.

"I'm sorry to hear about your mom."

"It happened a while ago."

"So you don't want to work?"

"Nah. If I did, I wouldn't get my check."

"Yeah, but will your check get any bigger?"

"Nope."

"Oh."

"I don't even have a diploma. What job could I get?"

He kicked a pebble off the stoop, reached into his pocket, and pulled out a cigarette and started smoking.

"Wait right here. I have something to show you," I said.

A few minutes later, I came back outside and held something behind my back.

"Okay, close your eyes."

Barry smiled and closed his eyes and held out his hands. I slapped a giant GED book in his hands.

"I got this for you."

Opening his eyes, a huge grin spread across his face.

"Really? For me?"

"Yeah. We can start it whenever you want."

He seemed excited and flipped through some of the pages and pointed to various sections. I had not expected such a happy response.

"I'm only good at the math stuff," he said flipping through the pages.

"Then I will help you with the English."

"It's kinda big," said Barry, looking daunted.

"Yeah, but I bet you know most of it."

Taking it out of Barry's hands, I flipped rapidly through the huge tome until I came to a review page. It happened to be a comprehensive summary of several chapters of mathematics. I scanned them briefly, I found that they were among some of the more complicated problems on the test. Deciding it was way too difficult, I went to turn the page, but Barry's scab-covered hand stopped me.

"Wait."

"What?"

"I want to try."

"Are you sure? It's kinda --," Barry interrupted me by calling out answers. Picked off the review questions, one by one, with surprising speed. I raced to do the problems myself, checking them as quickly as I could, but I wasn't as fast as him.

"Barry," I said in disbelief, "You almost got all of them right."

"Really? Which ones did I get right?"

"All of them except one, the one about—

I looked at the question again and caught my own mistake. Barry's answer was right, and I was wrong. He could tell by the expression on my face and smiled gleefully.

"I told you I was good at math."

Then I heard Barry's stomach growling and realized that I, too, was starving.

"I'm hungry. Let's go check on the food," he said.

He got up and disappeared into the house, but I sat on the stoop for a few moments before heading in. Still in shock at his mathematical prowess, I slowly folded up the book, shook my head and thought, *that just happened.* He was smarter than he let on, at least in math. This was good because I wasn't that great at math, and I probably couldn't teach it all too well. My imagination started getting carried away again, and I could see exactly how everything was going to play out. I would make him complete all the practice questions, study at the library, and take practice tests. I would explain challenging concepts repeatedly until he could explain them back to me. Then he would take the test, and probably fail, but we would not be discouraged. I would have him review vocabulary, grammar, and reading comprehension. Then he would take the test again, but this time he would pass with flying colors. Shortly after, he would find a good paying job; and in his spare time, he would volunteer to teach kids how to write and read well. I liked this vision, and I gave the study book a motivational slap before placing it prominently on the bookshelf.

In the kitchen, open cans of corn, beans, carrots, and salmon meat lay empty on the counter next to an army of pots and pans cooking on the stove. It was an interesting mix, but who was I to judge? I glimpsed the empty cans only for a second before Cheryl threw them into the trash. Her hands moved so quickly, it appeared as though the laws of physics did not apply to them. At any given moment, she was adding spices, adjusting heat ranges, or flipping salmon burgers while simultaneously stirring fresh sweet tea and wiping down the counters. She always did love a perpetually clean kitchen.

"Wow, that smells so good," I said, reaching to grab a piece of one of the patties while Barry attempted to fish out some corn. Cheryl's eyes narrowed as if to say how dare we invade her space, touch her food, and interfere with her art! With lightning reflexes, she slapped our hands away with a large wooden spoon. Each whack was solid and made a loud thud as the spoon cracked against our knuckles.

"Stop, boys. Wait until I'm finished," she yelled, slapping her spoon on the counter.

"Okay, okay."

Rubbing our arms and hands, we tended to our wounds and retreated out to the back porch to see how the bike repairs were coming. Outside we found all sorts of gears, screws, and bolts lying all over the deck. The sun was setting, and it was becoming harder to see the tools scattered around two upside-down bicycles. Paul and Skippy sat between them covered in oil, grease, and sweat. They were tightening the bolts on the gears. On the ground next to Paul's leg was a broken wrench, a wrench that was not previously broken. I had never seen such a thick piece of metal broken into so many pieces, and I was extremely curious to know how something like that could happen. But I didn't ask. I found it was best not to dig too deeply into how things got broken.

"Eh, Paul, hand me that hammer over there," said Skip.

"Aright."

"How's that food comin?" asked Paul as he handed the hammer to Skippy.

"It smells good."

"Does it taste good?"

"Cheryl won't let us touch it."

"Well, you know, Cheryl, always wantin' everythin to be just right."

"Yeah, I know."

After another hour of messing with the bikes, both Skippy and Paul determined that it was hopeless. The gears couldn't be fixed without new parts. So they packed up their tools and sat with us under the ceiling fan in the living room. We turned the fan up high and relaxed under its cool breeze. The food smelled so good that we were almost drooling in our seats. In the next few minutes,

Cheryl appeared holding several dishes piled high with salmon cakes, corn, and a light summer bean salad.

"This is amazing," I said with a full mouth.

"Yeah, she cooks good," said Barry.

"How did you make them taste like this? Didn't this salmon come out of a can?"

Barry was about to speak when Cheryl stopped him.

"Barry, don't tell him the secret," she said.

"Why?"

"He won't like 'em otherwise."

"Cheryl, tell me the secret."

"No way."

"They're good. I'll still like 'em."

"No, you won't."

"C'mon, Cheryl!"

"Nope."

"Barry, tell me." I said. I was beginning to get worried. I could only imagine what cooking tips Cheryl picked up from the homeless camp.

He just looked at Cheryl.

"Tell me."

"Italian salad dressing."

"Gross!" I yelled, scrunching up my face. Though I was just kidding. I was extremely relieved she hadn't been more creative.

We laughed and ate seconds. Well, actually, I had thirds when no one was looking because the food was so damn good. After dinner, we retired to the front porch for a night cap. Cheryl walked over and bought a couple of 40's to split among the group, except for Paul.

Sitting back on the top step, I tried my best to soak it all in. An unconscious smile grew on my face as I reflected on our, from most perspectives, ordinary gathering. A breeze played with the leaves as a frosty beer cooled my hands. Neighbors were out on their porches, the drunken Irishman was still drunk, and the bar was sparsely crowded with regulars. But this night was anything but ordinary. In my head, triumphant and victorious music played in the background, announcing a great victory. This was what I had been waiting for. All of us were eating and drinking together without agendas, without plans. Just sharing stories, laughing, and sitting there – sitting there together. We were one people, one community, one house, experiencing the same moment, together. Through the most unusual events, our impossibly separate paths had collided on this stoop. On this stoop in the middle of a West Baltimore ghetto, we ate the same food, breathed the same air, and enjoyed the same drunken Irishman entertainment. Together we had become rich, if just a few moment. If the job search was a language, a vehicle of communication, then this moment was the thing communicated, the point. They were called out from under a bridge, among the city's outcast, to be here and to be told that they were worthy of being hung out with. They were invaluable and priceless, and I wanted to be with them to remind them that no matter how dark things got, change for the better was always possible. If there could be one moment like this, then surely there could be another, and another, until they ran together in continuous succession. I wasn't sure if they saw what I saw in this moment, but I hoped that maybe one day they would.

After everyone had finished their food, I gathered up some of the plates and took them inside to be washed. I noticed that Lil' Barry had disappeared, which was bizarre considering the small size of the house.

"Hey, Cheryl."

"Yeah?"

"Where'd Lil' Barry go?"

"Oh, I think he walked upstairs to use the bathroom. But that was twenty minutes ago."

"That's strange."

"I'll go check on him," she said.

She put down her cigarette on the stoop and walked upstairs.

I set to work cleaning the dishes, but ten minutes later, I noticed that Cheryl had not come back either. Paul and Skip were messing with the bikes outside, leaving me alone on the bottom floor. The house was eerily quiet, especially in the wake of so much activity. I decided to check on Cheryl. Quietly, I crept up each step and poked my head over the top stair. I looked down the darkened hallway and noticed the bathroom door was wide open, but the bathroom itself was empty. A pit formed in my stomach, as my instincts told me that our fun loving cookout had probably come to an end. I could see light coming from under Cheryl's closed door, and then I heard unnaturally low murmurings. To hear clearer, I tried holding my breath, but they spoke too softly, as if they didn't want to be heard. The sudden unlocking of the door knob startled me. I felt adrenaline shooting through my veins, and I convulsed in fear.

Before the door opened, I jumped into my bedroom and turned off the lights. What the hell were they doing in her tiny room? I left my door open just enough so that I could peek through and watch the hallway unseen. Could he actually be attracted to her? She's at least 25 years his senior. Goosebumps formed on my arms and back. Barry and Cheryl emerge from the room and, as I watched, little hairs pricked through my shirt. They walked down the hallway single file and had weird looks on their faces. I held my breath as they passed by. Why did this have to happen today? How could Cheryl ever think about doing anything with Little Barry? He was practically a son to her. I wondered if Cheryl ever thought about the consequences of her actions. What if they had a kid? She couldn't even take care of her 12 and 13 year olds, which her oldest son was now raising. Everything had been going so well, so perfectly well, and now this. It made me question everything, but I did my best to keep those thoughts out of my mind. I tried to focus on all the good that had happened that day. I tried to keep myself from thinking about it, but I couldn't undo what I had seen.

Chapter 17: Smoke and Mirrors

Seven months had passed, and things had progressed much better than I ever imagined. Cheryl continued to do well at the medical center; and though Paul still spent all his time on the corner, he somehow found side work gutting a neighbor's kitchen. We were even able to successfully remove John. This was no easy accomplishment and required the assembly of a small army including Paul, Skippy, Cheryl, Lil' Barry, Mitchum, and a few neighbors to regulate the eviction process. John brought over his own goons to "help" move his trash bag; and after a minor standoff, everything ran smoothly. The other neighbors were so impressed that they later informed Cheryl, who told me, that this was the first eviction seen without police involvement. Furthermore, we escaped detection from the landlord, never went hungry, repaired the shower, survived John, and befriended the neighbors – all without missing a single day of work. Well, at least *I* didn't miss a single day of work. Things were going so well that I forgot about my own warnings to myself.

From the beginning, I knew that this wouldn't be easy. I knew that things were going to go horribly, horribly wrong. Well, not wrong, but badly because for no other reason than they had to go wrong. Nothing good ever comes easily, and I didn't think this was any exception. Three weeks before moving in, I went so far as to write it down in my journal – *Things will go badly*. I had done my homework on the homeless population, and I learned that people don't end up chronically homeless without good reason. There was always something that brought them there; and more importantly, there was always something that kept them there.

Around the middle of September, I came home and found Cheryl on the front stoop. The leaves on the trees had already started falling while the remaining leaves turned bright red, yellow, and orange colors. Puffy bags hung under Cheryl's eyes, and her golden brown hair hung crookedly across her face.

"Cheryl."

"Yeeeah?"

"You don't look so good."

"I know, hon."

She grimaced as she shifted on her seat and groaned. Rubbed her back and the hung her head in her hands.

"What happened?" I asked.

"All I know is that I jus' was carryin' the vacuum upstairs and then my back started hurtin.'"

"Your back?"

"Yeeeeah."

"Oh. I'm sorry to hear that."

"Now every time I move, it hurts."

She took deep breathes in between words as she spoke. And closed her eyes as she exhaled as if in pain.

"You gotta get this checked out."

"I will."

"What do you think it is?"

"Maybe a slipped disk?"

I considered this an unnecessary setback. She had a job, a good one. We had established a schedule, and she had been going to work daily. Incident free. We had come so far and overcome so many excuses. I expected that like all the others, this excuse, too, would be surmounted. None of them could withstand my persistence and pestering.

"Why do you insist on doing this vacuuming? I have never asked you to do that."

"Because, hon, I wanted to do it."

She gripped the stair railing tightly to help herself stand up.

"Why?"

"The carpets were getting dirty."

"Dirty?"

"Yeah, dirty."

"Couldn't you wait for me to do it? The hallway's not that big, and I could've done it in two minutes."

"Hon, you know how I am."

"Yeah, I know, but now look at yourself."

"What?"

"You're hurt because of some stupid dirty carpets that no one cares about!"

The sun had started setting earlier and shortened the days. Winter was coming, but it was still warm enough to wear wife beaters outside. The factory where Mitchum worked had cooled slightly, but they still kept the fans on for morale. My faded blue t-shirt ruffled in the breeze as I sat on the stoop and looked out at the neighborhood. A few of the younger kids were walking over towards the bar. I recognized one of them. His name was Trey. Trey was a 17-year-old drug dealer. Many a day I came home to find him on my stoop. Again, most of the time, the people sitting on the stoops didn't actually live in those houses, and Trey was no exception. Not only was he a drug dealer, but he had recently called a hit out on two people who had broken into his house and stolen his television. The thieves took it right off the wall. The funny part was that he watched it all happen. They came right through the unlocked front door, but Trey's gun was lying on the other side of the room out of arm's reach. The two guys pulled their guns on him, took his gun, and then took his TV, laughing as they went.

Afterwards he threw a temper tantrum, which was justifiable, as it had taken him almost a month of drug dealing to earn the money to buy it. It wasn't *just* a T.V. It was a 65" flat screen with 1080i resolution with a glossy black border, a quality machine by any standard. So, in pursuit of justice, he ordered a hit out for them; but after a week, the guys responsible were still alive and his TV was still not returned. Trey complained that the hitmen, especially in our area, were money hungry mercenaries and were essentially worthless because they gave their targets an opportunity to buy them off. This made them very expensive and very useless against wealthier people. After hearing about this hit situation, I made sure to be extra nice to Trey and even allowed him to use our living room to store his bicycle when he went to the bar. Of course, I explained that drugs weren't allowed in the house or on the stoop, but I didn't tell him personally; I made Cheryl tell him. I didn't want him to become annoyed with me and then, as they say in the ghetto, bust a cap in my ass. But surprisingly he was agreeable to my request and understood well my fear of cops, especially considering the landlord situation. He liked us, but he didn't think very highly of the other neighbors, one of whom was his father. Apparently he hated his dad and wanted to punish him for the woes of his childhood. I couldn't believe this little teenager was a real live drug dealer. He was so dangerous yet so small and friendly, always sure to wave at me and Cheryl on his way to the bar.

In between whimpers, Cheryl complained about one of her co-workers. One in particular embarrassed her to tears in front of the entire office. It turns out that this co-worker, Tamaqua (I'm not sure of the spelling), had recognized her from the corner during her panhandling days. At first she mentioned to Cheryl that she looked familiar but wasn't sure from where. A few days later, Tamaqua remembered. She started telling everyone in the office that Cheryl was homeless. What! I was outraged. Cheryl explained that she tried to defend herself but didn't do a very good job. Tamaqua started laughing, and so Cheryl started cussing at her to make her quiet. Then the woman paraded around the copy room telling everyone that Cheryl panhandled on the street. It turns out that this whole ordeal had been going on for a few days until yesterday, when it finally ended with a shouting match in the cafeteria. During the altercation, Cheryl dropped several f-bombs, and it quickly got out of hand from there. They were both brought before their supervisor, whom they nicknamed Hitler, for disciplinary action. I couldn't believe my ears and just started slowly shaking my head. Hitler gave them a verbal warning and explained that their meeting served as the first strike towards dismissal.

"I can't believe this happened," I said.

"I know. Neither can I."

"Well, what are you going to do to change things? You need to find a way not to fight with Tamaqua."

"I figured I'd just wait for her in the parking lot after work and punch her in the face."

I didn't respond to her plan.

"I'm just jokin. I don't got a clue what I should do."

"Listen," I said.

"What?"

"Invite her over to dinner, and when she sees--

"I don't want that woman in my house!"

"Oh, come on. Just give it a shot. She's not going to accept."

"Of course not. She hates me."

"Well, then, that's great."

"Why is that great?

"Because then you'll be the bigger person, and you won't even have to bring her over."

"I guess," she sighed.

"If it doesn't work, just go ahead with your parking lot plan."

"Okay."

After hearing about her co-worker dissatisfaction, I started pushing Cheryl to apply for other forms of work just in case. Now that she had a job, it would make getting a second one much easier. Maybe she could finally start working in restaurants again like she always wanted. In fact, I had already gone down to the Inner Harbor to inquire about openings. But she needed to take the initiative if it were to succeed.

"Did you find any new job postings today?" I asked. Cheryl slowly got up.

"I actually found some rooms. I'll be right back."

She hobbled back into the house, returned with the daily newspaper, and spread out the "for rent" section all over the stoop.

"I can afford most of these rooms now."

"And they're nearby," I said, pointing at the addresses.

"I could easily do this with a second job, too," she said, circling some of the rooms in red. This was music to my ears.

"Paul can bring home the food he makes panhandling," I said.

She looked up from the newspaper. Her eyes wandered as if she were distracted by a heavy thought, but I knew what she was thinking. I could read it right off her face.

These days Cheryl talked more and more about leaving Paul. She would always say that it was something she had to do to be reacquainted with her family. I wanted nothing to do with this decision. It was not my place to become involved with other people's marriages.

The days dragged on, and she continued to whimper almost continuously. Though I noticed that when she spoke of the daily injustice inflicted by Tamaqua, she became enraged and flailed her arms without any sign of pain.

The next few days Cheryl complained that her back was getting worse. She had gone to the hospital for an evaluation, and they sent her home with painkillers. Tired from work, I slowly walked down the block towards the house. Days had passed, but Cheryl still groaned with every movement. She was smashing the butt of her cigarette on the stairs when I came around the block. By then, twilight had fallen and the air felt almost cold. Every time the temperature dropped, it reminded me that winter was almost here and we were running out of time. Renewing the lease was not an option because from my perspective, it was going to work in the time we had or it would never work.

Cheryl had probably been on sick leave at least three times since her start date. I could not imagine a company continuing to grant her this time off without consequences. It was unlikely they'd be this lenient in the first place, and it suddenly occurred to me that I had never seen a single paycheck, pamphlet, or scrap of paperwork. She claimed that she had given the pay stubs to her father. The father I had never met. Cheryl told me that sometime after she received her pay stub, her father would take her to lunch and then they would go deposit the stub into a safe account. An account that could neither be frozen by her medical debts nor looted by Paul.

"How was your day, hon?"

"Fine."

"Work is goin good, isn't it?"

"Yeah, it is."

"Will you get any tickets to them Ravens' games?"

"I know your scheme. You just want those crab cakes in the Ravens' box."

"Well, yeeeahhh....'course."

"Those are very popular games."

"Aww shucks. Well, try anyway."

"I always try."

Over the next couple of weeks, I had fresh reasons to question things, and I started devising little plans to test my theories. Earlier that day I had set up one such experiment. The experiment involved the spare change on my desk, which I had recently been misplacing. I suspected that there might be more to blame than just my overloaded memory so that morning before I left for work, I cleared everything off the top of my small particleboard desk, the only piece of furniture in my room. On the center of the desk I placed a bible, upon which I laid about a dollar's worth of quarters. From the beginning, I had asked them not to go into my room. There was no reason for them to be there. Everything that I had of value I had already given to them.

Later that day when I reentered the room, I found that all of the coins were gone. The cover of the bible was completely cleaned off. Though I did feel slightly violated, a feeling of relief overpowered my sense of betrayal. I was relieved because of the foresight not to keep anything in my room. My suits were hidden at work, my car in the industrial park, and my computer at my parents' house.

Shaking my head, I closed the door and made my way back downstairs. Cheryl came hobbling out of the kitchen with a broom. Horrified, I demanded she explain herself. I was certain that no matter how big the mess, it could wait until her back healed. She claimed that the doctor wanted her to sweep because it would help work out the kinks in her back. I thought this was absurd.

"Cheryl, that's not something injured people volunteer to do."

"Hon, the doctors told me that I need to move around."

At this point, the conversation had become nonsensical, and there was no point in arguing. My choice was either to continue the conversation and become angry, or not and just stew. I chose to stew.

While stewing, I decided to sit on the couch and watch out the window at Cheryl tending to the sidewalk. She was slowly sweeping the copious amounts of garbage into a trash bag. The house sat only a few feet away from the neighborhood storm drain which, during rainstorms, flooded after being clogged with trash that floated down the street gutters. Cheryl hated how chip bags, newspapers, banana peels, and other discarded food always ended up in front of our stoop. She moved like a slow robot that badly needed oil, as if she had an acute case of arthritis in each of her joints. I found myself getting angrier after every sweep of the broom. I couldn't tell if I was angry because I thought she was lying, or if it was because I thought this was an unnecessary setback, or if it was because I didn't like to see her in pain.

Frustrated, I went across the street to Carl's bar. Betty, the forty-something blonde bartender, greeted me warmly. The other patrons were lively debating the outcome of the Steelers and the Ravens game, which wasn't much of a debate. I kept a low profile and pulled up a dark, wooden stool on the empty part of the bar, the part closest to the window. The countertop was made of dark wood with a very thick shiny gloss that had several nicks and scratches which added to its character. Slowly sipping my beer, I watched the house from a small window. Cheryl was almost finished sweeping and slowly bent down to pick up the last remaining coke cups and some Wendy's fast food cartons covered in barbeque sauce. Betty came over and asked how my "mom" was enjoying her new job.

"She likes it, I think."

"That's a good spot, that is."

"I know. I'm happy she got it."

Betty smiled, "Looks like you're running empty. You want anything else?"

"Just another beer, please."

When I looked back a few minutes later, Cheryl had completed her work, and I watched her tie up the trash bag. She still moved as if the bones in her body were broken, and I wondered if I should talk to her doctors and get her some better medicine. I don't know what she had done to her back, but it looked bad. She took a few limp steps before looking behind herself, as if checking to make sure she wasn't being followed, and then trotted off as normally as ever. She had been faking her injury the whole time. I slapped my hand on the bar and knocked my beer over. Furious, I decided to confront her immediately.

But by the time I paid for my beers, Cheryl had disappeared so I sat on the stoop and cracked my knuckles as the minutes passed. I only had to wait a short while before Cheryl reappeared with a 40 in hand. Chickening out at the last minute, I decided against open confrontation and took a more passive aggressive strategy. Feigning excitement, complete with cheerful tones, I said, "Cheryl, you're not limping any more. It's a miracle!"

She hid a flash of surprise before shrugging and said, "That's what the doctors said would happen."

I was so angry that I wanted to break something. It felt like I was playing some sick twisted cat-and-mouse game with her. We both knew there was a problem, but somehow we couldn't talk about it.

"I must have loosened my back up when I did the leaves," she continued.

I produced a hollow smile and nodded.

"Of course, you did."

The next couple of days I made up excuses to stay later at the office. Sometimes I worked on assignments weeks in advance. In fact, there were times when I stayed so late that I was often the last one on the floor and possibly the last in the building. Upon arriving home, I fell into the habit of immediately going up to my room. I didn't say much more than a few words and relished it when they looked hurt as a result.

Impossibly, we had lived together for almost a year, and there were so many points of success, so many improbable things achieved. Yet Cheryl's one complex, intricate lie, flawlessly executed with a straight face had in

261

an instant destroyed all that was beautiful about this experience. The more I thought about things, the more they drifted away into fiction.

After another few days, my reclusive lifestyle started to bother her. She missed our conversations on the stoop. Every day she came back, excited to share stories about her day, but I stopped listening. One night, she waited up for me, and I could see her perk up on the stoop when I came into view. I was trudging along in no particular rush and dragged my feet along the uneven concrete sidewalks. She asked if anything was wrong, which was not the best question to ask. I knew I wasn't ready to confront her in a mature, constructive way, but I couldn't resist an opportunity to vent.

"Cheryl, things aren't adding up," I said, throwing my bag on the ground.

"What do yuh mean, hon?"

"Well, among many other things, your medicine doesn't work yet you still take it."

"My back hurts, hon."

"Things just don't make any sense," I said, shaking my head.

"Yeah, you're absolutely right. I'll go back to the doctors tomorrow after work."

"Why? They didn't do anything for you before. What makes you think things will be different now?"

"Well, maybe when they see that this medicine isn't working, they'll have something different that might work better."

"I want the names of these doctors, the medicine, and their exact diagnosis."

"Aright, aright ,I'll write it all down for yuh," she said, nodding.

I didn't say anything more. I just walked in the house and slammed the door behind me. My mistrust in Paul and Cheryl crippled my ability to carry on genuine conversation anymore. Sometime after the first days of Cheryl's back pain, I had begun to draw away from them.

Switching off the light, I locked the door, rolled up in my blankets, and buried my feet in the corner clothes pile. I drifted in and out of sleep, tortured by the idea of their lying to me and betraying my trust. I had known this would happen from the beginning, and I desperately needed to remember why I started this in the first place; otherwise, I would never be able to finish it. Outside the blue light from the full moon came in through the window and reflected off my mirror. In my annoyed state of insomnia, I reached up and pulled the cord to lower the blinds. Right before falling asleep, I realized that if anything, now was the time when I needed to draw closer to them no matter how uncomfortable or unpleasant that might be.

As if I wasn't having enough trouble sleeping, sometime around one o'clock in the morning, something loud woke me up like the breaking of a plate or the slamming of a door. I woke up and heard two sets of heavy feet stomping around on the downstairs floor. Then the shouting started. I lay there awake listening, but I didn't dare make a noise. Slowly, I sat up and put my ear against the wall to hear better. I could make out Paul and Cheryl's familiar voices yelling very unfamiliar things. Between their thick Baltimore accents, the dry wall, and sleep grogginess, I had trouble understanding what they were yelling about. Next thing I knew, the front door slammed open and someone stormed out of the house. Then I heard Cheryl and Paul yelling in the streets. Scrambling across the room, I rolled the blinds up and opened the window slightly. A warm breeze blew some dust in my face and my eyes watered. Between the moon and a few street lamps, the deserted street was well lit, and I watched Paul hobble down the street carrying a red duffle bag. He didn't say very much at all, but Cheryl had plenty to say. She was standing on the stoop in her boxer shorts and a long t-shirt.

In between sobs she was yelling and screaming at Paul.

"Are you gonna leave me! You leaving me? Answer me! Answer me!"

Hearing was no longer a problem, and now I wished I had slept through the night.

She went on, "You goin to see that whore again, aren't ya? You gonna see that whore!"

Paul had walked his bike halfway up the block and was getting close to turning the corner. The wind blew harder, and dark clouds blocked out the bright moonlight. The farther he walked, the angrier Cheryl got, and she yelled louder and louder.

"You gonna see Tammy? You gonna see that Tammy whore? Answer me!"

The wind picked up, and I could hear the trees swaying. She yelled so loudly that she woke up some of the neighbors. Bedroom lights sporadically lit up windows on the other side of the block.

"You gonna go smoke some crack? Smoke your life away on that crack! Is that what you're gonna do! Answer me! Answer me!"

Somewhere between the hookers and crack pipes part of Cheryl's tirade, Paul got upset and turned around. His face was darkened with shadows, but I could tell he looked angry. He hobbled back towards the house. After exhausting her other insults, she just started screaming "I hate you! I hate you!" over and over again. She kept repeating herself louder and louder while Paul said nothing. By now he was already halfway back to the house. At this point, I decided that it might be a good idea to reinforce my sleeping barricade. Dragging some heavy suitcases from out of the closet, I put them up against the door. Then I dragged my desk over behind the suitcases for good measure. I locked and relocked the knob just to make sure.

Then I opened the second window just in case I needed to jump.

By the time Paul and Cheryl stomped back into the house, my barricade was reinforced with dumbbells, clothes, suitcases, and blankets. Cheryl continued her tirade and hate shouting while Paul stomped up and down the stairs. I heard bags scratching against the walls and the clinking of duffle bag hooks, and I figured he must have been moving his things out of the house. For the most part Paul was silent, but occasionally he would yell, "Shut up...Shut up!" They yelled so loudly that it sounded as if they were in my room with me. I could hear Cheryl sobbing, and I could just picture her makeup running down her face and onto her t-shirt.

There was so much pain on the other side of my bedroom wall, I could almost feel it. I wanted it to stop, but there was nothing I could do. They wouldn't stop shouting at each other. I tried to block it out by putting my hands over my ears. It didn't work. At some point my arms got tired, and I knelt down and just put my hand on the wall.

After another twenty minutes, Paul again started his journey down the block. Cheryl ran outside and started wailing, "Are you leaving me? Are you leaving me?" Though this time something was different. Before, when she yelled at him, she sounded furious, but now she sounded scared and screamed until her vocal cords ran raw. As she stood on the stoop in bare feet screaming, her voice became raspy and started to crack. Paul turned the corner, and she let out a bloodcurdling cry as if someone was torturing her right there on the stoop. Then everything stopped and went silent. Death-like silence. The door shut, and then I didn't hear anything more for the rest of the night.

My hand, now shaking, remained plastered to the wall until finally I fell asleep and collapsed on the ground next to my barricade. The next morning, I made my way downstairs to check on any fight induced property damage. Everything seemed fine, more or less, except that I found Paul snoozing on the couch. This was most bizarre and only raised more questions, but I decided not to wake him up. I never did find out where Paul went, what he did to make Cheryl so angry, or why he bothered coming back. I was pretty sure that I didn't want to know any of those answers. Later when I came home, I found Paul giving Cheryl a satisfying back scratching on the couch. She groaned sighs of pleasure, and no one ever brought up the fight from the previous night. We all acted as though it never happened.

On my walk to work, I reflected on how things had changed and how I had lost control of the situation. Common sense told me that the end was near and that I should increase my distance from them to make things easier. I spent a long time praying and sitting in front of my decision mirror trying to figure out what to do. Then finally it came to me, and I decided that common sense be damned! My will was still under my control, and I resolved to reopen channels of communication. I'd pull out all the stops to undo the bad things that I saw happening. Maybe I'd even take Cheryl to lunch during her afternoon break. This brilliant idea occurred to me on one of my morning walks to work. I rounded the corner to my office and knew that this was a good plan.

Powering up my laptop, I cancelled my afternoon plans for the day and blocked off an hour to hang out with Cheryl. I wanted to make sure that I had enough time for a long conversation, and so I called her pay-as-you-go phone to schedule a meeting time, but she didn't answer. No problem. It was still early so I decided to go down to her work and meet her on her way in. It would be easy because The University of Maryland Medical Center was only a few blocks from where I worked. I figured I'd just wait outside the front door and find out what time she was available for lunch. I arrived 30 minutes earlier than her start time to make sure I wouldn't miss her. But she didn't show up. I waited and paced and watched the mid morning traffic die down, but Cheryl was nowhere in sight. After another thirty minutes, I figured that she wasn't coming at all. Clearly something very urgent, surely more important than work, had come up, and I dragged my feet back to the office. On my walk back, I could hear my common sense whisper, *"I told you so."*

That night, I had a brief chat with Cheryl about her day and discovered that our window of success had all but closed. She claimed that I didn't see her because she went in through an alternate entrance. A strange, random, and unusual decision, as that entrance would have required her to walk an extra block. I considered this an unlikely choice for a rotund fiftyish-year-old smoker who frequently got winded going up a single flight of stairs.

Somewhere in the middle of her explanation, I stopped listening. This must have bothered her because she stopped talking. My patience was running out as I was faced with falling temperatures, a fast approaching winter, and a quickly shrinking number of weeks left in the lease. I was having trouble figuring out what the next steps should be. And then, quite randomly, through a few choice words, Cheryl convinced me that maybe, just maybe, there was a chance that everything could be salvaged.

"Guess what!" she said.

"What?" I answered in a detached monotone.

"My family is getting together for a big celebration."

Staring blankly, I replied with a faint nod.

"They want to meet you. It's in three days at Scott's place."

"Scott's place?" I said skeptically.

"Yeah."

"Huh, okay, I'll go."

It would have been wrong of me to accuse her of lying because I didn't really have any proof of her lying in the past. What historical evidence could I bring up? There weren't any past trends to justify my suspicions. She would be hurt by my mistrust, and I didn't want to harm our relationship without proper facts. I decided to get some facts so I could once and for all confront the truth. And so it began.

I explained to Cheryl that in order to extend all the niceties of the polite receipt of a dinner party invitation, I would need the phone number and address of her son.

"Why do you need that?" she asked.

"First, I need directions; and second, I want to ask him if I should bring anything."

"Oh, okay."

So without any further hesitation, she wrote out his number and address on a slip of paper for me. Then I casually had her tell me things about his house. She explained that it was near the water of a very nice neighborhood and how there was a slip to put boats in the water just a few blocks away from his house. Not that her son could afford a boat, at least not yet. Pleased with these tidbit descriptions, I felt I had enough to verify the address.

At work, I looked up the address on the internet to research her son's address. The website loaded, and I accessed the satellite pictures to verify Cheryl's description: a quaint little house located right on the water. Almost falling out of my chair, I was overcome with shock. The pictures perfectly matched Cheryl's description and convinced me that she was telling me the truth. Giddy, I did a little shake dance right in my cube. Her family was a crucial part of a successful rehabilitation, especially after we moved out of the house. If they could only see her, they'd know how much work she'd done to get back on her feet. No matter what she'd done in the past, I wondered how they could not take her back considering her progress. Just as I was getting used to being overcome with relief, the phone rang. It was Cheryl.

"Uh huh, uh huh.---- Too many people? --- Reschedule to Monday.---Your brother's house? Well, that's fine. You know the drill, address and number."

A few minutes later, I was back on the computer researching. Again, everything lined up. The address she gave me was only a block away from Scott's house. Apparently they wanted to reschedule and move it to her brother's house which was bigger than Scott's place. They probably didn't expect us to accept, and now that we did, they would need a bigger venue. Yes, of course, this made perfect sense.

Everything was great for the next couple of days. I watched TV with Cheryl and played cards with Paul. There was still never any mention of their shouting match from the week before and certainly no evidence of marital strife. Cheryl's back still hurt her, but soon I didn't even notice her whimpering. Things were going well again, almost too well, and that's what got me thinking. I remembered the old saying about things that seemed to good to be true. So the day we were to attend this party, I decided early in the morning to launch a preemptive attack. If anyone made any phone calls today, it would be me. I picked up the number Cheryl had given me for her brother Ryan who would be hosting us later that night.

"Good morning. Is this Ryan?"

"Yup."

"Hi. I understand that Cheryl and I are coming over for party at your house."

Uncomfortable silence followed. I decided to keep speaking.

"I just wanted to see if you needed me to bring anything. Like a bottle of wine or something."

269

A full thirty seconds of silence later, Ryan responded, "Umm, I have no idea what you're talking about."

"Oh, well, isn't Cheryl your sister?"

There was another long pause, and I decided to prompt him with, "Hello?"

Ryan answered in a shaky voice, "I severed connections with her a long, long time ago,"

"Oh. So no party?"

"I told you, I don't know what you're talking about. Goodbye."

"Okay. I'm sorry for disturbing y--"

The phone went dead.

I put the receiver down and fell back in my chair. There it was, the incontrovertible proof I was looking for but never wanted to find. It definitely stung. I never thought I'd have such clear-cut evidence that she had been playing me for a fool, and I felt like I just got hit in the face with a dump truck. I needed to go outside and get some air and clear my head. Before I could get up from the desk, the phone rang. It was Cheryl. It turned out that she was calling to push the knife in farther. I picked it up. Frantically, she explained that the party had been cancelled because Ryan's daughter just had a baby boy and, therefore, the family needed to attend to its needs, and the party would have to be rescheduled.

After all we'd been through I'd never once shown anger or lack of patience, but that could all change right now. I needed to hang up that phone before I said something stupid. Overflowing with the injustice and unfairness, I struggled to detach myself from the conversation, but she just kept speaking. and I couldn't help myself from indulging in one last round of passive aggressiveness.

I spoke in an upbeat tone, "That's wonderful news!"

"It is!" she said, laughing nervously.

"What are they going to name it?"

Cheryl broke out into more laughter right before blurting out, "Hon, you're not gonna believe this, but they're naming him Matthew."

She was right. I couldn't believe this.

"Uhh, umm. It's after my father's name," she muttered.

For the author of such sophisticated tales, was there no other name she could have come up with? Thanking the Lord that this phone conversation didn't take place in person, I just hung up.

Chapter 18: Dragon Boats and Charity

Early in the morning of a cool August day, water lapped against the edge of the cement wall of the Inner Harbor. The water was a muddy brown from years of city run off, oil leaks, and discarded trash. A plastic cup floated in the river past a very decayed log covered in brown slimy gunk. If you happened to fall into this water, it would probably be worse than being covered in radioactive fallout from an unusually harsh nuclear winter. A single open wound, even one the size of a paper cut, would allow pollutants and other assorted toxins to infiltrate your system, resulting in your untimely death, probably within a matter of seconds. If somehow you managed to survive the water, then you would need to be stripped naked and sprayed down with a fire hose, while hazmat-suit-wearing Department of Defense officials brushed you down with large thick-bristled brooms. Your clothes, obviously, would be burned. But all of these complications from falling into the water were nothing compared to the catastrophe that would happen on top of it. Yes, it was on this water that I was about to have one of the most embarrassing moments in my time of being a human.

Despite the toxicity of the water, the surrounding buildings and harbor are beautiful. It probably ranks among the most scenic city centers in the country. Million-dollar yachts bob up and down in their wooden slips as they glisten in the sun. The wealthy dock their boats and leave to go tour Baltimore and eat, shop, and relax. The harbor is surrounded by a large brick walkway lined with restaurants and shops with green shrubbery and flowers growing everywhere. On the far end, people play volleyball in several large sandpits which are lighted for night games. From the harbor, one can see the entirety of the city's skyline filled with glass skyscrapers bearing the names of Fortune 500 companies.

Its prestige, size, and proximity to water made the harbor the perfect venue to hold one of Baltimore's largest and most well-known charity events – the Dragon Boat Races. The proceeds would benefit Catholic Charities, and almost all the major corporations sponsored teams. Races were held every 20 minutes or so starting at 8:00 A.M. and ending around 4:00 P.M. Thousands of family members, supporters, and spectators turned out for the event and crowded the large brick walkways. Megaphones were erected that blasted music from all day concerts, which were interrupted regularly by race commentary and general announcements. The event was so large that it took almost two years to plan, and, thus, this event was held only once every two years.

The dragon boats themselves were basically large wooden canoes with dragon heads affixed to the front. These boats held about 22 people, comprised of twenty rowers, a drummer, and a steerer. The drummer sat facing the rowers, and it was his or her job to keep a steady rhythm by beating a drum at the desired pace. The steerer stood at the back of the boat on top of a very narrow platform, and it was his or her job to cut the shortest path to the finish line. If anything went awry, it was also the steerer's job to command the boat to speed up, slow down, or stop, whichever the situation required. I had rowed crew in college; and so being one of the few with actual boating experience, I was nominated to the steerer position. I argued against this, explaining that my experience was really in the actual rowing part, not the steering part, but no one listened. No one seemed to care that in crew the rowers row backwards with their backs to the front of the boat. I had no experience facing forward, navigating waterways, or anything of the like.

273

Considering that this event was very high profile, we started training three months in advance. In the past, we had never done well, but this year would be different. According to the long time employees, our boat was much younger and stronger than it had been in any other year. But our practices humbled us because we realized that though we might have above-average athleticism, we were not very well coordinated. Oars were going in the water at all different times, rocking the boat back and forth, sometimes violently. Not only that, but the left side of the boat was more powerful than the right side, and I found myself struggling to avoid going in circles. On a surprising note, I will boast that over the course of three months of practices, I had not a single steering incident; and though it was rocky when I first started, I felt confident in my abilities on race day.

Despite our coordination issues, we were decent, and we hoped not to embarrass ourselves in front of all of Baltimore. Lucius Muccino and the other heads of the Maryland region were supposed to be in attendance, and we wanted to give them something to cheer about. I was told that every other year our team had done a mediocre job, but this year, my first year, we were going to put on a show and maybe even win. At least, that's what we trained to do.

As if the pressures of racing in front of thousands of people wasn't enough, there was also the prospect of my parents showing up, more specifically my ghetto self-proclaimed parents. Yes, Cheryl and Paul wanted to come out and cheer me on. They had heard about the adventures of my practices for the past couple of months and how against all odds I had learned to steer the boat. They had heard all about my teammates and the funny things that happened during our practices. I got them excited about the races to the point where they begged to be allowed to come and watch them in person. The funny part was that I told the same stories at home to my biological parents. They, too, were excited and demanded to come see the races. And, of course, they told me this over the phone the morning of the race. I wanted to argue against this, but I could tell that they wouldn't listen.

After I got off the phone with them, I collapsed to the ground and huddled into the fetal position under the weight of this impending awkwardness. I could not imagine the chaos that would ensue upon the mixing of my co-workers, family, and formerly homeless roommates. We would all be in the same racing tent, in broad daylight, in front of thousands of people. Yes, everything in me felt the urge to prevent this from happening or to somehow cancel the race. But then I got to thinking. Would it be so bad to have everyone meet? We had coexisted in harmony for almost a year at this point and had nothing but good times to report. Surely this was the best of all times and the most dramatic of all venues for the story to be told.

With all these thoughts swirling in my head, I took my place on the small narrow platform at the back of the boat which had just taken its spot at the starting line. Holding the giant wooden oar, I bent my knees slightly and waited for the bang of the starting gun. My teammates lowered their oars in the water. We sat for a few seconds perfectly balanced, and I readjusted my grip. BANG! We were off to an okay start. I gripped the rudder tightly as the nasty harbor water splashed up on my feet and hands. The other boats had gotten off to better starts and were a few seats in front of us, but it didn't matter. Our team was a rowing machine. With disciplined, powerful strokes, we caught up to the other three boats. By mid race, we had half a boat length on them and soon had open water. We won easily, and I suspected that the other teams, which we had yet to race, looked on in fear.

There was an hour break after that race, and we were encouraged to sit and relax and regain our strength. It was during this break that I received a phone call from home. It seemed that my dad was having car trouble, something to do with a flat tire, and they would not be able to make it. And so ended my nervousness about the intersection of parallel universes. I scanned the crowds for Paul and Cheryl but couldn't find them. Before I knew it, we were summoned for our next race, and I struggled to inhale what was left of a bagel and cream cheese platter before joining my team on the docks. Just before we gathered into the boat, our team, which was in the middle of a motivational cheer, went silent. Lucius and another Firm executive had appeared among us out of thin air. Lucius held up his hands and said that he was just here to wish us luck. He thanked us for participating in this charity event and said that whatever we can do to make an impression in the city would please him greatly. He would remember us. Unfortunately, making an impression was exactly what we were about to do.

Everything happened in the same exact way as the first race. We got up to the starting line, I found my balance, gripped the oar tightly, and waited for the gunshot. Every team had their oars in the water, and we sat in suspense, which was heightened all the more by the awareness that executives were waiting for us at the finish line. A gunshot rang through the air, and in an instant, all those feelings of suspense were transformed into adrenaline. In all of our practices, scrimmages, and races, we had never had such a start as this one. It was so strong that I lost balance and almost went flying out of the boat. Luckily, I had hung onto the oar with a tight enough grip to regain my footing. I looked over, and within the first twelve strokes, we were already in the lead by four seats. I figured that this would be a good time to motivate my teammates so I let out a mighty battle cry to spur them onward. I felt the boat pick up speed and did my best to steer us on the shortest path to the finish line.

Unfortunately, midway through the race, something started to happen to the boat. We began doing mini slalom turns in our fairly narrow lane. It became harder and harder for me to control it. Then disaster struck. All of a sudden, on a very straight course, the boat decided to take a sharp right turn. No one else could see what was happening; and if I had been thinking logically, I would have called for the rowers to stop. But I didn't. Instead I decided that I could surely steer us out of this death course. I put my entire weight onto the oar by hanging my body out the opposite side of the boat. My plan was to bounce our boat off of the boat the next lane over, hopefully launching us back into our lane and back into the lead. It would be just like Apollo 13 when Tom Hanks used the gravity of the moon to slingshot the orbiter back on course. Except this would be more like slamming into the moon and hoping it would bounce us back to Earth. Whatever. This was my plan, a plan that was developed in a few hundredths of a second, and I was going for it. Unfortunately, it did not go well at all. I suspect there were more special effects in Apollo 13 than logic, something I didn't consider.

By the time we were in the next lane, our boat was completely perpendicular to the course where we were promptly T-boned by not one, but two boats. Their oars clashed with our oars, and everyone was shouting profanities. All three boats then drifted off course out of all the lanes and slowly headed toward the piers off the harbor walls. It was truly horrible. The next thing I knew, there were two splashes. I checked my boat to make sure none of our people were missing, but everyone was securely in their seats. Then I saw it: two dragon boat heads with bits of debris next to them slowly floated past us. The three boats were still locked together, and the rowers tried to push off one another. The outside rowers still kept rowing, splashing water on us all. Finally we broke free and slowly made our way back to the finish line. There was very little cheering, and the race commentator made a backhanded comment about what lane we were in. Usually, when boats finished, the commentator would announce the name of the company and their race lane. But for us, he announced our company and then said something about how at one point we were in all lanes.

As I mentioned before, each boat carried twenty-two people; and after doing the math, I realized that we were involved in a sixty-six-person collision. Not only that, but I was the sole person responsible. We found out later that it was the worst collision in years on the basis of head counts. After I got out of the boat, Lucius wandered over and pulled me aside. I don't remember this part as clearly, but I think he said something to the effect of what the hell was that? I just shook my head and reminded him that I was just trying to make an impression. Well, I actually didn't say that. I was much too embarrassed. But I should have. Instead, I think I just turned red and stood silently. Though I will say that I redeemed myself, to the degree that I could redeem myself after a sixty-six- person crash, by steering straight lines for the remaining three races. I didn't really speak that much for the rest of the day and tried as hard as I could to keep a low profile.

The next day when I returned to work, I found a large flier taped to my desk. It had a picture of the Titanic printed on it with a caption that read *Bjonerud's other boat.* Normally I would have put something like that up on my cube wall, but I wasn't in the mood and stuffed it into the bottom of one of a drawer. Cheryl and Paul never showed up for the race. They didn't have a very good excuse, but that was okay. I wasn't particularly proud of my performance anyway.

Chapter 19: The Smoking Gun

The time for confrontation had come and could be delayed no longer. I came home and found penny rolls scattered all over the kitchen table. The lights were switched off, and the living room was lit only by the television. I slammed the door loudly, took a seat on the couch and waited. I didn't hear any noise so I decided to take a look upstairs to see if Cheryl and Paul were gone or just napping and turned on the hallway lights. From the top of the stairs, I could see that her door was shut and the lights were off. It didn't look like anyone was home, but I figured I'd check just to make sure.

On my way to her room, I glanced into the guest room and almost wet my pants. In the shadows I saw what looked like a contorted body resting uncomfortably, half on the bed frame and half on the floor. Who the hell? I wasn't sure if he or she was awake or asleep, dead or alive. How could this have happened? There was no movement as I walked past so I quickly made my way to the bathroom as if everything was normal. Once inside, I bolted the door and leaned my back against it. A few weeks ago, a dead hooker was found in a field about fifty yards from us. I remember feeling a bit unsafe when I heard about it, but having a dead guy in my house was just ridiculous. I figured that if I was threatened, I could jump out the window, though it would be a tight squeeze and a worse fall, but I would live. I needed a weapon or a pipe or something to defend myself in case this person was alive and hostile. Rummaging around, I found one of the pipes I had bought to replace the broken shower. Perfect. I gripped the pipe and stood facing myself in the mirror. I was a warrior ready for battle, and I wished I had some war paint; but after opening all the drawers, all I found was

Cheryl's makeup. No matter, my lead pipe would be intimidating enough.

I couldn't figure out how this happened. Where were Cheryl and Paul? After about twenty minutes of silently standing in the bathroom, I decide that I couldn't live the rest of my life there, though I might like to try. I needed to make sure the hallway was clear for me to escape. I dropped down on the linoleum tiles and looked under the bottom of the door. It looked clear. So I threw the door opened and ran down the hallway past Cheryl and Paul's room, past the guest room with the dead person, and down the stairs. Then I unlocked both the back door and the front door to make sure I had escape options. After all the preparations had been made, I sat on the end of the couch. From this vantage point I could see the stairs, the front door, the back door, and outside the window. I concealed my pipe behind the couch in such a way that I could grab it quickly. This would give me the element of surprise or maybe just the illusion of innocence. From all appearances, it would look like I was just relaxing on the couch.

So in an effort to look normal, I turned up the television volume and pretended to watch the news. After about 45 minutes of waiting, I heard creaking from the upstairs hallway. Silently I waited and felt goosebumps rise up on my arms. The creaking got louder, a door opened and shut, and then I saw a foot appear on the top stair. The foot looked strangely familiar.

"Cheryl?"

"Yeeahhh."

"You napping?"

"Yup, yuh guessed it."

By now she had come all the way down and plopped herself into the dish chair.

"There's a guy in the guest room," I said casually.

"Oh, that's just a friend of Paul's."

"Well, what the hell is he doing here, Cheryl? We talked about this. Don't you remember the last time one of Paul's friends stayed here? Don't you remember John?"

"I know, I know, but listen. I told him he could stay here. He didn't want to, but I made him."

"Why would you say that?"

"Because, he was all hopped up on valium."

"Valium?"

"Yup."

"Well, why the hell was he doing drugs here?"

"Not here; somewhere else, but I took his keys so he couldn't drive home."

"You stole his keys? Weren't you just in court for grand theft auto last month?"

"Yes, I know, but…"

"Damn it, Cheryl, you need to learn to stay away from people's cars!"

"Matt, he had nine valiums. If he drove home, he'd be dead."

"Nine? Isn't that dangerous?"

"Yeah, I think."

"Cheryl, you should go check on him. He looks dead now."

"Really?"

"The way he's sleeping, it looks like he already has rigor mortis."

"Why do yuh say that?"

"His elbow is in the air, his legs are weirdly crossed, and somehow he's lying in an M shape," I said, starting to get angry.

"I'll check him."

"Thank you."

After another fifteen minutes, she came back down, but she was still acting groggy. She explained that he was leaving first thing in the morning and that there was nothing to worry about. Even in the dim lighting, I noticed the large bags under her eyes and puffy lips as she innocently asked me about my day. I ignored her questions.

"Why are you so tired?" I asked.

She explained that the doctors gave her a new prescription for her back. Apparently the new medicine had double the strength of her old prescription.

Her brown hair was all tangled, and she awkwardly fumbled at her pink t-shirt. She tried to sit down on the couch next to me, but I stood up and wandered into the unlit kitchen. Trying to compose myself, I pretended to rummage through the cabinets for some snacks. Cheryl stepped outside to puff on a cigarette. Twilight had already set in, and the streets were unusually quiet for such a warm night. I put both my hands down on the counter and hung my head as I thought -- it's now or never. Confrontation was not one of my strong points, and I tried to avoid it at all costs.

I walked back into the living room and then out the front door. I folded my hands behind my back as I walked down the stoop. Then I paced up and down the sidewalk to compose my thoughts. I stopped, and she looked at me curiously. It was time to begin the prosecution proceedings.

"Do the doctors think you're getting better?" I asked.

"They think it will take more time. There's really nothing they can do."

Carefully choosing my questions, I tried to get answers in such a way that would bind her tongue and shed light on the truth.

"Why bother with the stronger meds then?"

"It's the only thing they could do to relieve the pain."

As she answered, I continued to pace back and forth.

"It doesn't make sense to me."

"What doesn't?"

"The idea of just increasing the strength of the medicine. If it wasn't working, then why bother?"

"I guess, but I figure that the docs know what they're doin."

"Can I see the prescription?" I asked.

"Oh, sure, hon. I'll write it down for you."

"Umm, do you think I could see the label instead?"

"Huh?"

Visibly uncomfortable, she lit up a cigarette and started smoking. I could tell she was thinking about how to get herself out of this. I didn't want to give her time to make up new stories so I carried on.

"Usually, the medicine you're given has a label on the pill bottle or the box," I explained.

"Oh, I ain't got it filled yet, hon."

"Then what did you take to make you groggy?"

"I got a sample from the doctors. They do that, yuh know."

"Oh."

I cracked my knuckles and briefly cleared my throat.

"Well, we should go get the prescription filled."

"Okay, but not right now. I'm in too much pain to walk to the pharmacy," she whined.

"How far away is it?"

"'Bout five blocks."

Flashing a smile, I fumbled for my keys.

"Cheryl, I have my mom's car today. I can drive you."

"Nah, I don't wanna."

This was quickly becoming one of those Discovery Channel specials. The type of specials where photographers venture out into the African countryside to document lion hunts. For those who haven't seen them, they all follow the same basic pattern. They shoot video of lions working to alter the direction of the herd until a few straggler zebras are left on their own. Then the lions close in on the smallest one and surround it before pouncing. Once they have their fangs in the zebra's side, it's game over. Try as it might, it's pointless for the zebra to run.

"Why?"

"The co-pay is too expensive."

"How much is it?"

"Eight dollars." I was pretty sure I had just heard the sound of a zebra collapsing.

"I'll pay the co-pay, Cheryl. It's no problem."

"I don't even think they're working. Let's just forget it."

"You don't think it works?"

"No, it doesn't do anything. I'm not even going to get it filled."

"Then why wouldn't you tell the doctors that?"

"I don't know. I don't know!"

I just shook my head in feigned frustration. In actuality, I was quite pleased with myself and my newfound lawyer skills. If consulting didn't work out, then I figured I could try my hand as a litigator. Ah yes, Esquire did have a nice ring to it.

By now it was almost 8 P.M. She put out her cigarette and hobbled back into the house to watch "Deal or No Deal." Probably sensing my lack in sympathy, she whimpered extra loudly as she moved. I just sat deep in my dish chair and watched her. I folded my hands together and leaned my chin on them as I watched. I tried to speak several times but couldn't bring myself to open my mouth. I could feel my face turning bright red as I tried. Once I opened my mouth to say something, but no words came out. At the start of the next commercial break, Cheryl slowly got up, announced that she was going to grab a 40, and bounded out the door. Alone with my own thoughts, I paced uncomfortably and decided that I should be the one getting myself a 40 Cobra.

The night before, I had consulted with a college friend, Erin Devlin, about how to handle this situation. I wanted her ideas on what questions I should ask to get Cheryl and Paul to confess. But she refused to give me any questions and said I was going about it all wrong. She was right.

"Just don't give Paul and Cheryl any more chances to lie," she said.

"But why? They need to fess up to what they've done."

"You already assume they're guilty. Why bother?"

"Because. I need them to know that I know. It does no good if they go around thinking that I don't know. They'll think that they're pulling one over on me."

"Well, you can let them know without asking any questions."

"How?"

"In your head, pretend that they confessed to you. Then just start speaking from there."

"Of course!" I gasped. "Erin, you're a genius!"

Cheryl came back quicker than I had expected and startled me. I jumped out of my seat but covered it up my nervousness with feigned excitement that beer had finally arrived.

"Hey, can I grab a glass of that?"

"Oh, sure, hon."

She walked over and handed me a glass before plopping down on the couch. Two gulps later, my glass was empty, and I hid it behind my chair. Luckily, the television was the only light on in the room which meant that she wouldn't see my flushed cheeks.

"Cheryl, I know what's going on."

She shifted her attention from the television over to me.

"What do you mean?"

I sat upright with my head resting on my folded hands.

"Cheryl, things haven't been adding up."

Silence. The silence made me nervous, and I lost control of my thoughts. I just started blurting out anything that came into my mind.

"You're continuously hurt; the doctors' medicine doesn't make any sense; I've never seen a pay stub nor a single scrap of paperwork from the hospital; there's an almost dead guy upstairs; you can't produce a prescription; you haven't been to work in the past couple of days; and you still insist on doing yard work, even with excruciating back pain."

Sitting silently, she got really still and didn't even blink.

I continued, "You guys now have two phones, when originally it was like pulling teeth for you to put minutes on the one phone I bought you. Random names on pieces of paper are showing up all over the house. You haven't been to work in two weeks. Paul stays out late every night and--."

"Matt, if you ever suspect Paul of anything, please tell me. I check his things every night. I'm worried he might start --

I cut her off, "Cheryl, please let me finish."

Her mouth snapped shut.

"Cheryl, this house was created to be a springboard for people who had fallen down on their luck. It was designed to help those who only needed housing and some support to get back on their feet."

"And it's working wonderfully," she said.

"No, it's not."

At this point, her face started to get all contorted.

286

"I know about the addiction."

"Paul's?"

"No, the addiction I'm referring to is not Paul's and definitely not mine."

Tears began streaming down her face. She started fidgeting with her hands. No backing down now. I had to keep going. This had to be resolved tonight.

I was surprised by a slight desperation in my own voice, but I continued, "Cheryl, I am not equipped to treat addictions. I have neither the experience nor the training."

In between sobs and sniffling, she said, "You're so smart. I don't know why we thought you wouldn't figure it out. You're so smart."

She got up from the couch, grabbed her cigarettes and light from the mantle, and moved out to the stoop.

"We're not done here," I said, walking outside after her.

"I'm so glad you brought this up. It's been eating at me and making me miserable. I'm so glad you brought this up."

Tears formed rivers down her cheeks as she opened the front door. I followed her out.

"I couldn't bear to hide it from you anymore," she said.

Outside I stood facing her and tried to make eye contact.

"I need to search your room," I said.

"Okay, yeah, that's fine," she said in between sobs, "Tomorrow."

I involuntarily chuckled. I tried not to, but it was just such an unexpected comment.

"That's certainly not going to happen. I need to search it now."

"Matt, it's a mess. Let me clean it first." She spoke firmly now, almost angrily.

"Don't care."

"I have my bloody period rags everywhere."

I cringed at the thought. Good Lord, woman, why would you say that?

"I think I'll bite the bullet on this one."

"Paul's gonna be really upset."

"If anyone, anywhere should be upset, it should damn well be me."

Still sniffling, she wiped her face, finished her cigarette, and then, in silence, we grabbed a trash bag and proceeded upstairs towards the room. When Cheryl opened the door, I could hear the fan above us spinning slowly, but I couldn't see much. The room was lit only by the black and white static of a boxy 13" TV. Cheryl flipped a switch, and I was stunned. The place was a dump. The light, which was nothing more than a naked bulb, dimly lit the room; and in the middle of the floor, I saw a thin queen sized mattress, which looked like it had come straight from the homeless camp. It had cigarette burns all over it and took up almost all of the floor space in their shoe box shoebox-sized room. Stacked bowls filled with cigarette butts and plates crusted with old food were piled between the mattress edge and the wall. Old worn out shoes and boots were scattered on top of their piles of crap, which were just mounds of used clothing, jackets, and old magazines. Against the other wall were towers of Tupperware containers filled with trinkets, which I assumed were collected from the side of the road or from dumpsters.

The room smelled of stale cigarettes, beer, and bad body odor. The fan did nothing more than to mix the smells and spread them around the room. The only visible carpet was directly under the path of the door where I now stood. I remembered how proud I was to give them these brand new carpets, but I wasn't proud anymore. I looked down and winced as I saw their light cream color had turned a smoky black as if they were welcome mats to a coalmine. I did my best to remain calm.

Glancing over at the wall above the mattress, I noticed a huge gouge that exposed the wooden studs. It appeared as though they were storing things inside, but I pretended that this was perfectly normal. I simply couldn't bring myself to do any more confronting that night.

The next fifteen minutes were straight out of "CSI Miami" or "Law and Order SVU," as I conducted my first ever drug bust. Ignoring the hole, I began searching the bags of clothes and plastic containers that covered the floor and the bed. Considering the size of the room and the number of people inhabiting it, there was an ungodly amount of tattered clothes, broken bowls and chipped cups. Surprisingly, there was no contraband in plain sight; however, when I lightly tapped one of their piles, pills rolled out onto the floor in mini avalanches. In the closet, I found each shelf bare except for neatly arranged sets of needles and pill assortments. One set per each of the seven shelves. From rummaging through all of their stuff, I had collected a small heap of drugs in the middle of the floor. I never yelled; I never sighed; nor did I show any signs of disappointment through this whole ordeal. Instead, I spoke in upbeat logical tones as if talking to a kindergartner, saying things like, *well, what do we have here?* and *Oh, dear, this doesn't belong in this room, does it?* and *Oh my, you have been mighty busy, haven't you?*

By the end of the raid, I had collected several bags of pain pills, heroin, crack, and weed. Not only that, but I also had found a crack pipe and sixteen heroin needles. It was enough to stock a CVS for a week, that is, if CVS sold illegal drugs and associated paraphernalia. There were so many more drugs than expected, and I was completely perplexed as what to do with it. Originally, my plan was to flush it all down the toilet. But there was too much. It would have clogged the pipes, and I couldn't figure what I would tell the plumber. Before coming to my senses, I considered saying things like:

"It's so hard to find a good plunger these days"; or They don't build toilets like they used to"; or, "This always happens when Paul stops taking his laxatives."

No, no, none of those things would work. Surely, the plumber would pull the drugs up and have us all arrested.

Seeing no viable explanation for a drug-induced stoppage, I let my emotionally charged instincts take over. Barreling out the front door, I sprinted into the streets wearing red mesh shorts and a bright yellow t-shirt as if begging to be shot at. I used to wear those shorts all the time but was encouraged to stop a few weeks after moving into the ghetto. One of my neighbors was kind enough to inform me that I shouldn't wear them outside, explaining that red was a gang color. But at this particular time, I was too emotional to be worried about such things.

I carried the drugs out in front, with both arms fully extended, as I rapidly moved deeper and deeper into the ghetto. Finally I stopped about two alleys back from where the cops had recently found the dead hooker; and at this point, I was too scared to go any farther. In the back alleys, ferocious dogs growled as they jumped up against their chain link fences. They started barking viciously and scared me half to death. Some lights turned on in the houses behind them, and I knew I didn't have much time. Like watching a bad tennis match, my head bounced from one trashcan to another as I frantically tried to figure this out. Selecting the fullest trashcan around, I dumped all of its contents onto the ground, stuffed my drug heap into the can, and replaced the original garbage. Wiping my hands together, I scanned the area to make sure I wasn't followed and then sprinted all the way back to the house. I was a fast runner and knew that if Cheryl had followed me, she would never have beaten me back home.

At the house, I found her smoking cigarettes on the stoop. Just as I was about to tell her that the drugs had been destroyed, Paul rode his bicycle up to the stoop. He dismounted and planted a kiss on Cheryl's cheek. His beard had grown back, and it tickled her face. She laughed briefly as she handed him some of her cigarette to smoke.

"Honey, Matt has something to tell you."

I guess that was as good a cue as any.

"Paul, take a seat," I said.

Clearing my throat, I faced them both, placed my fists on my hips, and in a deep superhero voice I said, "Paul, I know what's going on. I've found the drugs and destroyed them all. From the beginning, you knew this was against the rules, and I can't allow this to continue."

After I ended the sentence, Paul did something I had never seen him do. He started pacing and looked as if he were actually thinking for the first time in his life. He even stroked his beard, just like a little homeless philosopher.

"Cheryl, what's wrong?" I asked.

"He'll tell ya, hon," she said in a resigned voice.

Paul stared intently at the sidewalk as he paced.

"Paul, what's up?"

He came back and faced me, but I wasn't afraid. I expected him to be furious, but he looked more worried than angry.

"I understand that we weren't supposed to be doin this," he said.

"Good."

"But I really wish you hadn't gone an destroyed 'em."

"What would you have had me do?"

"Anything else."

"Why?"

"Cause now we've gotta pay back the dealers."

"Dealers?" I gulped, "Why would you need to pay them?"

"We didn't own all those drugs ourselves; we just held 'em."

And that's when I realized that I had unwittingly done one of the most dangerous things I could possibly do. I had violated the first and only rule of the ghetto which should never be broken, not under any circumstances. The rule: do not cross the drug dealers. It's a surefire way to get yourself killed.

"The drugs are gone. What's done is done," I continued with feigned stubbornness. I couldn't tell if he was lying or if it was a ploy to get me to lead them back to the drugs. Paul shook his head and started walking back inside to assess the damage.

"We're not finished," I said and made Paul come back outside.

Still in my deep superhero-like voice, which exuded maturity and responsibility, I announced that I was going to give them three choices. Smoking rapidly, fresh tears formed in Cheryl's eyes, and I guessed that the finality of what was happening had begun to sink in. I straightened my back against the black night sky as puffs of her grey smoke dissipated in front of me. The lamp across the street was very bright, but my shadow covered Paul and Cheryl and made it hard for me to read their facial expressions. Not that it mattered. I would continue on with my plan. Enlisting the use of my hands for emphasis, I outlined the choices before them.

"Choice number one: I will allow you to remain here with me. But, effective immediately, all drug use will end. Your room will be searched three times a day, and I will search both of you every time you come in and out of the house. All contraband will be destroyed, regardless of ownership."

Paul and Cheryl just stared ahead and sort of nodded.

"Choice number two: Rehab. I have already called and gotten the details and location of the Baltimore Behavioral Services. It's a rehab center only a few miles away. They will house, feed, and medicate you for an entire year. And, the great news is that your Medicaid covers it all. I hope you choose this option. I believe it's the only one with a future.

"However, if neither of these options appeals to you, then you may choose to go back to the woods where I found you. I've heard that once you're addicted to heroin, it's almost impossible to break free. I don't know enough about it to make proper judgments. Please know that I am not disappointed in you. I'm just not able to help you. If you do choose this option, then I will personally move you, buy you a tent, and help you build your camp."

Paul stood up and faced me.

"I know we disappointed you. I'm sorry."

Then he gave me a hug, which was probably the most unexpected thing of all.

"I've learned a lot, and I don't want it to end," I said. "We've had a lot of good times, and I guess now, some not-so-good times, but I am happy I got to know you, whatever you choose."

Cheryl came off the stoop and gave me a hug, too.

"Do you need us to be out tonight?" asked Paul.

"No, heavens, no. I already called BBH. They can receive you as early as Monday at 7:00AM. That's four days. I'm giving you until then to make up your mind."

They just sat in silence staring at me.

"Again, I hope you choose rehab," I said.

Weird, I was neither frustrated nor angry, but I knew I should be furious. I mean, they took advantage of me, didn't they? But they did it to keep a roof over their heads and food on the table. How could I be angry with that?

After the chat, Cheryl and I walked over to the corner store. She slid her arm through mine and said she was going to treat me to an ice cream. She kept saying how happy she was that everything was out in the open. She told me that she wanted to go to rehab. She said she wanted to leave Paul. She told me that she loved me, and I was caught off guard. It all happened so fast that I couldn't really respond.

We reached the corner store, and I picked out a chocolate chip ice cream sandwich, my favorite. Even at ten o'clock at night, the old ladies were sitting out in their lawn chairs smack in the middle of the sidewalk. It was the most dedicated neighborhood watch I had ever known. They smiled and waved to us as we walked by.

Sleeping was difficult after such an emotionally strained evening. I sat up in my pile of blankets and thought of how these next days would be the most dangerous days ever spent in the ghetto. Paul and Cheryl had angered the drug dealers, incurred un-payable debts; and now with the end of the house on the horizon, they had nothing to lose. Truly desperate people have no honor, no code of ethics, no loyalty, and I realized that this was the last night I would sleep in that room.

Lying in bed, I remembered how Paul and Cheryl told me that before they lived under the bridge, they lived out of a van and used to sell scrap metal to make ends meet. And now at their new level of desperation, I figured it was just a matter of time before they threw caution to the wind and tore out the metal pipes from my house. Obviously, they wouldn't just take the pipes; they would take the appliances, fixtures, wires, air ducts, everything. I couldn't believe it, but Father Lorenzo's prediction would come true, and the realization made sleeping very difficult over the next couple of nights. Now is when they would steal everything, and I needed to make sure the house was protected. So I decided to start going home for lunch.

I knew something was wrong the second I came through the door. They were both home, camped out in the living room. Something that never ever happened. Paul usually spent his whole day out on the corner making money; and in our whole time together, I had never seen him in the house during afternoon hours. Now here he was, curled up in the chair, clutching my lead pipe.

"Cheryl, what's going on?"

"Why are you home, hon?" she asked me, as if I needed to explain myself.

"I was hungry and figured I'd take you guys to lunch."

"Oh. That's nice."

"Why are you all here?"

Paul wasn't speaking and just sort of dozed in and out of consciousness.

"Because of last night," she said.

"I don't understand."

"Well, he didn't sleep at all last night. Paul's scared. We're scared."

"Why?"

"'Cause they called."

"Who called?"

"The drug dealers."

"Drug dealers?"

"Yeah. They put a hit out on the house," grumbled Paul.

"A hit?"

"Yeah, a contract, a bounty, a hit, yuh know."

"Why the hell did they do that?"

"They don't believe us."

"They don't believe what?"

"They think we used 'em."

"The drugs?"

"Well, what are you gonna do about it?" I asked in a tone that I would use to discipline a five year old.

"Lock the doors, stay inside."

"Won't they come to the house?"

"Yeah, but we'll just pretend we're not home."

"How long will that last?" I asked.

"Long enough for us to make another plan."

I pretended to give off the perception of aloofness to avoid getting sucked into this problem.

"Okay, well, it sounds like you have everything figured out," I said, opening up the fridge. There was nothing but expired food, moldy leftovers, and some water jugs. Things had really started going downhill.

"Well, hit or not hit, I need to eat. Paul you want anything?"

"No thanks," he said.

"Cheryl, you coming?" I asked.

"Where?"

"Across the street."

"Carl's Bar?"

"Yeah, Carl's Bar."

"Okay, I'll come."

The wooden door swung open and the daylight streamed in. Those sitting at the bar squinted and yelled for me to shut the door. Cheryl and I grabbed two large stools and waved Betty over.

"Fancy seein ya here this time a day."

"Yeah, I figured I'd stop over for lunch."

"That's a nice shirt you're wearin, hon."

"Oh, uh, thanks Betty. It's my work shirt."

We ordered cheeseburger subs and sodas.

"What's the matter, hon?" asked Cheryl. "You don't seem all there."

"Oh, sorry, I'm just thinking."

"You're worried about the hitman, aren't you?"

"Yeah, a bit. What do you think'll happen?" I asked.

"Don't worry about it. Paul has a plan."

"A plan? Enlighten me."

"He's gonna get a guard dog, a knife, and then he's going to build a bunker in the forest."

Almost spitting out my soda, I slowly repeated, "A knife and a guard dog?"

Cheryl started laughing, "Stupid, I know."

"Cheryl, that's the worst plan I've ever heard."

"What do you think will happen when the hitman comes?"

"Oh, don't you worry about that," she said. Then she explained the timeline. Any day a hitman will, in fact, show up on our front door, probably in the middle of the night. She went on to say that generally they don't want to make trouble as long as they get their drugs back. I asked her what would happen if they didn't get their drugs. She gulped before saying that they would probably start killing.

"How's the food?" asked Betty.

"It's great," I said, even though I hadn't eaten a bite.

Betty smiled and walked over to service the others at the bar.

"So, have you and Paul decided what you're going to choose?"

"I don't wanna go back out there. I don't."

"I don't want you to."

"I'm gonna go to rehab, but Paul won't come."

"Figures."

"I'm gonna have to leave Paul. I'm gonna leave him."

"Cheryl, you're not choosing to leave him; you're choosing to get well. If he doesn't follow you, then he's choosing to leave you."

Cheryl just nodded as tears formed in her eyes.

"I'm going to miss him. I love him, and I will worry to death about him out in those woods."

"None of these decisions are easy," I said, looking at my plate of food.

"I know," sobbed Cheryl.

I put $20 on the bar to cover the food and sodas.

"Cheryl, I'm proud of you, and I think you're making the right decision."

"I know, hon." She smiled.

Generally I don't think that throwing money at problems is the best solution; however, in the case of this hitman, it might be the best solution. I figured that money would be an acceptable substitute for the drugs so I stopped off at an ATM before returning to work. Pulling out several hundred dollars, I stuffed it into my wallet and hoped that it would be enough for a down payment. Of course, I kept my cash wad a secret from Paul and Cheryl. I figured that telling them would be the equivalent of dressing up in raw steaks and jumping into a bear pit.

Friday night I went back to my parents' house. Sitting in the kitchen, surrounded by granite countertops, I explained to them that my adventure was coming to a close. We all sat at a large pinewood kitchen table covered in Mom's favorite green placemats. Mom and Dad expressed relief, probably because I made no mentioned of the hitman contract. Dad then insisted that he help me move them out on Sunday. I tried to argue against this, but I honestly needed the help.

Chapter 20: The Purple Sea

At about eleven o'clock on Sunday morning, my dad and I arrived in a twelve- foot, bright yellow Penske moving truck. I didn't realize it yet, but this was probably one of the worst of all times to conduct any type of moving operation. I suspected as much after getting stuck in hours of bumper-to-bumper traffic on the way over. Finally, we arrived at the house but barely had enough room to open the truck doors. We were completely engulfed in a sea of purple fans tailgating for the Ravens game. I correctly deduced that this was going to make moving damn near impossible. Being only about fifteen blocks from the stadium, the neighborhood was overrun with fans of all kinds. Cops, posted at every intersection, did their best to direct traffic, motor and pedestrian, and I immediately became paranoid. I realized that after three days since the drug bust, Paul and Cheryl had surely restocked their supply. All it would take is for one cop to get curious and we'd be done.

The sun was out, and though winter was on its way, it still hadn't arrived. It was an unusually warm fall day, and the heat was unbearable. I was sure that Dad regretted wearing his slacks. Even though this was basically the end of my adventure, I didn't want to appear well off. I still wanted to present a needy image to fend off any last-minute lawsuits. I specifically told him not to wear any fancy button-down shirts, designer slacks, leather shoes, and especially not the Rolex. He agreed not to wear the watch or the shoes but demanded to wear slacks and the button down.

I opened the front door to show my dad the house that he had heard so much about. As we walked up the stoop, I realized that the neighborhood had looked infinitely less scary with thousands of normal, purple-wearing football fans wandering around, but I figured we could always come back later for a proper tour. Excited to introduce him to my roommates, I fumbled with the door handle and finally got it open. Cheryl greeted us in the living room. Well, I guess it was more that we found Cheryl in the living room. She looked as if she had recently been hit by a train and tried unsuccessfully to hide the empty beer bottles lying in her lap. Her breath reeked of alcohol, and her khaki capri pants were covered in wet beer stains. The strands of her hair were frizzled, yet greasy, as if she had lathered her head with butter before sticking her finger in an electric socket. Her makeup still had not worn off from the day before, and her oversized plaid shirt was covered in cigarette ashes. She sat up, surprised by the sudden entrance, and became slightly embarrassed when she realized she was in the presence of my dad. It was here that I realized that the decision to go to rehab couldn't have come a moment too soon.

The bottles in her lap knocked together and made loud clinking noises as she shifted her weight on the couch. She sneezed and gracefully wiped snot all over her unrolled sleeves. Then Dad and Cheryl exchanged niceties and broke into some sort of conversation, which really surprised me. Sitting on the couch, still rubbing her puffy eyes, she thanked him for helping with the move. They tried to talk over the TV, blaring commentary on the recent presidential debates, which Cheryl and Paul watched avidly. Cheryl lowered the volume,and Dad asked a casual question about which candidate she preferred. Cheryl responded, and soon they were going back and forth outlining political plans that were necessary to fix the country and the world. I made a mental note to contact Joe the Plumber's agent. It was only fair that I let him know that he would have some unexpected competition in 2012.

Dad was surprised to find that she was a conservative Republican, and they went on and on about each of the candidates' strengths and weaknesses. I started packing while they talked and kept glancing out the window at the cop on our corner. He made me nervous.

I couldn't believe how much Cheryl and my Dad had to say to one another. I had never seen her in such bad shape before, and I was truly impressed at how coherently she was able to express her ideas and debate politics and current events. I had met many functioning alcoholics in my day but very few functioning alcoholics who were also heroin addicts. Though I didn't think Dad knew of her heroin addiction, I could tell that, considering her appearance and smell, he was still surprised at her ability to present logical arguments to justify her opinions. Finally, after some time, their conversation died down, and I set Dad to work. His first job would be to pack up the kitchen and put all the pots, plates, and silverware into boxes. As was part of the furniture bargain, everything that could be salvaged would have to be returned to my buddy Russ.

After packing several boxes, we walked out to the back porch and surveyed the torn-up sections of counters that needed to be hauled away. This was left over from the side job Paul found gutting a neighbor's kitchen. Of course, I was proud of him for finding the work, but I was unsure why he had to store the debris in my backyard. It had sat there for almost two months, and it was only fitting that Paul was nowhere to be found when we finally cleaned it up. Not only that, but he had leaned these extremely heavy counters up against our wooden fence which couldn't support the weight. The wooden planks broke loose from the beams and cracked under the pressure. Ignoring this, I lifted some of the heavier counter sections and began bringing them outside. Sometime after the truck was already half filled with furniture, clothes, and boxes, Paul returned home from panhandling. He jumped right into the mix and helped load the remaining bed frames, boxes, and Tupperware containers full of trinkets.

After another hour, the truck was filled up. It overflowed with counter pieces, beds, chairs, mattresses, clothing, boxes of trinkets, and various other personal belongings. By using creative packaging skills, we were able to make it all fit. It took a while, and Dad's face dripped with sweat by the time we finally secured the back hatch. Then the three of us piled in, but there were only two seats. Dad volunteered to sit on the floor. No one was arguing with him, but he justified it anyway by reminding us that I needed to drive and Paul had bad knees.

Paul's park of choice was only about one-and-a-half miles away from the house, and the drive over should have taken no more than three minutes. Unfortunately, navigating through thousands of drunken tailgaters is no easy task, and we arrived an hour-and-a-half later. Paul made his park preference painfully clear, claiming that only one park in the entire State of Maryland would meet his needs. I thought this was outrageous and offensive, but Paul wouldn't have it any other way. So we scoped it out and found that it was surrounded by parking lots which were guarded by armed policemen and flooded with drunken tailgaters. It was almost physically impossible to fit our truck into a parking lot where the cars were parked so close together. The few remaining paths through the lot were narrow and unforgiving. It would have been a challenge getting a bicycle in there, much less a bulky twelve- foot- long moving truck. So we pulled next to a large sign, that read "LOT FULL" in big black letters, and that's where we debated our options.

"Paul, where else can we go? We're not getting in here."

"There's no wheres else."

"What the hell does that mean? Of course, there's someplace else," I said.

"Nah. Let's pull over. We can walk the stuff in."

Paul scratched at his beard and prepared himself for the feat.

"Paul, that would take hours!" I yelled.

Our debate grew so lively that we didn't notice that a police officer had wandered over to our truck. He claimed that we were blocking the entrance which was very hard to argue. I stopped fighting with Paul and began frantically trying to come up with something believable to tell this cop. Amidst my disjointed thoughts, I heard Dad's voice.

"Officer, we have a bit of a situation here," said Dad.

"Oh?"

"Paul is homeless. And, due to some very unusual circumstances, we are trying to help him relocate."

The cop shifted his glance from my dad sitting on the floor to me, and then over to Paul.

"Paul desperately wants to move into the woods behind these parking lots," Dad continued. Stepping back from the window, the cop observed the full length and girth of our giant moving truck and then looked back at us.

"How long?" He asked.

"Twenty minutes, max," I said.

"Okay. If you can get this thing in there, you have half an hour," said the cop, waving us through.

Drunk people swarmed through the parking lot. Most stood around little grills, while others lounged in beach chairs. Everyone seemed to be having such a good time that they didn't really pay much attention our moving truck. For a moment, I relished the thought of joining them but figured that if I lived through these next few days, I'd be joining them soon enough.

We parked the truck next to the forest and surveyed the task at hand. An extremely sharp four-foot incline of earth, tree trunks, and brambles separated the lot pavement from the beginning of the woods. Dad and Paul pushed their way through the thicket of vines, brush, and thorns to find the perfect spot. While they went exploring, I started to unload the truck. About 15 minutes later they reappeared.

"Did you find anyplace good?"

"Yeah. It's only about 35-40 paces in through the woods," Dad said, pointing into the forest.

"But there's no actual path so it's gonna be tricky," said Paul.

"Oh," I said, scratching my head.

"So it won't be easy getting this stuff through."

"We'll just have to be persistent, I guess."

"Yeah."

Dad and Paul got on opposite sides of a heavy mattress and began carrying it up the steep berm. The vines were thick so they had to basically ram it through and weave in and out of trees. I followed behind them with the drawers to the desk and a folded tent. The bright white furniture in the green forest looked as unnatural as polar bears roaming through Kansas, but everyone around was drunk, and I doubted they would care.

Awkwardly pushing past a few squatting drunk girls, we finally reached the spot. After setting down the tent bag, I began to quickly assemble the pieces. Paul and Dad joined in, and soon it was fully constructed, standing up over six feet tall with the capacity to sleep five people.

"See, Paul, your own personal 'Four Seasons'!" I said.

"Does it come with a tarp?" Paul asked.

"Oh, yes. It's still in the truck. I'll go get it."

When I came back with the tarp, I found Dad and Paul discussing the slope of the land and arguing about the best way to avoid water damage. Then we made twenty to thirty more trips back to the truck to haul out the rest of the furniture, clothes, and boxes.

After an hour, the truck was empty and the campsite was fully established. We were exhausted, and nothing would have been more refreshing than cracking open a few beers and lounging around the shaded campsite. Unfortunately, we couldn't stay to admire it. The policeman was getting antsy, the Ravens game was about to start, and the truck needed to be returned.

On Monday, my alarm went off at five o'clock in the morning. I was at my parents' house and needed to move quickly if I was to make everything on time. Jumping into my mom's beat up old car, I sped all the way to Baltimore. This was the only car I felt comfortable taking into the ghetto. Dad bought it almost twenty years ago, and it's had plenty of literal wear and tear. Rust ran down the back side of the car where a tree had fallen and bent the metal. Every leather seat had rips in them, and the bottom of the car continuously leaked oil. Every fifty miles or so, I had to put a quart of oil in the engine which was no easy task on account of the worn out hydraulics. To keep the hood open, I had to prop a broom underneath it which I kept stored in the trunk. It was never a graceful procedure. A few years ago, the antenna lost a fight with a low tree branch leaving only some black frayed cables dangling out the top of the car. As if all this wasn't enough, the handle of the driver's door had broken off leaving a razor sharp edge on the rest of the handle. You needed to exercise extreme caution whenever entering the driver's side, or else you could lose one, possibly two fingers. Thus, even though it was a Lexus, it was the perfect car for the ghetto.

Today was the day Cheryl was going to rehab, and I was happy for her. I felt like she would get the help she deserved there; and, if it worked, she might finally be reunited with her family and her children. The sun still had not yet risen when I parked the car outside the house. Coming through the door, I found Paul and Cheryl asleep on the floor of the living room. They lay on cushions. I slapped my forehead. I felt stupid for taking *all* of the mattresses to the woods without leaving anything for them on their last night. What was I thinking? The floor was covered with trash and dirt from the move. A few needles and a crack pipe lay on the floor next to my foot, and pills were scattered everywhere, like Legos on the floor of a child's nursery. With a heavy heart, I woke them up with as firm a voice as I could muster.

"It's time."

Cheryl went upstairs to gather up the belongings that she wanted to take with her. The rehab program lasted for one year. She wouldn't need to bring much, just a few sets of her clothes. In fact, they'd prefer she not bring much else at all.

The house looked like a war zone, completely different from one week ago. While waiting for Cheryl, I walked around the kitchen and looked at the old cigarette butts that littered the counters. Trash and half eaten containers of food sat floating in the clogged sink. The fridge was practically bare, and the whole house smelled like cigarette smoke.

The funny part is that this is what I had expected the house to be like from day one. I was prepared to handle it at the outset, but I was not ready to handle it now. Loud snoring noises from the living room got louder as Paul drifted back to sleep. Collecting myself, I walked over to Paul who was bundled up in extra clothes and sleeping soundly. I reached over and switched off the TV.

"Paul, it's time to go."

Grunting, he sat up.

Almost whispering, I said, "This is your last chance. It's either rehab or the park."

"Nahh, park, park."

I sighed loudly enough for him to hear. Paul nodded with half open eyes and silently stuffed his remaining things into a backpack.

Finally with tears running down her face, Cheryl came downstairs carrying a small grocery bag of clothes which couldn't have fit more than one pair of pants and a t-shirt.

I asked her if she thought she might need at least a few more clothes for the year, but she just shook her head. As far as I was concerned, the writing was on the wall. Now all that was left was the humiliating task of formally extending her the benefit of the doubt. We hugged Paul goodbye and got into the car. I watched as Paul rode his bike toward the wooded campsite; and shaking my head, I turned the ignition. It rumbled to a start, and we were off.

Fifteen minutes later, we ended up at the rehab center. It was 7:00AM. The rehab center was also in the ghetto which was just stupid. I could see what looked like drug dealers hanging out near the entrance of the center. It was beyond me how anyone could resist falling back into drugs with dealers hanging around the front entrance. It was almost comical to see the type of environment this "rehabilitation" was supposed to take place in. Stopping at the door, I hugged Cheryl goodbye and told her that I'd be sure to visit. She thanked me for everything and then walked into the waiting room. I waited a few moments and watched her through the outside window. When I saw her filling out paperwork, I decided it was time to leave.

I was proud that she actually went inside; and to be honest, I was genuinely surprised. Back in the car, I turned off the radio and drove in silence. I was having a hard time believing that it was finally goodbye. It was kind of like at the end of "White Fang" when the guy sends the dog to be free into the wild. A sad ending, but everyone knew it was for the best. In a last- minute decision, I pulled an illegal u-turn and sped to the nearest CVS. This went against my better judgment, but at the time, I figured that cigarettes were better than heroin, and anything better than heroin should be encouraged. Running in, I grabbed a pack of her favorite brand, hopped back into the car, and sped over to the center. I hoped I could catch her before she left the waiting area.

"Excuse me, miss," I said to the receptionist.

"Yes?"

"I'm looking for Cheryl. The big plump woman."

"Excuse me?"

"Oh, I'm sorry, the big plump white woman."

"A patient?"

"I guess. She just signed in about ten minutes ago."

"Why do you need to see her?"

"I have a gift for her," I said, excitedly holding up the CVS bag.

"I'm sorry, but she's not here."

"Yes, I can see that, but which room is she in now?"

The woman was just silent and looked at me as if I were a bit slow.

"Or should I just leave this here with you?" I asked.

"Sir, I think you misunderstood."

"What?"

"She's not here at all."

Clearly this lady was confused, and I needed to make her understand.

"No, no. I just dropped her off ten minutes ago."

"Yes. And she left five minutes after that," said the woman, becoming annoyed.

"Oh."

I stuffed the cigarettes back into my pocket and got back in the car. A few blocks from the house, I found Cheryl hightailing it back towards the park. She had been moving pretty fast and was sweating profusely. I pulled up beside her and rolled down the window.

"Cheryl, cut it out. And get in the car!"

She got in and strapped on the seatbelt.

"I told you I wouldn't be upset. I'll take you back to the park and --

She cut me off with, "They wouldn't let me in because I didn't have an inhaler."

I didn't acknowledge this excuse with a response and so we sat in silence all the way back to the park.

We both got out of the car and faced the woods. The trees were still thick, and it was not possible to see deep enough to even get a glimpse of the red tent. Cheryl gave me a big hug and thanked me again for everything. She then made her way up the steep berm in front of the woods. Back at the car, I realized that I'd forgotten something.

"Cheryl wait."

Already on top of the berm, she turned back towards me.

"What?"

"Catch!"

She held out her hands as I lobbed the cigarettes up in a perfect arch. The rotating pack reflected glimmers of sunlight before it descended into Cheryl's outstretched hands.

"Be sure to share them with Paul!"

The next morning, I had to drive in from my parents' house. I arrived almost an hour earlier than normal, partly because I couldn't sleep and partly because I wanted to beat the traffic. Ironically, I ended up parking in the same garage where I had spent so many months changing in and out of my ghetto attire, but it was still too soon for me to feel any emotion or nostalgia. This was the first day back at the Firm since "the move," and I was ready to be distracted by work. Climbing the stairs, I quickly reached the top in no time at all, took a few steps into the plaza, and then stopped.

Maybe it was because it was so early in the morning, or maybe it was because I had never bothered to look, but I saw something that I had never seen before. In the midst of a swarm of pigeons was a little old man with long grey hair, squinted eyes, and a slightly hunched back. Around his arm he carried a shopping bag, one of those reusable ones for environmentally minded shoppers. Placing it on the ground, he bent down on his knee and started tending to something in the bag. I thought he was just getting out some bread to feed those damn birds, but I was wrong. From inside the bag, he produced another pigeon. It looked to be injured, and I thought I saw something of a bandage wrapped around its leg. The man carefully took it out and placed it among the others. He wiped some dirt off its feathers and patted it lightly before picking up and inspecting a few of the bird's friends. I noticed how he inspected the heads, wings, and feet in a specific order. He did this several times. They never flapped in his hands and just sort of went limp, as if they trusted him completely. I noticed that one of them had a badly damaged wing. I watched the man scoop it up in his hands. He held it between his fingers, rolling the wing to see if anything was broken. I could tell by the way he handled them that this man cared about these birds. He was so careful with them, so thoughtful with the way he folded back their feathers and ran his fingers softly over their feet. I knew he loved them dearly; and from that moment on, I could never looked at those pigeons the same way again.

As I watched the man slowly hobble out of the square, I thought about all the things that had happened over the past year. I thought about what I had learned and I wondered if I had made any difference at all.

I had never set out to find a model of solving homelessness, but rather I was looking for someone to be an example. I wanted to find someone who had fallen off the proverbial cliff of despair because this person needed to be relevant to the homeless population. Thus they needed to have a similar mentality and outlook as the majority of the others who had become homeless. If Paul and Cheryl were able to find a way to climb out of their wretched situation, then I could have used their story, and perhaps even they themselves to help me free others from the bonds of homelessness. They were supposed to be symbols of hope; they were supposed to be living light that could show others the way out. Alas, everything I had put into this situation was not enough; I realized far too late that I was not enough.

The way I see it, is that even if someone is mentally ill, addicted to drugs, or an alcoholic, they can still love and be loved. Their humanity and thus their value cannot be diminished by any choices they have made or have failed to make. Though their capacity to make good decisions may be all but gone, I know that they can still *feel* just like you and me. And so, I cannot believe that a single act of love or kindness is ever pointless or wasted. Even if lasting change didn't immediately happen. Even if lasting change never happens. Love is still love and kindness is still kindness and Paul and Cheryl knew it. Just because it was not enough doesn't mean that it was not good.

I don't know when homelessness will finally end, I don't know specifically how it will end, but I do know that now it's personal.

Chapter 21: Just Getting Started

The thuds of air were audible through the thick metal doors as the elevator rocketed through floors towards the executive level. I stepped out onto the white marble and brightly lit corporate foyer, furnished with modern white leather chairs, mahogany tables, and plasma televisions displaying a smattering of stock graphs, pie charts, and ticker symbols. I felt the heat of a giant screen as I rushed down the long narrow hallway lined with glass encased in Asian style dark wood frames. I got to a large door and could see the figure of Carlyle Mansfield behind a wall of frosted glass. I had been called down to his office twice already in the same day, which was very unusual. His boss had been on the phone a couple of times about my extra curricular "projects". Carlyle sat behind a large polished desk bordered by matching wood bookcases and cabinets with bronze fixtures. Oil paintings with thick paint and faded gold frames hung on the walls. I remember I used to be intimidated by the office, but over the years the intimidation gave away to familiarity. Today, however, I reminded of the intimidation I felt by the look on Carlyle's face.

He grimaced and his eyes darted back and forth as if trying to figure out what to say. His hands nervously gripped the lip of his desk and he uncomfortably shifted in his chair. The phone was ringing but he ignored it, which was something he never did. From outside one of the three executive receptionists called, "Carlyle, it's --."

"I know who it is!", Carlyle called back, "tell him anything you want, I can't talk to him now." I knew who was calling. It was his boss. He was calling about what to do with me. I hated to hear the phone ringing. The meetings, the incessant phone buzzing, the frustration was all because earlier that day corporate ethics found something. They found out that I was a part owner of a company that, in their uninformed opinion, might be a conflict of interest with the Firm or at the very least could be extremely distracting. Corporate ethics immediately sent out alert emails to my boss, my boss' boss, and me. It's a violation to secretly have other employment with another firm. Carlyle slid the ethics form across the desk and said in panicked tone, "What exactly do you think you're doing?"

The company wants their employees who will be committed 100% of the time and they want it to be perceived that way too. This is especially true of those who are out in the city making an effort to be visible for the purposes of generating business for the Firm. This last point is important because employees could be immediately terminated if they are found to use the company's networks for sales of another employer. Carlyle had me explain to him the business concept, which only convinced him further that this was a massive violation that was all but indefensible. Carlyle asked, "Why wouldn't you sell this service to the Firm's customers? That's exactly what I would do, if I were you. And that's exactly why this is a big problem." He spoke as he paced around the office, clearly upset about this discovery. And the problem was that it was all true. I was the co-founder of a company. It wasn't much more than a glorified lemonade stand, but it was a company nonetheless. If the roles were reversed, I would have been just as upset after making discoveries that had been hidden from me. I probably would have overreacted and I would have assumed that my employees might be putting my entire portfolio of customers at risk because of some part time job. I would have been confused and then furious as I'm sure Carlyle must have been. And yet, though everything he had found out was true, it was certainly not the whole story. It was all part of the plan to end homelessness.

It's a bad bet for America to continue to gamble the salvation of the homeless on the charity of a handful of saintly citizens. Instead I success lies in leveraging our strengths: America's ambition and its industrial muscle. We need to find jobs that are labor intensive, can never be outsourced to India or China, and can never be automated. We need jobs that are more than just a cashier at convenience store. Jobs that turn into careers and don't require an ivy league education to make money. Those types of jobs are hard to find. So, I have set out to create them myself.

It was a cold January day and the year 2011 was still very young. I had spent the past three years trying to move on from my time with Cheryl and Paul. I missed what it was like to be hopeful and so I busied myself with the comings and goings of climbing the corporate ladder at the Firm. I had graduated out of my analytical rotation and I had officially entered into the business development side of the company. I was out in the community drumming up new deals and wining and dinning some of the most influential business leaders in the city and state. And yet despite all the baseball suites, black tie gala dinners, and multi million dollar contracts, I couldn't help but try and find new ways to solve homelessness. Lately, I had found myself covered in grease more often than not. On a particular night, I was wedged underneath an almost twenty year old Lexus LS 400. A beauty in it's day, she had come to what I had believe was her final resting space in the back corner of my parents garage. The garage was filled with large mahogany desks, brass end tables, soccer balls, skis, Persian rugs, and piles of shoes. Bikes hung from large hooks on the ceiling and cobwebs lined the top corners.

314

Everything, literally everything, was covered in a thick yellow dust and several layers of dog fur. The garage probably would have killed anyone with allergies. I looked at the car sitting in the clearing of furniture and boxes and remembered that this was the same car that I had used three years ago to drive Cheryl to rehab, and then that same day, to drive her to the park.

"I can't see it." I said, coughing as grit and dog fur had fallen into my mouth.

"Here, use this," said Derek sliding a large wrench under the car into my hand. It was funny to see Derek in this setting. He was a friend of mine from the Firm, who had recently been recruited away to work in the corporate finance division of a billion dollar energy company. He had a look of privilege about him, always dressed as if he'd just stepped off a yacht with boat shoes, polo shirts, khaki pants, and colorful belts. His closet overflowed with preppy Brooks Brothers' clothes. His closet was a mini Brooks Brothers. His blond hair was perfectly cut and his face always clean-shaven. Not that he could have grown a beard if he had wanted. His baby face wouldn't have allowed it, which amused me because he was older than I, yet I had no trouble with facial hair. I made comments when he bought razors and annoyed the hell out of him. I would tell him it was a worthless investment. Stupid. Wasteful.

"I think we have to take off this entire protective cover. It has 12 bolts to undo," He said.

"Ugh. This is such a pain," I said sighing.

"Hurry up, the timer is ticking," complained Derek, "We have to make this work."

"I'm unscrewing those bolts as fast as I can!"

My back was pressed up against the freezing cold concrete floor. The temperatures couldn't have been much

315

above 20 degrees, but I was happy to at least be inside the garage. Outside was literally impossible to perform any kind of car maintenance. I knew because my fingers had turned numb from the cold, not that it would have mattered because even with the use of my fingers I wouldn't have been able to see. The winter days are short and it night sky had already turned pitch black. We had no portable lights because we had not considered ample lighting as a problem. We were very new at this and set backs were to be expected. We did get some work done on the truck outside, but we didn't last very long before we gave up and moved into the garage, where we at least had light.

"Boys! Dinner!" Called my mom from inside the house. Her voice had a way of carrying through locked doors. I shouted back that we would be just another couple of minutes. A few moments later she appeared in the garage carrying a wooden tray filled with sandwiches and Gatorades. She stepped into the garage and I'm sure saw my legs sticking out form under the car, Derek's oil covered face and clothes, and the strewn about tools, before she let out a big sigh.

"You both are in high level finance at companies that are already successful."

"Yeah mom, we know," I mumbled from underneath the car.

"You should be day trading in your spare time, not changing oil!"

I chuckled, because I knew day trading wasn't going to save the world. Changing oil, however, just might.

You see, changing oil is one of those recession proof, labor intensive industries, that can never be outsourced. It's a job where employees can earn a livable wage and also provide an opportunity for advancement. In an oil change company, there is no requirement that employees have college degrees to be able to perform an oil change or manage others performing oil changes. We have drastically altered the typical auto -maintenance business model to maximize scalability, efficiency, and dramatically reduce our fixed costs compared to competitors such as Jiffy Lube and gas stations. Since this initial change in early January of 2011 we have formed an LLC entity, setup merchant services, and performed a successful six month trial phase with a large network of family and friends with each customer inviting us back for repeat service. The plan is to build the customer base up to a point where it could support one homeless veteran. When Carlyle understood the motive for this company, relief swept across his face. He was able to successfully lobby for an official approval from the Firm on the formation and operation of my company.

About two weeks after my meeting with Carlyle, I was contacted by someone I had not expected. It was Cheryl and it had been about three years since we had last spoken. I saw her name flash across my email inbox and I wasn't sure what to think. I had mixed emotions about everything and I assumed she and Paul had remained spiraling further into homeless and addiction. I was sure that she was writing to me from her deathbed. But I was wrong.

Things had worked out better than I or anyone could have ever imagined. She explained that she had gone back to rehab for a few months, but it was miserable. She left and returned to the park where she and Paul were thrown out by city officials, who had deemed the park a health hazard. But from what I've been told, the city was merciful in their eviction and provided the homeless with temporary housing and instructions on how to apply for HUD housing.

Cheryl was fed up with drugs and fed up with living in the park. She missed her family and so she took steps to get back into housing. Once her family heard of her plan and her efforts, they all jumped to support her and Paul. Now, she tells me that she and Paul have been clean for over 2 years. She lives near her family and receives SSI, which affords her the time to take care of her aging parents. I was shocked to hear that Paul finally found a job with a forgiving contractor, who employed him to work various construction jobs. Cheryl tells me that Paul goes to work every day and has developed more friendships than she has at their local church. She couldn't be happier and told me that she had a small modest car that she could use to help give me a ride if I ever needed it.

She and Paul have reintegrated themselves with her family and with society. I couldn't believe my computer screen was displaying the words in her letters. I was overwhelmed as I remembered the Wall of Want. Everything she had written down, she had received. It had all come to fruition, better than planned even. The idea of Paul going to church was beyond my comprehension. I thought of all the months, all the years that had gone by where I thought I had failed. I thought of everyone who told me it couldn't happen, from the priest, to my friends, to acquaintances and family. All those individuals who told me this would never work got the satisfaction of getting to say, "I told you so". Now I finally had a chance to respond with Cheryl's own words, "Thank you for being there for Paul and me, you're efforts was'nt in vain."

END

Acknowledgements:

Even after writing several hundred pages of this story, I still do not have the capability to express in words the gratitude I have for those I had mentioned here and the many more who I have not.

I wanted to acknowledge a few of those who are directly responsible for this specific adventure. Below are the names of those who have influenced me, inspired me, or helped me live this out whether they knew it or not. Julie Collins, Father David Collins, Dr. Stephen Ochs, Father Chris Steck, Father Stephen Fields, Father Otto Hentz, Kathy Piwko, Kate Burke, Chris Maloney, Richard Drozd, Bonnie Hanes, Andrew Mahr, Josh Bull, Erin Devlin, Kristen Whitworth, Lacey Campbell, Kaitlyn Edsall, Hutch Walbrige, Chris Badeker, Moira Kennedy, Sharon Olah, Grandpa Stan, Stephanie Novosel, Frank K. Turner, Krystal Covey, Hutch Walbridge, Colin Wilson, Stephanie Brown, Russ Watts, Phyllis Goldstein, Msgr. Luca, and Dan Rodricks.

I wanted to especially mention, Alex Rienhoff who voluntarily trusted and hired my roommates to paint her rental property in an effort to help me help them get back on their feet. My Aunt Marilyn for always being there for me along with my Mom, Dad, and my brother. Julie Collins for listening to me throughout the adventure and for the kindness she showed Cheryl. Peter Fargo who lent me his furniture, much of which never made it back. And Msgr. Luca, who convinced me that this story was worth putting up online.

About the Author

Matthew Bjonerud is a graduate of Georgetown Prep High School and Georgetown University's Business School. He is a member of the Catholic Community of South Baltimore. He serves as a member of Baltimore City's Leadership Advisory Board, which was convened to execute Baltimore's 10 year plan to end homelessness known as the Journey Home (http://www.journeyhomebaltimore.org/). In addition he serves as the Vice-Chairman of At Jacob's Well, a Baltimore non-profit that houses 40 mentally challenged homeless persons in the northern part of the city (http://atjacobswell.org/). He currently works for a Corporate Bank in the middle market corporate space.

.

Made in the USA
San Bernardino, CA
24 October 2016